Exogenous Data in Accounting and Auditing in the Rutgers Series in Accounting Information Systems

Exogenous Data in Accounting and Auditing in the Rutgers Series in Accounting Information Systems

EDITED BY

MIKLOS A. VASARHELYI
Rutgers Business School, USA

HANXIN (ALICE) HU
Kean University, USA

AND

ANN F. MEDINETS
Rutgers Business School, USA

emerald
PUBLISHING

United Kingdom – North America – Japan – India – Malaysia – China

Emerald Publishing Limited
Emerald Publishing, Floor 5, Northspring, 21-23 Wellington Street, Leeds LS1 4DL.

First edition 2025

British Library Cataloguing in Publication Data
A catalogue record for this book is available from the British Library

ISBN: 978-1-83608-735-9 (Print)
ISBN: 978-1-83608-734-2 (Online)
ISBN: 978-1-83608-736-6 (Epub)

Printed and bound by CPI Group (UK) Ltd, Croydon, CR0 4YY

Contents

About the Editors *vii*

About the Contributors *ix*

Introduction
Miklos A. Vasarhelyi, Hanxin (Alice) Hu, Ann F. Medinets and Steven Katz *1*

Part One Exogenous Data in Business Research

Chapter 1 Accounting's Resurrection: An Exploration of Future Business Reporting with Exogenous Data
Melissa A. Dardani *7*

Chapter 2 Exogenous Data Using Large Language Models like ChatGPT
Irina Jie Bao and Benita Gullkvist *25*

Chapter 3 A Survey on Cookie Disclosure and Practice
Hanchi Gu and Qing Huang *49*

Part Two Exogenous Data from Google Trends

Chapter 4 The Search Volume Index for Business Analysis
Fangbing Xiong *61*

Chapter 5 Two Studies Using Exogenous Internet Data to Assess Investors' Attention
Maria Guangyue Zhang *71*

Chapter 6 When Google Speaks: Unveiling Corporate Performance Through Google Trends
Xin Jin and Haoyun (Harry) Gao *89*

Chapter 7 Impact of the Fit for 55 Policies on the Response of Electric Vehicle Consumers in Germany: Stress Analysis in Market Trends from Google Trends
Maristela Roza, Leonardo Flach and Fabricia Silva Da Rosa 99

Part Three Exogenous Data from Social Media

Chapter 8 Beyond the Facade: Misinformation on the Internet and Identification of Paid Posters on Social Media
Shaoyu (Shawn) Liu 117

Chapter 9 Exogenous Data in Governmental Accounting: Expanding Auditing Practices
Huaxia Li 133

Chapter 10 An Exogenous Leading Indicator of Box Office Revenue: Piracy as a Consumer Proxy
Steven Katz 143

Chapter 11 A Conceptual Model for Mining Customer Reviews
Talha Afzal 151

Chapter 12 A Review of the Use of LinkedIn in Accounting Studies
Lanxin Jiang 157

About the Editors

Miklos A. Vasarhelyi is the KPMG Distinguished Professor of Accounting Information Systems at Rutgers University. He is a leading Researcher in continuous audit application with over 200 journal articles and 20 books published in the field. He is also Editor of the *Journal of Emerging Technologies in Accounting* and the *Artificial Intelligence in Accounting and Auditing* series. As Head of the Rutgers Accounting Research Center (RARC), the Continuous Auditing & Reporting (CAR) Lab, and the Rutgers AICPA Data Analytics Research (RADAR) initiative, he has worked on projects for Siemens, KPMG, Procter & Gamble, AICPA, CA Technologies, and Brazil's Itau-Unibanco.

Hanxin (Alice) Hu is an Assistant Professor in the Department of Accounting and Finance at Kean University. She holds a PhD in Accounting Information Systems from Rutgers Business School. Her research interests focus on financial reporting, audit risk assessment, and the application of artificial intelligence in accounting and auditing. She has published in peer-review journals, including *Accounting Horizons*, *Journal of Information Systems*, and *Journal of Emerging Technologies in Accounting*. She enjoys teaching financial and managerial accounting, audit analytics, and financial statement analysis.

Ann F. Medinets is an Associate Professor of Professional Practice at Rutgers University. Her paper "Say-on-Pay: Is Anybody Listening?" with Stephani Mason and Dan Palmon (*Multinational Finance Journal*, 2016) was featured on Harvard's Forum on Corporate Governance and Financial Regulation. Another paper "Disclosure Regulations Work: The Case of Regulation G" with Dan Palmon and Yu-An Chen (*Review of Quantitative Finance and Accounting*, 2022) received a Bright Ideas Award in Accounting. Other publications include "Giving Shareholders Real Rights, Reducing Excessive Executive Pay, and Reducing One-Size-Fits-All Regulation" with Dan Palmon and Gary Kleinman (Rutger*s Business Review*, 2022), "Developing Continuous Assurance at Siemens" with Jason Gross and Gerard Brennan (Audit Analytics and Continuous Audit: Looking toward the Future, 2015), and "A Theoretical Model of Cognitive Factors that Affect Auditors' Performance and Perceived Independence" with Dan Palmon, Gary Kleinman, and Asokan Anandarajan (*International Journal of Behavioural Accounting and Finance*, 2010).

About the Contributors

Talha Afzal is a PhD Student in the Department of Accounting and Information Systems at Rutgers University. His research interests include AI with a focus on neural networks and generative AI, as well as text mining. His co-authored article, "Fair Value Estimates for Illiquid Cryptocurrency," was published in the *International Journal of Accounting Information Systems*.

Irina Jie Bao is a PhD Candidate in the Department of Accounting and Information Systems at Rutgers University. She earned her bachelor's degree from Fudan University in China. Her research interests encompass a broad spectrum of areas, including environmental, social, and governance (ESG) criteria, artificial intelligence (AI), large language models (LLMs), auditing, the economics of regulation, accounting standards, and the gamification of accounting education. She is particularly focused on exploring the potential applications of LLMs in the ESG context, such as extracting and analyzing data from ESG reports and enhancing ESG assurance.

Melissa A. Dardani is a licensed Certified Public Accountant (CPA), Certified Fraud Examiner (CFE), and is pursuing a PhD in Accounting Information Systems from Rutgers University Graduate Business School in Newark, New Jersey. At Rutgers, she focuses on integrating artificial intelligence (AI) into business reporting, measurement, and assurance. Her research primarily investigates the applications of AI for continuous auditing and assurance, emphasizing a holistic, risk-focused approach to better preserve and protect business value. Bringing a decade of practical experience to Rutgers, her expertise includes forensic accounting, specializing in assisting businesses in distress due to fraud, mismanagement, and waste. She has conducted forensic audits and investigations and has designed and implemented systems of control for the finance function.

Leonardo Flach is a Full Professor in Accounting at the Federal University of Santa Catarina (UFSC), Brazil. His research interests include corporate sustainability and cooperative management.

Haoyun (Harry) Gao is a third-year PhD Student in Accounting & Information Systems at Rutgers University, with research interests at the intersection of auditing and emerging technologies. His work includes a published article titled

"Extracting Financial Data from Unstructured Sources: Leveraging Large Language Models" in the *Journal of Information Systems*.

Hanchi Gu is a Lecturer at the Shanghai University of Finance and Economics. He earned his PhD from Rutgers University in the Accounting and Information Systems program. His research focuses on artificial intelligence applications in accounting and auditing (e.g., large language models, outlier detection, and supervised-learning models), continuous monitoring, and other topics on accounting information systems.

Benita Gullkvist is currently employed as Senior Researcher at the University of Vaasa, Finland, after being an Associate Professor of Accounting at Hanken School of Economics, Finland, for over 10 years. She received her PhD degree from Abo Akademi University in 2005, where she was appointed as Adjunct Professor in April 2012. Her research interests include behavioral, social, and organizational issues related to accounting and accounting information systems. She is a Member of the editorial board of the *International Journal of Accounting Information Systems*, and she also serves as a Reviewer for journal and conference submissions. She has published in renowned journals such as the *European Accounting Review*, *Management Accounting Research*, and *Critical Perspectives on Accounting*. In addition, she has made contributions to several books and actively presented her research at international accounting conferences.

Qing Huang is an Assistant Professor at Marshall University. She earned her PhD in Accounting and Information Systems from Rutgers University and is a certified public Accountant (inactive) in China. Her research focus is on continuous auditing, audit analytics, outlier detection, graph neural networks, machine learning, and fraud detection.

Lanxin Jiang is a PhD Candidate at Rutgers University, specializing in archival auditing and accounting information systems. Her research centers on harnessing the power of machine learning to advance accounting and auditing practices, as well as leveraging emerging technology to enhance ESG reporting and assurance. Her ongoing projects include the application of machine learning to accounting research, audit data outlier detection, text mining of ESG reports, and blockchain- and lifecycle assessment enabled greenhouse gas (GHG) reporting. One of her dissertation chapters utilizes explainable AI to analyze audit partner characteristics extracted from LinkedIn.

Xin Jin is a second-year PhD Candidate at the Escola Brasileira de Administração Pública e de Empresas (Brazilian School of Public and Business Administration, EBAPE), which is part of the Fundação Getulio Vargas (Getulio Vargas Foundation, FGV) in Brazil. Her research areas include accounting, auditing, ESG reporting, and exogenous data. Specifically, her interests focus on corporate social performance, the correlation between firms' corporate governance and their environmental performance, and the use of exogenous data to predict firms' performance.

Steven Katz is an Accounting Information Systems PhD Candidate at Rutgers Business School. He has an abiding interest in natural language processing, corporate responsibility, and the future of ethical technological innovation. He has presented papers exploring the role of technology in governmental accounting and the automated extraction of information from corporate sustainability reports.

Huaxia Li is an Assistant Professor of Accounting in the Department of Accounting and Finance at the University of Michigan-Dearborn. He earned his Ph.D. in Management (Accounting Information Systems) from Rutgers, The State University of New Jersey. Prior to his current role, he served as a Researcher at the Rutgers Accounting Research Center and the Continuous Auditing and Reporting Lab. Huaxia's research interests include accounting information systems, accounting data accessibility, the application of emerging technologies in accounting and auditing, governmental financial accounting and disclosure, the municipal bond market and fiscal distress, and corporate social responsibility. His work has been published in the *Journal of Information Systems, Sustainability Accounting, Management, and Policy Journal*, and the *Journal of Emerging Technologies in Accounting*. He received his M.S. in Information Technology and Analytics from Rutgers, The State University of New Jersey, and his B.B.A in Accounting and Finance from the University of Macau.

Shaoyu (Shawn) Liu is a PhD Candidate in the Department of Accounting and Information Systems at Rutgers Business School. His research focuses on leveraging emerging technologies, such as large language models (LLMs) and robotic process automation (RPA), to explore strategic corporate disclosures and enhance financial reporting transparency. His work delves into the use of ESG disclosures as a strategic tool prior to earnings announcements, uncovering the impact of misclassifications in Form 8-K filings on market outcomes. His research has been presented at major conferences, including the AAA Annual Meeting. He is also interested in examining misinformation on social media, the detection of malicious content, and its influence on consumer behavior and stock returns. His work aims to enhance transparency in digital business environments and provide innovative solutions for distinguishing between genuine and manipulated content.

Fabricia Silva da Rosa has a PhD in Production Engineering. She is a Professor at the Department of Accounting Sciences and the Accounting Program at the Federal University of Santa Catarina (UFSC), Brazil, and she leads the Center for Studies in Innovation, Accounting and the Environment (NEIMAC).

Maristela Roza is a PhD Candidate in the Graduate Program in Accounting (PPGC) at the Federal University of Santa Catarina (UFSC) in Brazil where she is a Member of the Research Group on Work and Teaching in Accounting (NETEC). Her research interests include environmental sustainability, artificial intelligence, and electric vehicles (EVs), as well as public policy and regulations.

Fangbing Xiong is a PhD candidate at Rutgers University who specializes in information system design and LLM improvement based on her expertise in emerging technologies, such as text mining, data visualization, process mining, process automation, and retrieval-augmented generation. Her research includes the development of a digital role-playing game (D-RPG) that combines behavioral experiments and gamification to enhance accounting education. The first paper from this project has been submitted to *Journal of Emerging Technologies in Accounting* and received the Jack and Maye Stewart Student Project Award. Additionally, she is developing an LLM-powered AI agent framework for accounting and auditing using a design science approach. She explores advanced emerging technologies and their applications in business, aiming to benefit accounting education and practice through innovation.

Maria Guangyue Zhang is a PhD Candidate at Rutgers Business School. Her main research focus is on accounting information systems. Her work includes continuous monitoring for risk management and consumer privacy in the healthcare setting. She also studies financial accounting and disclosure using exogenous data sources, such as financial performance evaluation in multi-segment firms and cryptocurrency fair value measurement.

Introduction

Miklos A. Vasarhelyi[a], *Hanxin (Alice) Hu*[b], *Ann F. Medinets*[a] *and Steven Katz*[a]

[a]*Rutgers Business School, USA*
[b]*Kean University, USA*

Traditionally, accounting information has relied on data sourced directly from firms of interest. A host of elaborate and sensitive measures have been devised to parse endogenous data with the understanding that they were, to some extent, flawed. Reported earnings may be managed. Managerial disclosures and analyses may carefully omit relevant information. Earnings calls may be unnecessarily optimistic. All of these types of information share the same endogenous source and, therefore, are burdened with the potential for bias. However, the digital age has seen an enormous increase in the volume and variety of relevant data available from sources external to a given reporting firm. This exogenous data offers independent, timely insights into endogenous business outcomes, allowing for unbiased confirmation or contradiction of corporate claims. Exogenous data is also often voluminous, frequently updated, and varied in format, allowing for sensitive analyses conducted on demand using data that would be cumbersome to collect manually (e.g., Yelp reviews, compared to conducting a randomized survey).

Any source of information that is both external to an organization of interest and correlated with that company's reported outcomes can provide useful exogenous data. For example, social media posts, Google Trends, and weather data can all proxy for business-relevant factors (e.g., customer's impressions of products, broad social trends, and localized weather events that impact operations). Accountants can use these sources to supplement and substantiate their analyses with data that does not share the same inherent conflicts of interest carried by endogenous data. For example, if a firm reports making changes to its manufacturing process that minimize its factories' impact on the local ecology, satellite images of the environment surrounding those factories can be used to assure their claims (Gu et al., 2023). Similarly, a retailer's claims about sales revenue may be tested by analyses that use weather data to estimate likely customer behavior.

Exogenous Data in Accounting and Auditing in the Rutgers Series in Accounting Information Systems, 1–4

doi:10.1108/978-1-83608-734-220251014

If reported revenue does not match customers' expected behavioral patterns in the face of inclement weather, it may be a sign that revenue is being misstated (Yoon et al., 2024).

This book explores several innovative sources and uses of exogenous data, organized into three parts. The first part provides an overview of applications for exogenous data in business research. The second part focuses on extracting insights from analyzing search volume index (SVI) data, which represents how often specific phrases are searched for on search engines like Google. The third part explores the use of social media and public internet activity to infer users' sentiments, behaviors, and intentions.

Part One: Exogenous Data in Business Research

In Chapter 1, Melissa A. Dardani argues for the utility of exogenous data in modern reporting environments. She suggests that accounting analyses can be improved by combining vast exogenous data sources with data-hungry machine-learning algorithms that improve as they incorporate more input and that these analyses could theoretically be conducted on a continuous basis to create a nearly real-time assurance tool.

Chapter 2 by Irina Jie Bao and Benita Gullkvist discusses how Large Language Models like ChatGPT can be used to extract and analyze various types and sources of exogenous data. They demonstrate this process by using ChatGPT to obtain and use both endogenous and exogenous environmental data for ExxonMobil, laying out a step-by-step explanation of their procedure.

In Chapter 3, Hanchi Gu and Qing Huang examine published policies and actual practices related to corporate websites' distribution of traceable packets of internet data colloquially known as "cookies." Their comparison between official and observed practices suggests that there may be privacy concerns on corporate websites, adding a hidden cost to the use of this endogenous, non-financial information.

Part Two: Exogenous Data from Google Trends

In Chapter 4, Fangbing Xiong explores how firms and auditors can leverage search engine query frequency, commonly measured using the SVI in general and referred to as Google Trends specifically. Her paper reviews SVI literature and demonstrates how to use Google Trends to gather information about consumer habits.

In a related area, Chapter 5 by Maria Guangyue Zhang uses SVI to demonstrate that investors have shifted away from firms' annual financial reports toward newer, third-party intermediaries that offer more timely and digestible information. In addition, she shows that investors in the cryptocurrency market react materially to relevant news headlines, further suggesting that exogenous sources of information have tangible effects on financial markets.

In Chapter 6, Xin Jin and Haoyun (Harry) Gao predict Brazilian airlines' quarterly revenue using SVI statistics, both concurrently and for the subsequent quarter. They also use SVI to predict flight-related carbon emissions both in the same month and two months in advance, rationalizing that customers are likely searching on Google either for flights on short notice or for trips far in advance.

Chapter 7 by Maristela Roza, Leonardo Flach, and Fabricia Silva da Rosa examines the impact of EU policy changes on consumers in the German electronic vehicle market through the lens of Google Trends. She also uses Trends to proxy for consumers' stress in response to the policy changes, gaining insight into the psychology of a large population of potential customers.

Part Three: Exogenous Data from Social Media

Shaoyu (Shawn) Liu catalogs the different types of misleading reviews on social media in Chapter 8, including compensated endorsements and targeted slander campaigns in the context of past research on social media and the integrity of review systems. Detection systems struggle to keep up with innovative manipulators, suggesting that social media platforms and users alike should be prepared to grapple with widespread misinformation when conducting business online.

Chapter 9 by Huaxia Li describes exogenous data sources that may be useful in governmental accounting, with a particular emphasis on governmental environmental, social, and governance outcomes. This includes foot traffic data, geopolitical and economic data, and measures of public sentiment toward governmental policy. A case study uses text mining to extract negative sentiment in response to New York City street cleanliness, providing novel information that may have implications for future legislation and city planning.

In Chapter 10, Steven Katz discusses flaws in existing predictors for movies' box office revenue and proposes two potential exogenous leading indicators: illegal movie downloads and activity on piracy-focused social media websites. In this framework, legitimate consumers' intent to view is proxied by tracking downloads and uploads on illegal torrent streams, while piracy-focused social media posts can be mined for their sentiment and volume of discussion to represent interest and viewer response at large.

Talha Afzal proposes a framework for mining customers' textual internet reviews in Chapter 11 by decomposing them into topics using machine-learning algorithms. While numerical reviews are straightforward to process, incorporating the context offered by customers' stated opinions has the potential to yield much more informative analytics.

In Chapter 12, Lanxin Jiang reviews past studies that analyze different aspects of accounting employees' LinkedIn profile pages, including profile photos, number of connections, and individual characteristics. LinkedIn's unique status as a combined social media platform and professional hub creates an unusual convergence of data that can inform studies ranging from the financial to the deeply psychological.

We are all adrift in a sea of data. An incredible amount is being generated, stored, and lost every day. Exogenous data analyses present opportunities to supplement traditional analyses by pulling something relevant out of the great shifting sea of data. Realizing that potential will require ingenuity, passion, and scientific rigor. This volume is an attempt to demonstrate and inspire all three of these traits in this tentative analytical realm. The world is full of interesting, useful information if we are prepared to look for it.

References

Gu, Y., Dai, J., & Vasarhelyi, M. A. (2023). Audit 4.0-based ESG assurance: An example of using satellite images on GHG emissions. *International Journal of Accounting Information Systems*, *50*(C), 100625.

Yoon, K., Kogan, A., Vasarhelyi, M. A., & Pearce, T. (2024). External nonfinancial measures in substantive analytical procedures: Contributions of weather information. *Journal of Information Systems*, *38*(2), 143–162.

Part One

Exogenous Data in Business Research

Chapter 1

Accounting's Resurrection: An Exploration of Future Business Reporting with Exogenous Data

Melissa A. Dardani

Rutgers Business School, USA

Abstract

As the relevance and utility of traditional accounting data decline, emerging types of data are proving valuable for predictive analytics. The accounting profession must contend with this data's increased capability to enhance business reporting in the face of antiquated reporting methods and standards. Simultaneously, a disconnect between financial reports and stakeholder needs arises from inherent information asymmetry and conflicting reporting priorities among stakeholders. Management tends to focus on factors affecting share price, while investors may be concerned with the horizon and sustainability of an investment's value. When coupled with the subjective nature of accounting principles and the limitations of auditing practices, concerns about the reliability and usefulness of modern financial reports are exacerbated. Despite the potential of predictive analytics to enhance business reporting, the profession is lagging with respect to the integration of these new, valuable data sources. Not embracing exogenous data and artificial intelligence for their utility seems inconsistent with the conceptual framework for financial reports, which defines the characteristics of useful financial information. Bridging this gap requires accounting practices, standards, and frameworks to evolve. This chapter is designed to encourage the exploration of expanded data sources and analytical methodologies in accounting and auditing by outlining conceptual

Exogenous Data in Accounting and Auditing in the Rutgers Series in Accounting Information Systems, 7–23

Published under exclusive licence by Emerald Publishing Limited
doi:10.1108/978-1-83608-734-220251001

considerations for this proposed enhancement to financial reporting and assurance.

Keywords: Audit; accounting; financial reporting; artificial intelligence; data analysis; predictive analysis; exogenous data; big data

Introduction

As the value of accounting data is diminishing in terms of its usefulness, timeliness, and understandability, other types of data are emerging as valuable sources of predictive information. The modern problem with financial reports should be attributed, at least in part, to the inherent dichotomy among various groups of stakeholders and their conflicted reporting priorities. For example, organizational management is primarily concerned with attributes that impact share price, such as analyst ratings and institutional interest, while prospective investors tend to focus on a company's fair market value and ability to generate returns over time. Paired with the asymmetrical nature of business information, this problem should be of concern to the accounting profession, especially when considering the subjective nature of accounting principles and the limitations of auditing practices. Consequently, today's business filings have questionable usefulness for stakeholders.

The increase in data and the ease of access to analytical tools present an opportunity to improve the business reporting cycle with predictive analytics, a shift that is already driving business performance and market price discovery. Analytics are used internally by market participants, such as companies and analysts, for growth, profitability, strategy, and planning. Analysts also use a wide array of market-related financial and non-financial data to explore investment performance.

Yet accounting measurements, perhaps rightfully, tend to favor fair representation and consistency in reporting and have, therefore, been slow to incorporate these new sources of available information. It is argued that current financial reporting standards and their historical focus are hindering the reports' usefulness by excluding significant, even material components of value (Schmidt et al., 2020). The field of computer science is expanding the usefulness of data through the creation of predictive models (Kureljusic & Karger, 2024). These models require data that capture the predictive qualities surrounding the prediction target. For financial markets, these sources come in a wide variety, but for reporting purposes, these abundant data sources must be filtered to include only those impacting actual value, rather than reactionary attributes that cause fickle swings in market price.

In light of the widely accessible nature of exogenous data today, simply continuing to ignore these external predictive variables leads to an inexcusable information gap between market performance and financial reporting. For example, as of the date of this writing, artificial intelligence computing leader NVIDIA is trading at a remarkable 68.29 12-month trailing price-earnings ratio, representing a value at odds with market averages and indicative of a perception of higher quality earnings.[1] Due to the inarticulate nature of public filings, even a thorough understanding of the application of accounting principles and their limitations in financial reporting is insufficient to reconcile this knowledge gap, an idea that seems out of sync with the objectives of financial reporting.[2]

Motivations

Traditional accounting reports have long been evaluated and scrutinized with respect to their usefulness as a source of market information (Ball & Brown, 1968; Beaver, 1968) and have since fallen farther from grace (Lev & Gu, 2016). This shift may be attributed to the static and backward-looking nature of financial reports, which make them less relevant to stakeholders who require timely information to make informed decisions. The standardized approach to these reports, while intended to increase consistency and comparability, may not capture the nuanced operational dynamics and innovative activities of modern businesses, thus limiting their usefulness in assessing future performance and growth potential (Alles et al., 2021). Furthermore, the inherently conflicted objectives of the issuers and users of these reports only exacerbate the utility concerns (Healy & Palepu, 2001; Ronen & Yaari, 2008).

The nascent availability of data, technology, and advances in analytical methodologies present an unprecedented opportunity to enhance the reliability and accuracy of financial predictions (Alles et al., 2021; Dai & Vasarhelyi, 2017; Vasarhelyi et al., 2015). The integration of big data analytics, artificial intelligence, and machine learning into financial analysis and reporting processes can significantly improve the areas of financial reports that rely on forward-looking judgments. These technologies allow for the processing and analysis of vast volumes of diverse data sources – from market trends and consumer behaviors to media sentiment and global economic indicators – that traditional accounting methods may overlook (Cheong et al., 2022).

The reluctance or failure to incorporate modern data and technology into accounting extends beyond the immediate risks of fraud and financial misstatement. It represents a broader missed opportunity for strategic insight and decision-making by stakeholders of the reporting entity (Appelbaum et al., 2017; Griffin & Wright, 2015). In an increasingly complex and volatile business environment, the

[1]*Source*: Yahoo Finance, August 14, 2024.

[2]According to the Financial Accounting Standards Board's (FASB) Conceptual Framework for Financial Reporting, Statement of Financial Accounting Concepts No. 8, "the objective of general purpose financial reporting is to provide financial information about the reporting entity that is useful to existing and potential investors, lenders, and other creditors in making decisions about providing resources to the entity."

ability to leverage predictive analytics and advanced data interpretation creates a critical competitive advantage.

The accounting profession's failure to adopt these developments represents a balancing act of issues of faithful representation and information asymmetry between companies and their stakeholders. The result of this failure is inferior information given what is attainable with modern technology (Vasarhelyi et al., 2015). This can have significant implications, such as misaligned expectations about a company's performance and prospects, and stock price volatility. When this misalignment yields favorable share price surprises, we refer to it as the "market game" with a few perceptive or fortuitous winners. When this misalignment yields unfavorable share price surprises that indicate a more systemic exploitation, it risks becoming a catalyst for a market collapse (Laux & Leuz, 2009; Plantin et al., 2008; Ryan, 2008).

Conflicted Dichotomy of Financial Report Stakeholders

The evolution of the digital economy and the rise of intangible assets, such as brand value and intellectual property, exacerbate the gap between traditional accounting measures and the perception of value in today's marketplaces (Hand & Lev, 2003; Lev, 2001; Lev & Gu, 2016). The intrinsic value of these intangible assets is difficult to quantify with traditional accounting methods, leading to a widening discrepancy between a company's book value and its market value. As businesses evolve in complexity and operate in rapidly changing environments, the static and historical nature of traditional financial reporting struggles to remain relevant, rendering it less effective as a tool for predicting future performance and assessing real-time value (Cheong et al., 2022).

Consider, for example, fair value measurement. While intended to provide a standardized approach to disclose investment valuations, the resulting measurement requires significant judgment and estimation inputs (Landsman, 2007; Laux & Leuz, 2009; Ryan, 2008). This subjectivity arises from the challenges in determining the fair value of assets that do not have active market prices, particularly complex financial instruments and intangible assets (Merton, 1987). Estimations based on future cash flows, discount rates, and market comparables introduce variability and potential biases into financial reporting. This subjective area of accounting can also create variability in interpretation and the possibility of significant discrepancies between reported values and actual market conditions. The reliance on fair value measurements in a complex business environment emphasizes the need for rigorous valuation methodologies and transparent disclosure of assumptions.

The danger of subjectivity in accounting is enhanced by the conflict introduced by the agency relationship between a company and its stakeholders (Healy & Palepu, 2001; Ronen & Yaari, 2008). This conflict arises because managers (agents) may have different incentives and objectives than shareholders (principals), leading to potential manipulation of financial reporting. The subjective nature of certain accounting estimates, such as fair value measurements, provides managers with discretion in the valuation process. This discretion can be exploited to present a more favorable view of the company's financial performance and position. Moreover, the inherent information asymmetry between managers and stakeholders further exacerbates the problem since stakeholders may not have access to the same level of information to assess the reliability of subjective accounting estimates (Alles et al., 2021). The combination of agency conflicts and subjectivity in accounting can undermine the integrity and reliability of financial reporting, leading to potential misallocation of resources and erosion of trust in the capital markets.

The Value of New Data

By leveraging new analytical tools and data sources, financial analysts and companies can develop more nuanced and predictive models of business performance and valuation. For example, predictive analytics can identify emerging market opportunities and risks before they are reflected in financial results, providing a competitive advantage in decision-making. While this notion is formally introduced in the seminal works of Ball and Brown (1968) and Beaver (1968), developments in computing power, data storage, and accessibility make formalized techniques for predictive measurement possible. For example, machine-learning algorithms can improve the accuracy of forecasting by learning from vast datasets by identifying patterns and relationships that human analysts and traditional time-series methods may miss. The accessibility of this emerging capability commands the accounting profession to embrace these technologies to push the profession further.

Large and diverse data sets are required to obtain quality, applicable machine-learning models. Consider an analogy to the auditing profession, in which sufficient appropriate evidence is required to provide a reasonable basis for an auditor's opinion (AS 1105). Reliable predictive analytics require adequate amounts of relevant and reliable data to produce meaningful results that reflect the dynamic nature of the prediction target's environment (Domingos, 2012; Halevy et al., 2009; Vasarhelyi et al., 2015). In comparing various statistical and machine-learning algorithms for fraud detection, Perols (2011), Cecchini et al. (2010), and Fanning and Cogger (1998) demonstrate the need for large and diverse training sets for training and validating robust and generalizable models. Perhaps one of the greatest challenges in model development is accessing and preparing useful sources of information.

Insufficient, low-quality, or non-representative data can lead to biased, inaccurate, or unreliable outcomes. Internal data sources alone will not provide the circumstantial context of the economy, industry, and financial market behavior that must be considered for a holistic prediction model. This data quality consideration is exacerbated by the profession's general lack of understanding about machine-learning methodologies. Yet auditors' risk assessment mentality can aid in their ability to consider relevant sources of information required for robust analyses. This research introduces a framework for the incorporation of relevant data into the enhanced predictive reporting cycle.

Research has increasingly shown the utility of external, exogenous data in accounting analytics (Brown-Liburd et al., 2019; Cheong et al., 2022;

Li et al., 2024; Yan et al., 2023; Yoon et al., 2015). For example, Yoon et al. (2024) employ weather in substantive analytical procedures for revenue. The relationship between the sentiment of company disclosures via social media and earnings performance is studied by Kim et al. (2022). Bao et al. (2020) utilize news articles, analyst reports, and social media sentiment to enhance their model's ability to detect accounting fraud in publicly traded U.S. firms. Similarly, Bertomeu et al. (2021) use news articles and analysts' reports to improve their machine-learning model's performance in detecting financial misstatements. Other studies employ external data to assess various factors affecting accounting outcomes, such as job postings, employee reviews, CEO property records, luxury asset ownership, management education, and employment history (Bonsall et al., 2017; Bushman et al., 2018; Choi et al., 2013). These sources all have the potential to provide valuable insights and improve the predictive power of machine-learning models, but their predictive relevance should be assessed prior to incorporation.

The accounting profession may not yet be prepared to embrace the use of new data and methodologies due to a lack of a relevant framework and standards. Its professionals also generally lack the skills and expertise to interpret and apply the results effectively (Brown-Liburd et al., 2015). Thus, the shift toward predictive analytics for accounting requires a transformation in the role of accountants and auditors with assistance from professionals, such as data scientists, as part of the financial reporting or assurance team. While impossible to ignore given the context of this chapter, this highly relevant concern is acknowledged as a limitation but is beyond the scope of this research.

Preventative Action Against Future Failures

The accounting profession has historically seen progress in response to failures that shook public confidence. Following the onset of the Great Depression, the Securities Acts of 1933 and 1934 were passed through legislation to reset this perspective, leading to the conception of the Securities and Exchange Commission (SEC). In its own words, the SEC, which maintains the public record of company filings, has a mission to protect investors; maintain fair, orderly, and efficient markets; and facilitate capital formation.[3] The public company filings they maintain are guided by U.S. Generally Accepted Accounting Principles (GAAP). The savings and loan crisis of the 1980s led to the Financial Institutions Reform, Recovery, and Enforcement Act of 1989, which mandated, among other things, increased accounting requirements. Following the accounting failures of the early 2000s, the Sarbanes-Oxley Act of 2002 (SOX) and the Public Company Accounting Oversight Board (PCAOB) were formed to increase transparency and oversight in accounting and governance and to enhance the audit profession.

Table 1.1 outlines recent consequential modifications to GAAP, aimed at improving transparency and financial reporting. The goal of this chapter is to communicate the need for the profession to be proactive in adapting technology

[3]https://www.sec.gov/about/mission

that further the objectives for financial reporting and to promote education about these technologies. The value of data from endogenous and exogenous sources is its ability to enhance the predictive capability of accounting information, which depends on unfiltered, disaggregated data access (Alles et al., 2021). A modified reporting framework that emphasizes control-based, customizable analytics is introduced, and its intersection with the existing reporting framework, professional governing bodies, standards, and regulations is discussed.

Table 1.1. Recent Significant Changes to U.S. GAAP.

Topic	**Standard**	**Issue/(Update) Date**	**Description**
Entity Consolidation	ASC 810	(December 2003)[4]	Improves the transparency of reporting relationships with variable interest entities and provides more guidance on when these entities should be consolidated
Fair Value Accounting	ASC 820	September 2006[5]	Defines fair value, establishes a framework for measuring fair value, and requires disclosures about fair value measurements
Revenue Recognition	ASC 606	May 2014[6]	Replaces various industry-specific guidelines with a five-step model aimed to improve comparability and reduce complexity in revenue reporting across industries
Lease Accounting	ASC 842	February 2016[7]	Increases transparency and comparability by requiring lessees to recognize almost all leases on the balance sheet

[4]See FASB Interpretation No. 46 – an Interpretation of ARB No. 51 (Updated as ASC 810).
[5]See FASB Statement No. 157 – Fair Value Measurement (Updated as ASC 820).
[6]See FASB Update 2014-09 – Revenue from Contracts with Customers (Topic 606).
[7]See FASB Update 2016-02 – Leases (Topic 842).

Considerations for the Proposed Framework

The incorporation of data from varying sources into predictive accounting models requires a framework that supports the logical development of the model from data mining to machine-based outputs. These outputs include classifiers, predictors, dual-use supervised learners, pattern detection models, clustering models, and knowledge-based systems (Sutton et al., 2016). During the problem identification and data collection stages, the desired result can drive the selection of both data and models. These are particularly vulnerable points in the process because the objectives of stakeholder and management may be weighed against each other. Since each model employs different measurement techniques, the process of converting raw data from the Global Datasphere[8] may involve steps to parse and cleanse the data, normalize or standardize the scale of the data, or engineer new features from the data.

Machine-learning methodologies are employed through algorithms with various "settings" or configure options that impact the model's behavior. Thus, the accounting profession will need to expand its skills or make room for technical experts to aid in the process of providing some level of assurance for data quality and selection, as well as model validation. This assurance may include procedures, such as the review of a log of different decision points, the decisions made and the analyst's rationale, the appropriateness of the explanatory variables, and the model validation mechanisms and robustness checks, to name a few.

Stakeholder Objectives

Considering the inherent agency relationship that exists between company management and its stakeholders, data selection and model development should balance their priorities but should never subordinate its goal to the needs of either party. In determining the goal of machine-based accounting and assurance, the general objective will drive the set of professional standards on which insights can be drawn. This is not to suggest that existing standards and guidance are sufficient to handle the incorporation of these techniques into financial reporting since these areas are still ripe for development.

Multipartite Data

The International Data Corporation estimates the volume of data created, captured, and replicated in the world, or the so called Global Datasphere, to be 181 zettabytes[9] by 2025 (Statista). Within this data are external signals with varying degrees of predictive capabilities. It is important to be able to parse the Global Datasphere logically to identify these predictive signals. It is further important to be able to develop procedures to test the strength of the relationship between

[8]Defined by Statista as the total amount of data created, captured, copied, and consumed globally (https://www.statista.com/statistics/871513/worldwide-data-created/).
[9]1 zettabyte equals 10^{12} gigabytes.

those identified signals to rule out weak predictors or assign importance factors to those incorporated into a predictive model. While generally not trained in the computer or data sciences, the accountant or auditor may be well suited to imagine the universe of data relevant to solve business prediction questions.

To illustrate this point, consider the risk-assessment mentality required under the PCAOB auditing standards. AS 2110 requires the auditor to consider risks from various external sources when performing risk assessment procedures, including "conditions in the company's industry and environment, and company-specific factors, such as the nature of the company, its activities, and internal control over financial reporting." Here, the auditor can serve as a sort of financial architect in designing machine learning models. As such, the profession will require either accountants with specialized knowledge in data science or the assistance of another professional who possesses these skills.

Technological Capabilities and Accounting Processes

According to the FASB, the objective of general purpose financial reporting is to provide financial information about a reporting entity that is useful in making decisions about providing resources to the entity.[10] Useful information is that which is relevant and faithful in its representations. Usefulness is enhanced by its comparability, verifiability, timeliness, and understandability.[11] Machines can be used to substantiate human judgment for financial reporting, with their ability to efficiently produce superior predictive capabilities. Yet, the profession will need to mitigate the loss of understandability with education, training, and a new group of accounting support professionals.

Consider also the objective of auditing, which is to express an opinion on the fairness with which a company's financials present, in all material respects, the company's financial position, results of operations, and cash flows in conformity with GAAP.[12] The respective goals of analytical procedures are applied in the risk assessment and substantive procedures phases. During the risk assessment, the auditor seeks to provide a reasonable basis for identifying and assessing the risks of material misstatement due to error or fraud and design further audit procedures, while substantive analytical procedures involve evaluating financial information through a study of plausible relationships of both financial and nonfinancial data.[13] Both involve the analysis of relationships within the entity (endogenous) and external to the entity but within its economic, operational, or regulatory environment (exogenous) (Cheong et al., 2022).

---

[10]Financial Accounting Standards Board (FASB) Concept Statement No. 8, Chapter 1, The Objective of General Purpose Financial Reporting.
[11]FASB Concept Statement No. 8, Chapter 3, Qualitative Characteristics of Useful Financial Information.
[12]PCAOB AS 1001: Responsibilities and Functions of the Independent Auditor.
[13]PCAOB AS 2110: Identifying and Assessing Risks of Material Misstatement, and AS 2305: Substantive Analytical Procedures, respectively.

The Resurrected Business Reporting Cycle

Assuming acceptance of the notion that machine-based functions have a place in accounting and auditing, a framework is proposed to aid in understanding the overall process and for the profession to begin considering a logical update of and append to the existing sets of standards relevant to accountants and auditors. First, consider the proposed flow of information for a predictor model as shown in Fig. 1.1.

Data are extracted from multipartite sources that can be classified as either endogenous or exogenous. Endogenous data are generally easier to manage since the data collection can be controlled with validation checks or other similar measures and structured in a way conducive for the desired analysis. Mining techniques can be employed to identify and decipher relationships of the variables with the prediction target. Once the attributes are filtered to some degree and preliminarily preprocessed, they can be loaded into a database and utilized for predictive modeling. Here, formalized procedures to identify relationships in the data occur, and the analyst will be required to select model inputs and hyperparameters. The model development should include validation and robustness tests,

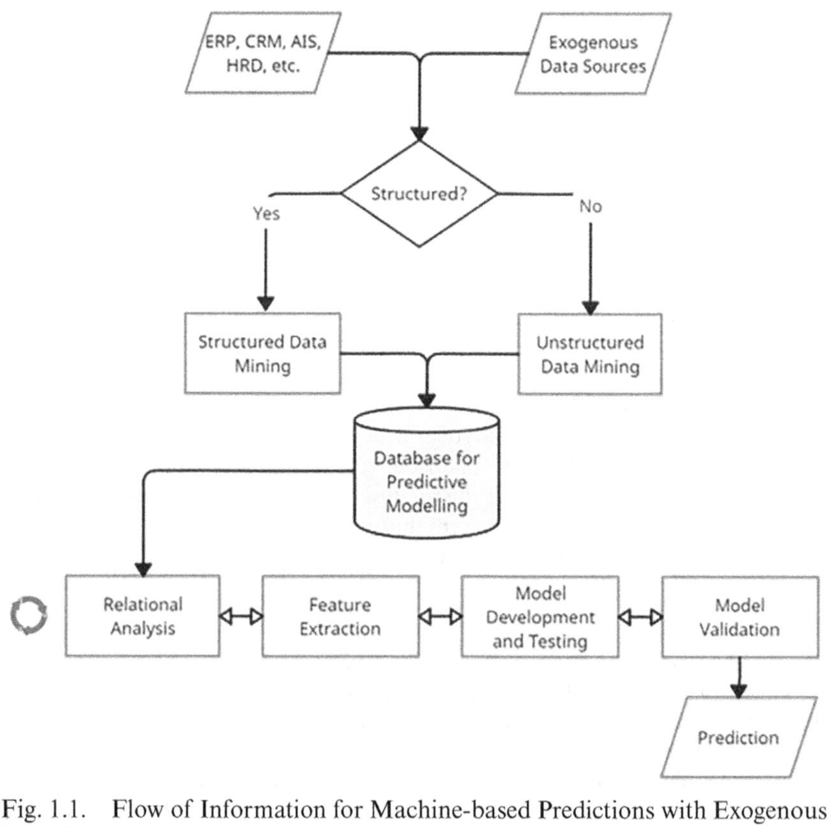

Fig. 1.1. Flow of Information for Machine-based Predictions with Exogenous Data Sources.

meaning that the model should be generalizable beyond the test set. This requires input variables that are significant to the prediction target and the use of appropriate methods for the given task.

Continuous Reporting

Alles et al. (2021) design a new framework for application-based reporting that is continuous and customizable to users' needs, such as mode of access, the ability to filter on relevant information, and a disaggregated view of the data. A static view of the machine-based environment lacks the relevance factors identified by Alles et al. (2021), such as a contemporaneous flow of real-time results. The quality of information produced in this data flow depends on the processes to collect and organize raw data from operations. A digital business environment with system interoperability, automation, and virtualization is the foundation for this type of data collection (Kagermann et al., 2013).

A more involved application of the machine-based environment is the incorporation of predicted asset or liability values on a continuous report of financial position. The methodology to produce these predicted values is an area in need of further research. Furthermore, if incorporated into financial reporting, the assurance profession will need to expand to assess data quality, model development, and validation to protect the integrity and guide the development of the continuous reporting framework.

Fig. 1.2 provides a continuum of information cadence orthogonal to the stakeholders concerned with the data. Certain data procedures are required to present data to stakeholders irrespective of the periodic or continuous nature to ensure that the business reports faithfully represent the financial activity and economic position of the company. Internal and external users are concerned with different types of information, and the sensitivity of external users should be considered when developing reporting and disclosure procedures.

Continuous reporting involves providing data on a contemporaneous basis in addition to periodic "snapshots." This continuous information would allow a user with basic training in understanding data and financial reports to bridge the continuous data to the periodic snapshots with limited procedures. This requires a level of disaggregated access, a sort of disentanglement of financial information that is currently lost in aggregated and consolidated report. The entity may rely on automated recording processes plus key performance and exception indicators to ensure that continuous disclosures coincide with reported figures as needed.

The valuation of certain assets or liabilities is not comprised solely of their current, measurable cash flows. Predictive models require a collection of interrelated variables to derive meaningful outputs. In these instances, exogenous data may be incorporated into the business cycle to enhance the predictive value of the company's internal data. A description of classifications of prospective exogenous data sources is described in Table 1.2, and a framework for predictive external signals in the business cycle is outlined in Fig. 1.3. The bracketed numbers in Table 1.2 correspond to the number labels in Fig. 1.3 and suggest use cases for the various categories of data in the business activity cycle.

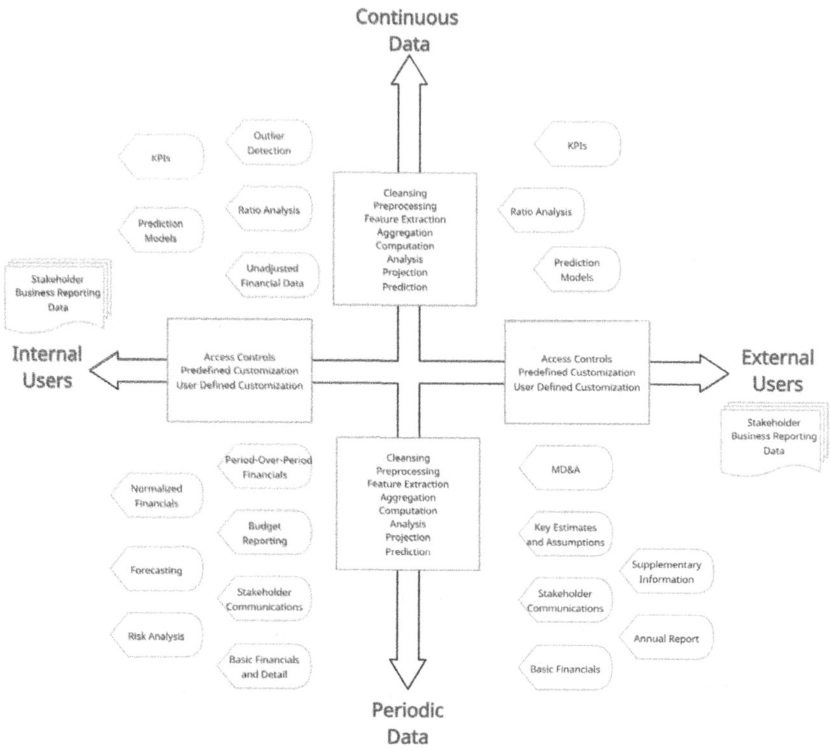

Fig. 1.2. Example Continuous Reporting Schema.

Table 1.2. Classifications of Exogenous Data Sources.

Exogenous Data Source	Description	Categorization(s)
Extended Internal Data	Extends the usefulness of internal company data	[1] Operational and Industry
		[2] People
		[3] Compliance/risk
		[4] Inventory/manufacturing
Specialized, Collected Data	Datasets collected for unique purposes	[5] Geospatial
		[5] Weather
		[5] Internet tracking
		[5] Other
Stakeholder Connection Data	Data that describe internal and external stakeholder	[6] Customer data
		[7] Social media
		[8] Market data
		[9] News data

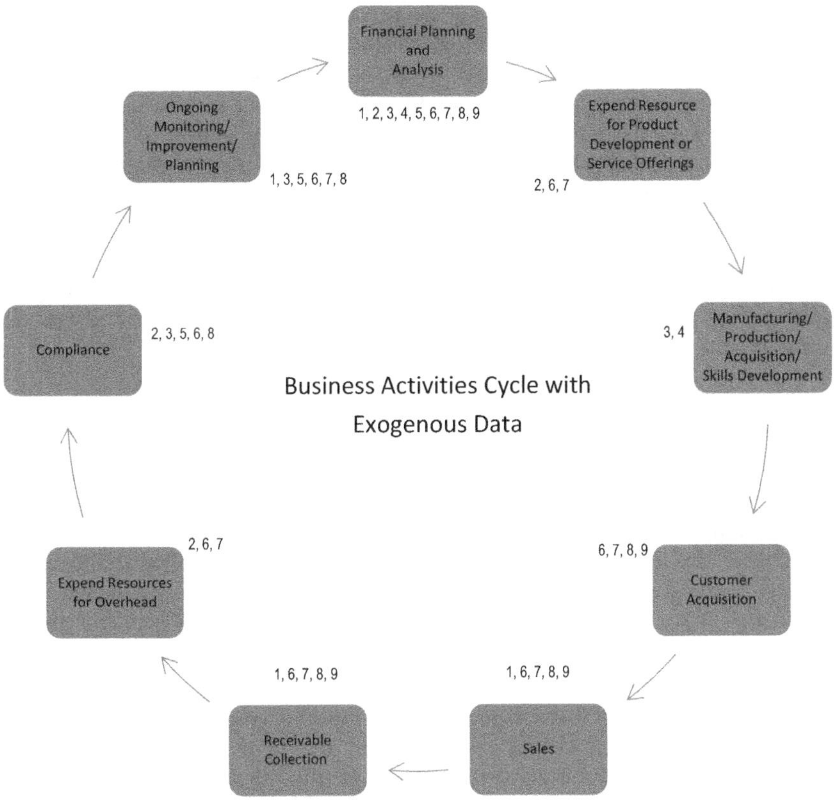

Fig. 1.3. Business Activities Cycle with Exogenous Data.

Continuous Monitoring and Assurance

With continuous data comes the ability to monitor continuously, and with continuous reporting comes the need to provide continuous assurance. Continuous monitoring, while traditionally used internally to flag anomalous transactions in real time and to track performance indicators, trends, and patterns, will have an expanded role under the proposed framework. Ensuring a fair classification of transactions in real time is necessary to ensure understandability in continuous reporting. This can be accomplished through knowledge-based systems, such as expert systems, intelligent decision aids, intelligent decision support systems, and intelligent agents (Sutton et al., 2016).

The Need for New Assurance

Since the framework calls for the incorporation of updated measurements, procedures involving exogenous and endogenous data sources and machine learning models, a new form of assurance is required to safeguard all interested parties. Given what is at stake with real time reporting and machine-based measurements, standards and guidance are necessary components to achieve some acceptable level of control by the profession. This must include procedures to determine data source veracity and appropriateness for inclusion in the model, model development including training and testing, and model validation on new, unseen data.

The machine-based models will diminish understandability of the outputs pushed to financial reports that are relied on by stakeholders. This clearly requires an extension of the accounting and assurance profession to include a new variety of skills or professionals. Yet, to develop and provide assurance surrounding machine-based accounting also requires an expansion of skills to aid in this process, calling for additional education and training. Accountants must either gain a new set of technical competencies that extend to data science or a new group professionals with this training will be necessary.

Conclusion

The utility of accounting data is moribund in an increasingly technical and digitized business environment due to its non-timely nature, lack of understandability and comparability, and backward-looking focus (Dardani et al., 2024; Lev & Gu, 2016). This is exacerbated by the inherent information asymmetry that exists between a company's management and its stakeholders. Given the increases in data accessibility, storage, processing, and predictive methodologies, the profession has an opportunity to improve the existing, antiquated reporting and assurance frameworks. This opportunity would wisely be applied to the subjective areas of the accounting framework while transitioning toward a real-time reporting and assurance mechanism as envisioned by Alles et al. (2021).

At the center of the framework proposed in this chapter is a consistent flow of data from internal and external sources. This will allow for contemporaneous updates to and refining of predictive models. All that considered, the incorporation of predictive models into a reporting framework will require a revitalization of the profession. The spirit of the standards may convey integrity and usefulness in the financial reporting framework, but more specific guidance must be given to ensure quality in data and model development. Furthermore, the technical competencies of accountants will either need to be extended to include principals of data science or a new variant of accounting professionals with this type of training and expertise is necessary.

References

Alles, M. G., Dai, J., & Vasarhelyi, M. A. (2021). Reporting 4.0: Business reporting for the age of mass customization. *Journal of Emerging Technologies in Accounting*, *18*(1), 1–15. https://doi.org/10.2308/jeta-10764

Appelbaum, D., Kogan, A., Vasarhelyi, M., & Yan, Z. (2017). Impact of business analytics and enterprise systems on managerial accounting. *International Journal of Accounting Information Systems*, *25*(May), 29–44. https://doi.org/10.1016/j.accinf.2017.03.003

AS 1105: Audit Evidence. (2010). *Translated by Public Company Accounting Oversight Board.*

Ball, R., & Brown, P. (1968). An empirical evaluation of accounting income numbers. *Journal of Accounting Research*, *6*(2), 159–178. https://doi.org/10.2307/2490232

Bao, Y., Ke, B., Li, B., Yu, Y. J., & Zhang, J. (2020). Detecting accounting fraud in publicly traded U.S. firms using a machine learning approach. *Journal of Accounting Research*, *58*(1), 199–235.

Beaver, W. H. (1968). The information content of annual earnings announcements. *Journal of Accounting Research*, *6*(2), 67–92.

Bertomeu, J., Cheynel, E., Floyd, E., & Pan, W. (2021). Using machine learning to detect misstatements. *Review of Accounting Studies*, *26*(2), 468–519. https://link.springer.com/article/10.1007/s11142-020-09563-8, https://doi.org/10.1007/s11142-020-09563-8

Bonsall, S. B., Holzman, E. R., & Miller, B. P. (2017). Managerial ability and credit risk assessment. *Management Science*, *63*(5), 1271–1656.

Brown-Liburd, H., Cheong, A., Vasarhelyi, M. A., & Wang, X. (2019). Measuring with exogenous data (MED), and government economic monitoring (GEM). *Journal of Emerging Technologies in Accounting*, *16*(1), 1–19.

Brown-Liburd, H., Issa, H., & Lombardi, D. (2015). Behavioral implications of Big Data's impact on audit judgement and decision making and future research directions. *Accounting Horizons*, *29*(2), 451–468.

Bushman, R. M., Davidson, R. H., Dey, A., & Smith, A. (2018). Bank CEO materialism: Risk controls, culture and tail risk. *Journal of Accounting & Economics*, *65*(1), 191–220. https://dx.doi.org/10.1016/j.jacceco.2017.11.014, https://doi.org/10.1016/j.jacceco.2017.11.014

Cecchini, M., Aytug, H., Koehler, G. J., & Pathak, P. (2010). Detecting management fraud in public companies. *Management Science*, *56*(7), 1146–1160.

Cheong, A., Duan, H. K., Huang, Q., & Zhang, C. A. (2022). The rise of accounting: Making accounting information relevant again with exogenous data. *Journal of Emerging Technologies in Accounting*, *19*(1), 1–20. https://doi.org/10.2308/jeta-10812

Choi, J.-H., Choi, S., Hogan, C. E., & Lee, J. (2013). The effect of human resource investment in internal control on the disclosure of internal control weaknesses. *Auditing: A Journal of Practice and Theory*, *32*(4), 169–199.

Dai, J., & Vasarhelyi, M. A. (2017). Toward blockchain-based accounting and assurance. *The Journal of Information Systems*, *31*(3), 5–21. https://doi.org/10.2308/isys-51804

Dardani, M. A., Gu, Y., Hu, H., Medinets, A. F., Palmon, D., & Vasarhelyi, M. A. (2024). Rethinking the standard-setting process: The role of intangibles. *Journal of Emerging Technologies in Accounting*, *21*(1), 9–28. https://doi.org/10.2308/JETA-2024-001

Domingos, P. (2012). A few useful things to know about machine learning. *Communications of the ACM*, *55*(10), 78–87. http://dl.acm.org/citation.cfm?id=2347755, https://doi.org/10.1145/2347736.2347755

Fanning, K. M., & Cogger, K. O. (1998). Neural network detection of management fraud using published financial data. *International Journal of Intelligent Systems in Accounting, Finance & Management*, *7*, 21–41.

Griffin, P. A., & Wright, A. M. (2015). Commentaries on Big Data's importance for accounting and auditing. *Accounting Horizons*, *29*(2), 377–379. https://doi.org/10.2308/acch-51066

Halevy, A., Norvig, P., & Pereira, F. (2009). The unreasonable effectiveness of data. *IEEE Intelligent Systems*, *23*(2), 8–12.

Hand, J., & Lev, B. (2003). *Intangible assets – Values, measures and risks*. Oxford University Press.

Healy, P. M., & Palepu, K. G. (2001). Information asymmetry, corporate disclosure, and the capital markets: A review of the empirical disclosure literature. *Journal of Accounting and Economics*, *31*(1–3), 405–440.

Kagermann, H., Wahlster, W., & Helbig, J. (2013). *Securing the future of German manufacturing industry: Recommendations for implementing the Strategic Initiative*

Industrie 4.0 – Final Report of the Industrie 4.0 Working Group. Federal Ministry of Education and Research. https://www.din.de/resource/blob/76902/e8cac883f42bf28536e7e8165993f1fd/recommendations-for-implementing-industry-4-0-data.pdf

Kim, J., Lim, J.-H., & Yoon, K. (2022). How do the content, format, and tone of Twitter-based corporate disclosure vary depending on earnings performance? *International Journal of Accounting Information Systems*, *47*, 100574. https://dx.doi.org/10.1016/j.accinf.2022.100574, https://doi.org/10.1016/j.accinf.2022.100574

Kureljusic, M., & Karger, E. (2024). Forecasting in financial accounting with artificial intelligence – A systematic literature review and future research agenda. *Journal of Applied Accounting Research*, *25*(1), 81–104.

Landsman, W. R. (2007). Is fair value accounting information relevant and reliable? Evidence from capital market research. *Accounting and Business Research*, *37*(sup1), 19–30. https://www.tandfonline.com/doi/abs/10.1080/00014788.2007.9730081, https://doi.org/10.1080/00014788.2007.9730081

Laux, C., & Leuz, C. (2009). The crisis of fair-value accounting: Making sense of the recent debate. *Accounting, Organizations and Society*, *34*(6), 826–834. https://dx.doi.org/10.1016/j.aos.2009.04.003, https://doi.org/10.1016/j.aos.2009.04.003

Lev, B. (2001). *Intangibles – Management, measurement, and reporting*. The Brookings Institution.

Lev, B., & Gu, F. (2016). *The end of accounting and the path forward for investors and managers*. John Wiley & Sons, Inc.

Li, H., de Freitas, M. M., Lee, H., & Vasarhelyi, M. (2024). *Enhancing continuous auditing with large language models: AI-assisted real-time accounting information cross-verification*. https://dx.doi.org/10.2139/ssrn.4692960

Merton, R. C. (1987). A simple model of capital market equilibrium with incomplete information. *The Journal of Finance*, *42*(3), 483–808.

Perols, J. (2011). Financial statement fraud detection: An analysis of statistical and machine learning algorithms. *AUDITING: A Journal of Practice & Theory*, *30*(2), 19–50. https://search.proquest.com/docview/869506859, https://doi.org/10.2308/ajpt-50009

Plantin, G., Sapra, H., & Shin, H. S. (2008). Marking-to-market: Panacea or Pandora's box? *Journal of Accounting Research*, *46*(2), 435–460.

Ronen, J., & Yaari, V. (2008). *Earnings management: Emerging insights in theory, practice, and research*. Springer.

Ryan, S. G. (2008). Accounting in and for the subprime crisis. *The Accounting Review*, *83*(6), 1605–1638. https://www.jstor.org/stable/30243808, https://doi.org/10.2308/accr.2008.83.6.1605

Schmidt, P. J., Riley, J., & Swanson Church, K. (2020). Investigating accountants' resistance to move beyond Excel and adopt new data analytics technology. *Accounting Horizons*, *34*(4), 165–180.

Statista. *Volume of data/information created, captured, copied, and consumed worldwide from 2010 to 2020, with forecasts from 2021 to 2025*. https://www.statista.com/statistics/871513/worldwide-data-created/#:~:text=The%20total%20amount%20of%20data,replicated%20reached%20a%20new%20high

Sutton, S. G., Holt, M., & Arnold, V. (2016). "The reports of my death are greatly exaggerated" – Artificial intelligence research in accounting. *International Journal of Accounting Information Systems*, *22*, 60–73. https://dx.doi.org/10.1016/j.accinf.2016.07.005, https://doi.org/10.1016/j.accinf.2016.07.005

Vasarhelyi, M. A., Kogan, A., & Tuttle, B. M. (2015). Big Data in accounting: An overview. *Accounting Horizons*, *29*(2), 381–396. https://doi.org/10.2308/acch-51071

Yan, Z., Appelbaum, D., Kogan, A., Vasarhelyi, M. A. (2023). Teaching predictive audit data analytic techniques: Time-series forecasting with transactional and exogenous data. *Journal of Emerging Technologies in Accounting, 20*(1), 169–194. https://doi.org/10.2308/jeta-2020-018

Yoon, K., Hoogduin, L., & Zhang, L. (2015). Big Data as complementary audit evidence. *Accounting Horizons, 29*(2), 431–438. https://search.proquest.com/docview/1695019756, https://doi.org/10.2308/acch-51076

Yoon, K., Kogan, A., Vasarhelyi, M. A., & Pearce, T. (2024). External nonfinancial measures in substantive analytical procedures: Contributions of weather information. *Journal of Information Systems, 38*(2), 143–162.

Chapter 2

Exogenous Data Using Large Language Models like ChatGPT

Irina Jie Bao[a] *and Benita Gullkvist*[b]

[a] *Rutgers Business School, USA*
[b] *University of Vaasa, Finland*

Abstract

This chapter explores the role and potential of Large Language Models (LLMs) like ChatGPT to process exogenous data for various applications through illustrations with GPTs and several useful plug-ins, as well as a practical use case. Exogenous data refer to data external to organization's traditional, usually internal, financial data collection processes and may include social media, online searches, networks, and news media. The aim of utilizing exogenous data in accounting and auditing is to complement traditional financial reporting and assurance methods by offering a more nuanced and comprehensive view of a company's activities, as well as enhancing the quality of reporting and audit processes. Stakeholders can improve their decision-making processes by integrating publicly available exogenous data into their analyses. Although exogenous data can provide valuable insights beyond traditional financial statements, acquiring such data might be expensive and time-consuming. Therefore, there is a need for effective tools like ChatGPT to facilitate the process of extracting and analyzing data.

Keywords: Exogenous data; large language models; ChatGPT; generative AI; financial reporting and assurance; ESG assurance; business measurement; fraud detection

Exogenous Data in Accounting and Auditing in the Rutgers Series in Accounting Information Systems, 25–47

doi:10.1108/978-1-83608-734-220251002

1. Introduction to Exogenous Data and ChatGPT

1.1. Exogenous Data in Business

The value of exogenous data is inevitably increasing (Brown-Liburd et al., 2019; Cheong et al., 2022). Scholars emphasize the importance of supplementing company-generated data with a vast quantity of exogenous data. A variety of exogenous data can be used for measuring and assuring businesses (for overviews, see Appelbaum et al., 2023; Cheong et al., 2022). Examples of exogenous data include social media data, videos from cameras and drones, weather information, online search trends, web traffic data, social network data, and data from news media. Exogenous data can be collected on a real-time basis from sensors, search results, and target advertisement history (Cheong et al., 2022). Below, we review contemporary research that focuses on the potential uses of exogenous data in financial reporting and assurance, ESG (environmental, social, and governance) assurance, business measurement, and fraud detection.

Enhancing financial reporting and assurance: Exogenous data, including social media, online searches, and news media, introduce new avenues for business measurement and information assurance. Auditors are encouraged to use exogenous data to perform their risk assessment (Appelbaum et al., 2023). The use of exogenous data also enables more dynamic and real-time financial reporting and assurance processes. For example, auditors may get a better understanding of material business events, such as hacking incidents, environmental disasters, and geo-political conflicts, when using exogenous data for real-time monitoring of business activities (Cheong et al., 2022). However, auditors should validate data veracity and data provenance when using exogenous audit evidence (Appelbaum et al., 2023).

Supporting ESG disclosure and performance evaluation: The use of exogenous data is proposed to complement sustainability reporting. Exogenous data may play a crucial role in evaluating companies' sustainability performance by offering insights into environmental footprints, social interactions, and governance standards (Appelbaum et al., 2023; Cheong et al., 2022). For example, external data from ESG ratings can be used as a supplementary audit reference in the evaluation of corporate sustainability performance (Appelbaum et al., 2023). Using social media data, environmental information near a factory could be obtained, extracted, analyzed, and further used as audit evidence to verify sustainability reports (Gu et al., 2023a). Data are also needed to measure a company's sustainable risks and to assess how well the company manages those risks. However, there are challenges related to fragmented and inconsistent data sources (Appelbaum et al., 2023).

Improving business measurement with real-time data: Cheong et al. (2022) argue that contemporary financial reporting and assurance have limited value in firm valuation in the digital world and that sources of more diversified, exogenous information facilitate new types of business measurement and information validation, such as continuous measurements of real-time processes (Huang et al., 2022). The emergence of various forms of exogenous data as proxies for business process measurement provides potential sources for state-of-the-art business reporting. For example, weather data could be used to predict sales revenue (Yoon et al., 2024), and social media posts could predict future changes in product sales (Dardani et al., 2024). Real-time exogenous data from sources like Google Maps and similarweb.com can assess business activities for both physical and e-commerce stores. Dardani et al. (2024) propose that new business measurements with future-oriented guidance could be developed based on exogenous data. Thus, business decisions are not only influenced by traditional financial information, but various exogenous information can also determine the decision-making process.

Fraud detection and misconduct identification: In cases of fraud or misconduct, internal data often provide insufficient evidence. Exogenous data, such as social network information, can reveal cash flows, transaction contexts, and connections to counterparties, aiding efficient detection (Cheong et al., 2022). Furthermore, exogenous data, such as satellite images from a third party, are less likely to be manipulated and could be used for assurance purposes in sustainability reports (Gu et al., 2023a).

Moreover, exogenous data enhance stakeholders' ability to make informed decisions by providing a more comprehensive view of the company's performance and risks. For example, auditors can leverage exogenous data in their assessments, especially for ESG disclosures, by verifying them against established audit goals and regulatory norms. Investors are interested in more than the information obtainable in publicly available 10-K reports (Alles et al., 2022). For example, information about the company's employees, employee turnover rate, and loyalty can be derived from job service sites like Indeed or Glassdoor.com (Alles et al., 2022). Thus, various stakeholders can enhance their decision-making process by integrating publicly available exogenous data, such as environmental footprint information, diversity and equality insights, and product popularity measures from various online platforms, into their analyses. Stakeholders can significantly benefit from using exogenous data to make informed decisions, predict market trends, and identify investment opportunities.

Overall, prior studies emphasize the growing value of exogenous data in financial reporting, investment decision-making, and ESG assessments in providing a more holistic view of a business's operations, sustainability, and market position. However, prior research also addresses the challenges involved in the collection, analysis, and integration of exogenous data with existing financial and non-financial data. While social media and other online sources offer real-time information, the tasks of cleaning, linking, and extracting useful information from exogenous data (big data) sources require significant computational resources and expertise. Duan et al. (2022) note that the voluminous, unstructured, and often textual nature of exogenous data presents a huge challenge for auditors in terms of quantitative analysis and integration of the data into the auditing workflow in a continuous manner. Furthermore, acquiring such data might be expensive and time-consuming. The case of Luckin Coffee (Cheong et al., 2022) illustrates that investigators collected exogenous data through labor-intensive manual processes. LLMs like ChatGPT could facilitate the automated extraction of exogenous data.

1.2. LLMs and ChatGPT

In 2018, the introduction of transformer-based architectures (Vaswani et al., 2017) marked a significant advancement in natural language processing (NLP). As a result, models like Google's BERT, OpenAI's ChatGPT, and Meta's LLaMa were developed. These LLMs use neural networks with billions and later trillions of parameters, and they are trained on vast amounts of text data through self-supervised learning to process and understand natural language. The algorithms learn semantic and syntactic relationships among words from a large volume of texts. This allows them to consider context, including other words in the same text and word sequences in summarizing texts (e.g., Huang et al., 2023). The LLMs are considered efficient and accurate in terms of understanding human language (Gu et al., 2023a; Huang et al., 2023).

In 2020, the introduction of OpenAI's GPT-3[1] was a significant developmental milestone for LLMs that advanced the field of NLP by providing a powerful tool for human–computer interaction through conversational dialog (De Kok, 2023; Zhao & Wang, 2024). ChatGPT by OpenAI has become a key player in the realm of LLMs and has revolutionized the field of artificial intelligence (AI) with its advanced capabilities in understanding and generating human-like text (OpenAI, 2023a). In 2023, OpenAI announced the development of a new multimodal model called GPT-4, which can process both text and image inputs to produce text output (Dong et al., 2023; OpenAI, 2023b). The advent of GPT-4 marks a new milestone in AI, offering functionalities that were once considered exclusive to human intelligence (Dong et al., 2023).

Scholars argue that LLMs underline the growing significance of data in today's economy and suggest that technologies like LLMs that are able to analyze and interpret large datasets could play a crucial role in extracting insights and making informed decisions (e.g., Li et al., 2024). Furthermore, the utilization of AI will likely transform accounting practices substantially, resulting in enhanced efficiency in leveraging accounting data for decision-making within organizations (Zhao & Wang, 2024). Accounting scholars emphasize the potential abilities of ChatGPT to reshape various accounting processes by automating repetitive tasks, enhancing financial and managerial reporting and analysis, improving auditing and tax practices, and simplifying client interactions (Dong et al., 2023; Zhao & Wang, 2024). They mention, for example, ChatGPT's capabilities to extract and analyze relevant information, identify anomalies, and track reporting patterns. Saini (2023) and Huang et al. (2023) describe various reporting analysis scenarios in which ChatGPT is used for sentiment analysis. ChatGPT's insights could also be used for cost budgeting, retirement planning, risk management, and investment analysis (Son, 2023; Zhao & Wang, 2024). In auditing, ChatGPT's capabilities could extend to risk assessment, compliance monitoring, and financial analysis. Gu et al. (2023b) propose the "co-piloted auditing" concept, indicating

[1]GPT stands for generative pre-training transformer. GPT is designed as an autoregressive model for language generation, and it works as a sequential language creation model predicting one word at a time (Dong et al., 2023).

a collaborative partnership between auditors and AI models. Eulerich and Wood (2023) show concrete examples of how internal auditors could use ChatGPT in the internal audit process. Furthermore, ChatGPT's ability to process and analyze large datasets, provide real-time insights, and predict market trends make it a useful tool for businesses that seek to leverage AI for strategic decision-making (De Kok, 2023; Dong et al., 2023). Moreover, using AI for data analysis is often more cost-effective than traditional methods (Noy & Zhang, 2023).

2. Sources of Exogenous Data Through ChatGPT

This section explores various sources of exogenous data and shows how ChatGPT can facilitate this process for each data type. We propose that incorporating ChatGPT into the extraction and analysis of exogenous data sources can substantially enhance the efficiency and effectiveness of data-driven decision-making for investors, auditors, managers, and other stakeholders.

One of the most innovative aspects of ChatGPT is its ability to integrate with various plug-ins and GPTs, expanding its capabilities beyond mere text generation. These plug-ins and GPTs allow ChatGPT to perform specialized tasks, access external databases, and interact with different web services. The plug-ins and GPTs listed in Appendix 1 are some samples of specialized tools that can enhance ChatGPT's ability to interact with and interpret exogenous data.

2.1. News Analysis

News is a vital form of exogenous data because it encapsulates a wide array of information that reflects not only current events but also the perceptions, expectations, and sentiments of individuals, organizations, and market at large. When it comes to making informed decisions in the business world – whether for management, investment, or auditing purposes – news can provide real-time insights into factors that may influence a company's performance (Cheong et al., 2022). This includes but is not limited to changes in the political landscape, regulatory shifts, technological advancements, market trends, and emergent risks. For example, a news article about new tariffs could signal potential cost increases for manufacturers, whereas reports on a data breach could imply future expenditures and reputation damage for a tech firm.

Recent studies underscore the significance of AI, particularly ChatGPT, in analyzing news to gain financial insights. For instance, research by Dong et al. (2023) highlight the scope of ChatGPT's application in accounting and finance. Zhang et al. (2023) reveals that sentiment scores from a GPT-3.5 model, based on *Financial Times* news titles and subtitles, predict stock market movements more effectively than traditional models like BERT. Comlekci et al. (2023) find that ChatGPT's forecasts for the financial performance and dividends of companies in the Borsa Istanbul 100 Index improve significantly when supplemented with recent industry news. These studies collectively illustrate how ChatGPT can be a valuable tool in transforming news into actionable business intelligence, aiding in strategic decision-making, investment analysis, and understanding the broader context of financial disclosures.

For example, by integrating plug-ins and GPTs shown in Appendix 1, ChatGPT could assist managers by summarizing the latest local or global news that could affect firms' strategic decisions, provide investors with an analysis of how recent corporate and economic events might affect stock performance, and aid auditors in understanding and assuring the broader context of a company's financial disclosures. For instance, the Bitcoin Sentiment plug-in could offer cryptocurrency investors insights into potential stock market movements based on media sentiment. By contextualizing news items, identifying trends, and flagging pertinent information, ChatGPT can act as a sophisticated aid to decision-making processes.

2.2. *Social Media Insights*

Social media has emerged as an indispensable source of exogenous data due to its immediacy and the direct user engagement that it captures. It provides a real-time pulse for public sentiment, trends, and the collective voice of consumers, investors, and industry commentators. The emergence of social media as a critical source of exogenous data is emphasized by Cheong et al. (2022), who discuss the increasing relevance of accounting information when combined with external data sources like Reddit, Twitter, Facebook, Instagram, and TikTok. Furthermore, analyzing sales trends across various products and the flow of textual data on social media platforms can provide early indicators of a product's popularity and potential issues (Vasarhelyi et al., 2015; Warren et al., 2015). Executives can refine their corporate tactics to align with customer feedback, investors can assess the collective mood to predict investment outcomes, and auditors can scrutinize online discourse for any signs of fiscal or reputational hazards. For companies, social media data can reveal insights into brand perception, the impact of marketing campaigns, customer satisfaction, and emerging market trends before they are encapsulated in traditional reporting metrics. This information is invaluable to managers, investors, and auditors because it can act as an early warning system for potential issues, as well as an opportunity detector for areas of growth and innovation.

Incorporating ChatGPT to analyze social media involves utilizing its advanced language models to process and understand the vast amounts of unstructured text data generated by social platforms. ChatGPT, enhanced with the specialized plug-ins and GPTs outlined in the Appendix 1, can interpret nuances in sentiment, track the spread of information, and identify the significance of social media discussions related to a specific company or sector. For instance, an analytics advisor plug-in can help to quantify the effectiveness of a social media strategy, whereas a sentiment analysis GPT can assist in understanding the public's perception of a recent corporate decision or product launch (shown in Appendix 1).

2.3. *Web Traffic Data*

Web traffic data stand as a beacon of quantitative insight, shedding light on user behavior, engagement levels, and the effectiveness of online content and marketing strategies. For a company, understanding the nuances of this data can lead to improved user experience, more targeted marketing campaigns, and ultimately, increased revenue and growth. Such data include metrics like page views, bounce rates, session duration, and conversion rates. When these data are analyzed, they can provide a comprehensive picture of how users interact with a company's online presence. In addition to the traditional web traffic metrics, the study by Cheong et al. (2022) expands the scope of data analysis by illustrating how real-time foot traffic data from sources like Google Maps can be instrumental in evaluating physical store performance.

ChatGPT can process web traffic data to identify trends, patterns, and anomalies. For instance, a plug-in like Avian could allow ChatGPT to pull in data from various advertising platforms and search engines, giving a holistic view of a company's online visibility and the performance of its marketing efforts (Appendix 1). With tools like AnalyticsAI, ChatGPT could use simple prompts to interact with Google Analytics, simplifying the process of complex data analysis for managers who may not have deep technical expertise. The integration of ChatGPT with web traffic analytics equips decision-makers with a powerful tool and allows for a real-time understanding of the digital landscape. Managers can utilize these insights to determine the return on investment for digital campaigns, ensuring that resources are being allocated to the most effective strategies. Investors can understand a company's online presence and influence, which can be indicative of brand strength and market position. Auditors can cross-check reported web performance against actual data.

2.4. Weather Data and Predictions

Weather data and predictions are crucial exogenous factors that can have profound impacts on a range of business operations. The relevance of weather information extends beyond its immediate effects on production schedules and logistics to its influence on consumer buying behavior, energy consumption patterns, and even financial markets. Yoon et al. (2024) demonstrate that the integration of weather data into substantive analytical procedures in audit testing can enhance the precision of revenue forecasts for companies whose operations are significantly influenced by weather conditions. In the retail sector, weather predictions can help companies anticipate changes in consumer demand for certain products, such as increased purchases of warm clothing during an unseasonally cold forecast. In agriculture, accurate weather predictions can inform planting and harvesting decisions, directly affecting crop yields and market supply. For investors, an understanding of how weather data correlates with market trends can inform investment decisions, especially in commodities, the agriculture and energy sectors, and insurance, where weather plays a significant role. Auditors can also use weather data to validate the influence of weather events on financial performance and disclosures.

By incorporating ChatGPT with weather data plug-ins and tools, businesses can access personalized and actionable weather-driven insights. ChatGPT can interact with weather analytics tools, like those mentioned in Appendix 1, to process current, forecasted, and historical weather data. This can help in creating comprehensive business plans that account for the impacts of weather. For example, using a plug-in like Weather Meteosource, ChatGPT can provide real-time updates on weather conditions, allowing a logistics manager to reroute shipments to avoid delays due to unforeseen weather disruptions. Similarly, a tool like the Business Plan Builder can integrate weather data into broader strategic plans, helping businesses in weather-sensitive industries to mitigate risks or capitalize on weather-related opportunities.

2.5. Other Sources

The current business environment is complex and multifaceted, with a myriad of exogenous factors that influence company performance and decision-making. Appendix 1 provides some examples of plug-ins and GPTs that could incorporate different kinds of exogenous data. For instance, AITickerChat, which extracts insights from SEC filings and conference call transcripts, offers valuable information on a company's strategic direction, market position, and management's perspectives. These data are critical for managers who need to understand their company's competitive environment and for investors who make decisions based on company performance and strategy.

Polygon provides a broad spectrum of market data, which is integral for understanding market dynamics and the interplay between different asset classes, including stocks, options, foreign exchange markets (forex), and cryptocurrencies. ChatGPT can use such data to help decision-makers discern market trends and develop timely investment strategies or risk assessments. Furthermore, platforms like Quiver Quantitative provide unique insights into the financial activities of political figures, offering an additional layer of understanding regarding potential upcoming regulatory changes that could affect certain industries or markets. In the case of PointsRecap, daily updates and trading insights gleaned from YouTube content creators can give a real-time sense of investor sentiment and market reactions, which can be particularly useful for investors and traders looking to capitalize on short-term market movements. Similarly, PortfoliosLab's analytics can support more long-term, strategic planning and investment by providing detailed performance, volatility, and risk assessments.

Data from external sources like satellite imagery, which is less susceptible to managerial influence, can serve as a critical tool to reduce the risk of greenwashing and corroborate the authenticity of ESG disclosures (Gu et al., 2023a). The Space Photo Explorer, with its access to extensive space imagery databases, could be leveraged as an exogenous data source to verify environmental claims independently and enhance the credibility of sustainability reporting. Finally, the Sustainability Assistant could help provide expert advice on ESG aspects, deliver updates on relevant sustainability regulations and trends, and help to prepare for future changes in ESG practices. It could also balance insights across environmental, social, and governance factors, offering non-binding, practical guidance tailored to specific company or industry needs.

3. An Illustrative Case

We illustrate what exogenous data and information about greenhouse gas (GHG) emissions can be found when exploring ESG ratings provided by rating agencies, as well as by testing some of the plug-ins (provided in Appendix 1), for the ExxonMobil Corporation. ExxonMobil was selected because of the recent news story in *Fortune* (2024) saying that two of the biggest shareholders want the oil giant to commit to more ambitious emissions reductions. ExxonMobil reacted by suing the Arjuna Capital and follow this investor groups, emphasizing that the social responsibility of the firm is to increase profits, consistent with Milton Friedman's famous 1970 essay (Friedman, 1970). Another motivation for our choice is that GHG emissions constitute a material aspect in ExxonMobil's business operations based on SASB's standards and Materiality Finder (2023). Moreover, Appelbaum et al. (2023) regard the physical risk, transition risk, and liability/legal risk levels of companies operating as energy providers and chemical manufacturers as high in all three risk categories. Given the high risk levels and materiality aspects, it is important for shareholders and other stakeholders to take a closer look at ExxonMobil's disclosures and complement reported financial and non-financial information with data derived from exogenous sources.

First, we explore what information shareholders can access by using available corporate reports. We asked ChatGPT to summarize the main issues related to emissions in ExxonMobil's 10-Ks (annual reports) for 2022 and 2023. The result is included in Appendix 2. The text includes information about (1) emission-reduction investments and strategies, (2) GHG emission targets, (3) financial impacts of emission policies, (4) risks related to lower-emission business opportunities, (5) climate change and energy transition, (6) regulatory and litigation risks, and (7) decarbonization technologies and policies. We also asked ChatGPT to summarize the main issues related to emissions in the sustainability report of ExxonMobil for the last few years. As shown in Appendix 3, we received a brief overview (excluding numerical information) related to the following issues: (1) GHG emissions data, (2) emission reduction goals and progress, (3) third-party assurance, and (4) forward-looking statements.

As Appelbaum et al. (2023) note, ESG ratings provided by third-party rating agencies are considered objective and informative exogenous data. We extract ESG and Emissions ratings from the LSEG Workspace (previously Refinitiv) for ExxonMobil and the peer firm British Petroleum (BP). Table 2.1 shows that ExxonMobil's ESG and Emissions scores are lower than the comparable scores for BP on a scale from 0 to 100. According to LSEG Workspace, a score of more than 70 is considered good, so the difference in scores seems not to be significant. Table 2.1 also includes other information related to emissions, but information about the total Scope 3 emissions is not available for either company. However, it is notable that the numbers provided by BP related to "Upstream scope 3 emissions Fuel- and Energy-related Activities" are very high and also much higher than the firm's total Scope 1 and 2 emissions, indicating that Scope 3 emissions are material to this industry sector. Finally, BP's target year for emission reductions is 2025, whereas ExxonMobil's latest target is 2030. While exogenous data

Table 2.1. Extract of Emission Information from the LSEG Workspace.

Emissons Data (LSEG Workspace)	**ExxonMobil**			**BP Company p.l.c**		
Year	**2020**	**2021**	**2022**	**2020**	**2021**	**2022**
ESG score	77.56	73.25	N/A	86.37	89.96	87.17
Emissions score	85.85	84.12	N/A	92.05	93.61	92.12
CO_2 equivalents emission direct (Scope 1)	95,000,000	96,000,000	N/A	41,700,000	33,200,000	30,400,000
CO_2 equivalents emission indirect (Scope 2)	7,000,000	7,000,000	N/A	3,200,000	2,400,000	2,100,000
CO_2e indirect emissions (Scope 3)	N/A	N/A	N/A	N/A	N/A	N/A
CO_2 equivalents emission total (Scope 1 & 2)	102,000,000	103,000,000	N/A	44,900,000	35,600,000	32,500,000
Upstream Scope 3 emissions fuel- and energy-related activities	N/A	N/A	N/A	327,600,000	303,600,000	306,700,000
Total emission intensity (total emissions per net sales)	0.571	0.372	N/A	0.247	0.225	0.127
Emission reduction target year	2050	2030	N/A	2025	2025	2025

available in databases like LSEG Workspace are easy to find and extract, users must usually obtain a license to get access to such databases, and data are updated only after considerable delay. Therefore, we further explore information that can be found using the plug-ins provided in Appendix 1.

We test the Sustainability Assistant and WebPilot plug-ins to explore whether additional information related to ExxonMobil's emissions and risks can be extracted. The results are found in Appendices 4 and 5. For example, we find more details related to risks that were not available in the corporate notes to 10-Ks or in the LSEG database. Risks mentioned in Appendix 5 are, for example, risks for additional costs-related legal actions against shareholders who demand faster climate action, risks for assets being at risk of impairment due to climate change, and overall environmental and regulatory risks that may affect the company's long-term sustainability and legal standing. ChatGPT also provides some guidance to shareholders. For example, as a shareholder of ExxonMobil, it is crucial to recognize the company's substantial efforts to enhance transparency and reduce emission, as detailed in its sustainability reports and ESG-related news. These efforts include significant investments in lower-emission technologies and carbon capture projects that align with evolving environmental and shareholder expectations. However, shareholders should remain vigilant about potential risks related to transparency, investor relations, and the company's adaptation to regulatory and market changes in the context of environmental sustainability. Thus, we maintain that using plug-ins and ChatGPT may provide complementary information to what is available in corporate reports and third-party databases.

4. Conclusion and Future Outlook

This chapter has explored the role and potential of LLMs like ChatGPT in processing exogenous data, as illustrated in the case of ExxonMobil. The evolving role of ChatGPT, particularly in the context of exogenous data, is characterized by its increasing capability to process and analyze data from diverse external sources. This study delves into an array of exogenous data types that ChatGPT can help stakeholders to leverage. It details how ChatGPT's integration with various plug-ins and GPTs can streamline the processing and interpretation of data from news, social media, web traffic, and weather predictions to aid in informed decision-making. The integration of a wide array of exogenous information into existing financial and non-financial data provides stakeholders with a competitive edge and the means to ensure that decisions are as informed and strategic as possible.

By using ChatGPT to assimilate and analyze diverse data streams, managers, investors, and auditors can gain a richer, more detailed picture of a company's context within its industry and the broader economy. ChatGPT can help to translate vast amounts of data into actionable insights, a process that is essential for effective decision-making in today's business environment. This signifies a shift toward a more data-driven approach in business, where AI not only supports but also guides strategic planning and operational decisions.

While ChatGPT and similar AI technologies offer significant benefits, there are also challenges and ethical considerations that must be carefully managed. One of the primary concerns with ChatGPT is data privacy and security. Since these models are trained on vast datasets, including potentially sensitive information, there is a risk of data breaches or misuse of personal data (Munoko et al., 2020; Zhao & Wang, 2024). The issue of transparency and accountability in AI decision-making is another area of concern (Dong et al., 2023). As AI models like ChatGPT become more complex, understanding how they arrive at certain decisions or outputs becomes more challenging. Despite their advanced capabilities, AI models like ChatGPT have limitations in understanding context and nuance, especially in complex or ambiguous situations. This limitation can lead to errors or misunderstandings (Li et al., 2024). Furthermore, ChatGPT has been found to generate factually incorrect or entirely made-up information, a phenomenon known as hallucination (Dong et al., 2023). However, regardless of whether the data are collected manually or using ChatGPT, the effectiveness and reliability of the exogenous data must be assessed continuously (Cheong et al., 2022).

As research continues, the capabilities of ChatGPT and similar models are expected to expand, enhancing their role in business intelligence and decision-making. Future research in AI, especially in the context of exogenous data, is expected to focus on enhancing the precision and contextual understanding of AI technologies. This means improving the algorithms' ability to pick out nuances and patterns in large data sets, thereby providing more accurate and actionable insights for businesses, accounting professionals, and other stakeholders. Addressing the challenges of data privacy, security, and ethical considerations in AI will also be crucial in ensuring responsible and effective use of ChatGPT.

Appendix 1. Examples of Sources of Exogenous Data Through ChatGPT

Sources of Exogenous Data	Name of Plug-ins/GPTs	Icon	Description of the Functions
News	News		The most popular global news app, digest 80,000+ trusted sources for the latest news, trends, and insights in a flash
	Alpha News		Alpha News provides access to >80k news sources, letting you search for topics, publications, and trending stories
	WebPilot		Browse Webpage/PDF/Data. Chat and write with one/many/none URLs. WebPilot.ai Powered
	NewsBreak		Learn about the most popular local or national news and find local businesses and events in the United States
	Risk Factors for listed companies		This tool analyzes real-time news against NASDAQ 100 companies' SEC-reported risks, aiding informed investment decisions
	Corporate OSINT & Competitor Analyst		Provides strategic insights into market trends, competitor analysis, and critical intelligence for business decisions
	Bitcoin Sentiment		Track the current price of Bitcoin and the market sentiment based on the last 20 news media mentions
Social media	Social Search		The Social Search provides access to tweets, users, followers, images, media, and more
	Social Media Analytics		Discover insights with social media analytics tools, social media monitoring tools, Facebook analytics tools, Instagram analytics tools, Twitter analytics tools, and LinkedIn analytics tools. Elevate your online strategy efficiently

(Continued)

Appendix 1. (*Continued*)

Sources of Exogenous Data	Name of Plug-ins/GPTs	Icon	Description of the Functions
	Social Media Analytics Advisor		Analyzes and interprets social media data to drive strategic decisions
	Sentiment Analysis GPT		Performs a detailed sentiment analysis on text to uncover hidden patterns
	Comments Analyzer		This tool analyzes YouTube comments in seconds, providing trend analysis, sentiment checks, and valuable feedback. It could be extended to other social media platforms for similar analyses
Web traffic data	Avian		Analyze & visualize data from 20+ platforms, including Google Analytics, Google Ads, & Facebook Ads
	Cloudflare Radar		Get real-time insights into Internet traffic patterns and threats as seen by Cloudflare
	AnalyticsAI		Connect to your Google Analytics and get data with AI using simple prompts
	A/B Analytics		A/B test and analyze data from Google Analytics, Facebook Ads, and more
	Cloudflare Radar		Get real-time insights into Internet traffic patterns and threats as seen by Cloudflare
Weather data and predictions	Weather Meteosource		Accurate weather for chat-based insights – current, forecasted, and historical. Updated in real-time
	Business Plan Builder		Assists with creating business plans that could include weather data as an exogenous factor, especially in industries like retail, where weather can significantly impact consumer behavior
	Weather		Get the weather forecast for a US city or zip code. Predicting, planning, and adapting to the weather forecast via contextualized chat-based insights

Appendix 1. (*Continued*)

Sources of Exogenous Data	Name of Plug-ins/GPTs	Icon	Description of the Functions
	Weather Report		Current weather data for cities and airports using METAR aviation feeds
	MixerBox Weather		Get real-time worldwide weather updates and forecasts, instantly
Others	AITickerChat		Retrieve USA stock insights from SEC filings as well as Earnings Call Transcripts
	Polygon		Market data, news, and fundamentals for stocks, options, forex, and crypto from Polygon.io
	Quiver Quantitative		Access data on congressional stock trading, lobbying, insider trading, and proposed legislation
	PointsRecap		Daily stock market updates, trading insights, and view points summary from YouTube traders
	PortfoliosLab		Stocks, ETFs, funds, crypto analysis: historical performance, volatility, risk metrics, Sharpe ratio, drawdowns, etc.
	Space Photo Explorer		Tool for exploring space through images including Mars Rover Photos, NASA image database, and space pictures of the day
	Sustainability Assistant		ESG and Sustainability helper that provides regulatory updates, industry news, and advice on creating a more sustainable organization

Appendix 2. Example Using GPT-4 to Extract Information from 10-K

Prompt: Could you read the file of ExxonMobil annual report 2022 and 2023 and summarize the 5–7 main issues related to emissions mentioned in the 10-K for these years? Please cite some original texts for each issue.

Answer:

Based on the 2022 and 2023 ExxonMobil annual reports, here are the main issues related to emissions:

1. *Emission–reduction investments and strategies*: ExxonMobil is increasingly focusing on lower-emission business opportunities, including carbon capture and storage (CCS), hydrogen, and lower-emission fuels. They expect environmental expenditures to rise significantly due to these initiatives, with estimated costs of about $7.3 billion in 2023 and $8.2 billion in 2024.
2. *GHG emission targets*: The company aims for substantial reductions in GHG emissions. By 2030, ExxonMobil plans to achieve a 20%–30% reduction in corporate-wide GHG intensity, a 40%–50% reduction in upstream intensity, a 70%–80% reduction in methane intensity, and a 60%—70% reduction in flaring intensity. They also target net-zero GHG emissions (Scope 1 and 2) from unconventional operations in the Permian Basin by 2030.
3. *Financial impacts of emission policies*: ExxonMobil's financial results are significantly influenced by government policies and market developments related to emissions. The company includes estimated costs for reaching its GHG emission-reduction goals in its financial assessments, even in areas without current GHG pricing policies.
4. *Risks related to lower-emission business opportunities*: The company acknowledges that the success of their lower-emission initiatives, like carbon capture and hydrogen fuels, is dependent on market growth and supportive government policies. Uncertainties in technology development and policy changes present risks to their business plans.
5. *Climate change and energy transition*: ExxonMobil is aware of the global shift toward lower-emission energy sources and net-zero scenarios. The company aims to adapt and lead in the energy transition while considering the uncertainties in technology, policies, and market developments related to climate change.
6. *Regulatory and litigation risks*: The company faces risks from changing environmental regulations and policies, which can increase compliance costs and affect business strategies. Government actions like carbon taxes, trade tariffs, and efficiency standards impact their operations and product competitiveness.
7. *Decarbonization technologies and policies*: The decarbonization of industrial activities is crucial, requiring advancements in technologies like CCS, hydrogen-based fuels, and lower-emission solutions. ExxonMobil emphasizes

the importance of supportive policies and technology development for achieving broader emission reduction goals.

These points highlight ExxonMobil's increasing focus on reducing emissions, the financial implications of these efforts, and the challenges and risks associated with transitioning to a lower-emission business model.

Appendix 3. Example Using GPT's "Sustainability Assistant" to Analyze ExxonMobil's Sustainability Reports

Prompt: Could you read the ExxonMobil's sustainability reports for the last few years disclosed information about emissions?

Answer:

In recent years, ExxonMobil's sustainability reports have provided detailed information on their GHG emissions, demonstrating their commitment to transparency in this critical aspect of their ESG performance. Here are some key points from these reports:

1. *GHG emissions data*: ExxonMobil's reports include comprehensive data on their Scope 1, Scope 2, and, where applicable, Scope 3 GHG emissions. This includes metrics like CO_2 and CH_4 emissions across different operational segments such as upstream, downstream, and chemical.
2. *Emission reduction goals and progress*: The company has been making concerted efforts to reduce its GHG emissions. Their 2030 GHG emission reduction plans are incorporated into medium-term business strategies. They include ambitious targets such as achieving net-zero emissions for operated assets by 2050 and substantial reductions in methane and flaring intensity.
3. *Third-party assurance*: ExxonMobil's GHG emissions inventory and performance data are audited for compliance with recognized standards like ISO 14064-3, providing an additional layer of credibility to their reported figures.
4. *Forward-looking statements*: The reports also contain forward-looking statements about future ambitions and goals regarding emissions reduction. However, these statements are subject to numerous factors such as market conditions, technological progress, policy support, and regulatory changes.

It's important for stakeholders, including investors, to understand that these reports are based on the best available data and methodologies, which continue to evolve. Therefore, the figures and projections should be considered in the context of potential uncertainties and changing market and policy landscapes.

For detailed information and specific data, you can refer to ExxonMobil's Sustainability Report and Advancing Climate Solutions Report on their official website.

Appendix 4. Example Using GPT's "Sustainability Assistant" to Extract and Analyze ESG-related News About ExxonMobil

Prompt: Could you tell me some ESG-related news about ExxonMobil in the past few years? If I'm a shareholder of ExxonMobil, do you have any further suggestions/takeaways for me?

Answer:

In recent years, ExxonMobil has taken significant steps in addressing ESG-related concerns. Here are some key developments:

1. *Investment in lower-emissions initiatives*: ExxonMobil announced plans to invest $17 billion through 2027 in lower-emission technologies and initiatives, including their Low Carbon Solutions business. This is a clear indication of the company's commitment to transitioning towards a more sustainable energy future.
2. *Focus on CCS*: They have been actively involved in projects related to CCS. Notably, ExxonMobil partnered with Shell and the Government of Singapore to create a CCS value chain. This kind of collaboration underscores the company's dedication to innovative solutions for reducing carbon emissions.
3. *Strategic corporate moves*: ExxonMobil has been evolving its business strategy to align more closely with ESG goals. This includes their merger with Pioneer Natural Resources in an all-stock transaction, which likely has implications for their approach to sustainable energy practices.
4. *Activist influence on board composition*: A significant ESG-related event for ExxonMobil was the successful campaign by Engine No. 1, an activist investment firm, to place three dissident members on ExxonMobil's board in 2021. This event highlighted the increasing influence of shareholder activism focused on ESG issues, particularly climate change.

As a shareholder, these developments suggest that ExxonMobil is actively responding to ESG pressures and is making efforts to adapt to a changing energy landscape. This transition includes investing in new technologies and reevaluating traditional business strategies.

However, as an investor, it's important to stay informed about the effectiveness of these strategies and how they align with overall market trends and regulatory changes. Balancing the potential risks with the opportunities presented by these ESG-focused changes is crucial for making informed investment decisions.

For more detailed information, you might want to regularly check Exxon Mobil's sustainability updates and press releases:

https://esgnews.com/esg/exxonmobil/
https://investor.exxonmobil.com/esg
https://hbswk.hbs.edu/item/esg-activists-met-the-moment-at-exxon-mobil-but-did-they-succeed

Appendix 5. Example Using Plug-in "WebPilot" to Extract and Analyze ESG-related News About ExxonMobil

Prompt: GHG emissions constitute a material aspect in ExxonMobil's business operations. Further, previous research regards the physical risk, transition risk, and liability/legal risk levels of companies operating as energy providers and chemical manufacturers as high on all three risk levels. Please read the ExxonMobil's related news for the last few years and tell me what you find about its risks. And if I'm a shareholder of ExxonMobil, what are the corresponding suggestions/takeaways? Please include the references you use.

Answer:

Recent news about ExxonMobil highlights several key risks and developments:

1. *Streamlining operations*: ExxonMobil has been restructuring to enhance effectiveness, grow value, and reduce costs. This indicates a strategic shift to improve operational efficiency and adapt to changing market conditions.
2. *Climate change acknowledgment and action*: There have been reports that ExxonMobil internally acknowledged the impact of fossil fuels on climate change while publicly downplaying these risks. This raises concerns about transparency and corporate responsibility.
3. *Legal actions against investors*: ExxonMobil has been involved in legal actions against investors who demand faster climate action. This suggests potential conflicts between the company's operational strategies and investor expectations regarding environmental responsibility.
4. *Asset risk due to climate change*: ExxonMobil has warned that some of its assets may be at risk of impairment due to climate change. This indicates a recognition of the physical risks posed by climate change to its operations.
5. *Advanced recycling initiatives*: The company has been investing in "advanced recycling" plants, which could be part of its strategy to address environmental concerns. However, the environmental efficacy of these initiatives has been questioned.

For a shareholder of ExxonMobil, these developments suggest several takeaways:

1. *Need for vigilance on corporate strategy*: The restructuring and streamlining efforts indicate that ExxonMobil is adapting to market and operational challenges. Shareholders should monitor how these changes impact the company's profitability and market position.
2. *Environmental and regulatory risks*: The issues around climate change acknowledgment and legal actions highlight the environmental and regulatory risks facing ExxonMobil. Shareholders should consider how these risks might affect the company's long-term sustainability and legal standing.

3. *Investor relations and corporate governance*: The conflict with investors over climate action underscores the importance of strong investor relations and corporate governance. Shareholders should assess how ExxonMobil manages these aspects and their potential impact on the company's reputation and shareholder value.
4. *Innovation and diversification*: Investments in advanced recycling and other new technologies indicate ExxonMobil's efforts to innovate and diversify. Shareholders should evaluate the potential of these initiatives to contribute to the company's growth and environmental goals.
5. *Long-term outlook*: Given the evolving landscape of the energy sector, shareholders should consider the long-term outlook of ExxonMobil, including how it plans to navigate the transition to a lower-carbon economy and manage associated risks.

Overall, shareholders of ExxonMobil should stay informed about these developments, assess their implications, and consider how they align with their investment goals and risk tolerance.

Here are the references for the information provided:

1. *ExxonMobil streamlines structure*: This information was derived from ExxonMobil's news release about their efforts to streamline operations to enhance effectiveness, grow value, and reduce costs.
   ExxonMobil streamlines structure to enhance effectiveness, grow value, and reduce costs.
   https://corporate.exxonmobil.com/news/news-releases/2022/0131_exxonmobil-streamlines-structure-to-enhance-effectiveness-grow-value-reduce-costs
2. *Climate change acknowledgment and action*: Reports indicating that ExxonMobil internally acknowledged the impact of fossil fuels on climate change while publicly downplaying these risks were found in news articles from sources like NPR.
   Exxon minimized climate change internally after conceding that fossil fuels cause it.
   https://www.npr.org/2023/09/14/1199570023/exxon-climate-change-fossil-fuels-global-warming-oil-gas
3. *Legal actions against investors*: Information about ExxonMobil's legal actions against investors demanding faster climate action was reported by NPR.
   ExxonMobil is suing investors who want faster climate action.
   https://www.npr.org/2024/02/29/1234358133/exxon-climate-change-oil-fossil-fuels-shareholders-investors-lawsuit
4. *Asset risk due to climate change*: Reuters reported on ExxonMobil's warnings that some of its assets may be at risk of impairment due to climate change.
   Exxon warns some assets may be at risk for impairment due to climate change.
   https://www.reuters.com/business/energy/exxon-warns-some-assets-may-risk-impairment-due-climate-change-filing-2021-11-03/

5. *Advanced recycling initiatives*: The Guardian provided information on ExxonMobil's investment in "advanced recycling" plants and the environmental questions surrounding these initiatives.
   Exxon's new "advanced recycling" plant raises environmental concerns.
   https://www.theguardian.com/us-news/2023/apr/10/exxon-advanced-recycling-plastic-environment

These sources were used to gather the latest information and insights about ExxonMobil's operations, strategies, and the risks they face, particularly in relation to climate change and environmental sustainability.

References

Alles, M., Palas, R., Vasarhelyi, M. A., & Xiong, F. (2022). The case for an app-based financial reporting system. *Journal of Emerging Technologies in Accounting*, *19*(2), 1–21. https://doi.org/10.2308/jeta-10827

Appelbaum, D., Duan, H. K., Hu, H., & Sun, T. (2023). *The double materiality audit: Assurance of ESG disclosure*. http://dx.doi.org/10.2139/ssrn.4367032

Brown-Liburd, H., Cheong, A., Vasarhelyi, M. A., & Wang, X. (2019). Measuring with exogenous data (MED), and government economic monitoring (GEM). *Journal of Emerging Technologies in Accounting*, *16*(1), 1–19. https://doi.org/10.2308/jeta-10682

Cheong, A., Duan, H. K., Huang, Q., Vasarhelyi, M. A., & Zhang, C. A. (2022). The rise of accounting: Making accounting information relevant again with exogenous data. *Journal of Emerging Technologies in Accounting*, *19*(1), 1–20. https://doi.org/10.2308/jeta-10812

Comlekci, İ., Unal, S., & Mehmet, A. O. (2023). Can AI technologies estimate financials accurately? A research on Borsa Istanbul with ChatGPT. *SSRN Electronic Journal*. https://doi.org/10.2139/ssrn.4545954

Dardani, M. A., Gu, Y., Hu, H., Medinets, A. F., Palmon, D., & Vasarhelyi, M. A. (2024). Rethinking the standard-setting process: The role of intangibles. *Journal of Emerging Technologies in Accounting*, *20*(2), 1–20. https://doi.org/10.2308/JETA-2024-001

De Kok, T. (2023). *Generative LLMs and textual analysis in accounting: (Chat)GPT as research assistant?* http://dx.doi.org/10.2139/ssrn.4429658

Dong, M., Stratopoulos, T. C., & Wang, V. X. (2023). *Scoping review of ChatGPT research in accounting and finance*. http://dx.doi.org/10.2139/ssrn.4680203

Duan, H. K., Hu, H., Yoon, Y. B., & Vasarhelyi, M. A. (2022). Increasing the utility of performance audit reports: Using textual analytics tools to improve government reporting. *Intelligent Systems in Accounting, Finance and Management*, *29*(4), 201–218. https://doi.org/10.1002/isaf.1526

Eulerich, M., & Wood, D. A. (2023). *A demonstration of how ChatGPT can be used in the internal auditing process*. https://doi.org/10.2139/ssrn.4519583

Fortune. (2024). *Exxon is taking its shareholders to court as the anti-ESG backlash escalates into a civil war between the proponents of shareholder primacy*. https://fortune.com/2024/02/08/exxon-shareholders-court-anti-esg-backlash-escalates-civil-war/

Friedman, M. (1970, September 13). The social responsibility of business is to increase its profits (pp. 122–126). *New York Times Magazine*.

Gu, Y., Dai, J., & Vasarhelyi, M. A. (2023a). Audit 4.0-based ESG assurance: An example of using satellite images on GHG emissions. *International Journal of Accounting Information Systems*, *50*, 100625. https://doi.org/10.1016/j.accinf.2023.100625

Gu, H., Schreyer, M., Moffitt, K., & Vasarhelyi, M. A. (2023b). *Artificial intelligence co-piloted auditing*. https://doi.org/10.2139/ssrn.4444763

Huang, A. H., Wang, H., & Yang, Y. (2023). FinBERT: A large language model for extracting information from financial text. *Contemporary Accounting Research*, *40*, 806–841. https://doi.org/10.1111/1911-3846.12832

Huang, Q., Vasarhelyi, M. A., & Mantelaers, E. J. (2022). *Toward a continuous measurement model*. In eKNOW 2022: The fourteenth international conference on information, process, and knowledge management. https://personales.upv.es/thinkmind/dl/conferences/eknow/eknow_2022/eknow_2022_1_40_68004.pdf

Li, H., Machado de Freitas, M., Lee, H., & Vasarhelyi, M. (2024). *Enhancing continuous auditing with large language models: A framework for cross-verification using exogenous textual data*. http://dx.doi.org/10.2139/ssrn.4692960

Munoko, I., Brown-Liburd, H. L., & Vasarhelyi, M. (2020). The ethical implications of using artificial intelligence in auditing. *Journal of Business Ethics*, *167*, 209–234. https://doi.org/10.1007/s10551-019-04407-1

Noy, S., & Zhang, W. (2023). *Experimental evidence on the productivity effects of generative artificial intelligence*. http://dx.doi.org/10.2139/ssrn.4375283

OpenAI. (2023a). *What is ChatGPT?* https://help.openai.com/en/articles/6783457-what-is-chatgpt

OpenAI. (2023b). *GPT-4 is OpenAI's most advanced system, producing safer and more useful responses*. https://openai.com/gpt-4

Saini, G. (2023). *ChatGPT for financial analysts: Advantages and some limitations*. https://unstop.com/blog/chat-gpt-for-financial-analysis

SASB. (2023). *Materiality finder*. https://sasb.ifrs.org/standards/materiality-finder

Son, H. (2023). *JPMorgan is developing a ChatGPT-like A.I. service that gives investment advice*. https://www.cnbc.com/2023/05/25/jpmorgan-develops-ai-investment-advisor.html

Vasarhelyi, M. A., Kogan, A., & Tuttle, B. M. (2015). Big data in accounting: An overview. *Accounting Horizons*, *29*(2), 381–396. https://doi.org/10.2308/acch-51071

Vaswani, A., Shazeer, N., Parmar, N., Uszkoreit, J., Jones, L., Gomez, A. N., Kaiser, L., & Polosukhin, I. (2017). *Attention is all you need*. arXiv:1706.03762.

Warren, D., Moffitt, K., & Byrnes, P. (2015). How big data will change accounting. *Accounting Horizons*, *29*(2), 397–407. https://doi.org/10.2308/acch-51069

Yoon, K., Kogan, A., Vasarhelyi, M. A., & Pearce, T. (2024). External nonfinancial measures in substantive analytical procedures: Contributions of weather information. *Journal of Information Systems*, *38*(2), 143–162.

Zhang, B., Yang, H., & Liu, X.-Y. (2023). *Instruct-FinGPT: Financial sentiment analysis by instruction tuning of general-purpose large language models*. http://dx.doi.org/10.2139/ssrn.4489831

Zhao, J. J., & Wang, X. (2024). Unleashing efficiency and insights: Exploring the potential applications and challenges of ChatGPT in accounting. *Journal of Corporate Accounting & Finance*, *35*, 269–276. https://doi.org/10.1002/jcaf.22663

Chapter 3

A Survey on Cookie Disclosure and Practice

Hanchi Gu[a] *and Qing Huang*[b]

[a]*Shanghai University of Finance and Economics, China*
[b]*Marshall University, USA*

Abstract

Privacy and cookies have become increasingly prominent topics in web research. However, few studies examine companies' privacy policy and practices. This straightforward survey collects privacy policies and practices on companies' websites, analyzes the details, and examines cookie policies and practices in order to explore privacy considerations from the perspective of companies' cookie usage.

Keywords: General Data Protection Regulation; internet cookies; internet privacy; internet policy disclosures; internet policy in practice

1. Introduction

Privacy is a significant topic of discussion in the area of public and scholarly disclosure, especially in the context of online browsing and digital interactions. On January 14, 2020, Google announced its plan to phase out third-party cookies on Chrome in two years (Schuh, 2020). This announcement has been a hot topic since then. Google plans to use a new privacy plan called "Privacy Sandbox" in which a set of privacy-preserving APIs (application programming interfaces) will replace existing tracking mechanisms like third-party cookies. The privacy policies articulated by various companies serve as a critical lens through which their approaches to addressing privacy concerns can be evaluated (Schuh, 2020).

Exogenous Data in Accounting and Auditing in the Rutgers Series in Accounting Information Systems, 49–57

doi:10.1108/978-1-83608-734-220251003

These policies not only reflect the level of importance that companies place on privacy issues but also highlight the diverse strategies they employ to manage these concerns. Despite the growing interest in how companies navigate privacy challenges, a notable gap remains in the systematic analysis of the differences between privacy policies and privacy practices among companies' websites. There is a need for updated evidence to extend the literature on existing e-commerce privacy practices (Jamal et al., 2005).

To bridge that gap, this chapter examines the cookie policies and practices of various companies. Cookie policies are essential documents that detail how companies collect, store, protect, and utilize personal data gleaned from their users. Importantly, these policies offer transparency regarding the mechanisms by which companies track user activities and preferences through the use of cookies. The term "cookie practices," as used in this research, refers to the actual methodologies that these companies implement in the management of personal data. Note that there can be discrepancies between the stated cookie policies and companies' actual practices. Such discrepancies could pose significant privacy risks to unsuspecting users.

To address these concerns, this research is structured around two primary objectives. First, we conduct a survey that focuses on the content of the cookie policies published by a broad spectrum of companies. This survey aims to disaggregate and understand the various dimensions and commitments outlined in these policies. Then, we compare the documented cookie policies and the real-world cookie practices of these companies. This comparative analysis is designed to identify any divergences between policy and practice with an emphasis on understanding the potential implications of these divergences concerning user privacy.

By undertaking this exploratory analysis, our research sheds light on the current landscape of cookie policy design and implementation across different companies. Our investigation aims to contribute insights into the consistency between what companies pledge to do in their cookie policies and what they actually do in practice. This study not only enriches the academic discourse on privacy policy analysis but also holds practical implications for policymakers, industry stakeholders, and users who are concerned about their online privacy.

In this research, we conduct a survey to investigate the current state of companies' cookie policy designs and practices as an exploratory analysis. Cookie policies, standard on most official company websites, outline the protocols that govern the collection, storage, security, and utilization of users' personal data. Understanding the alignment between stated policies and actual practices is crucial. While cookie policies delineate intended procedures, the term "cookie practices" refers to the real actions undertaken by companies in collecting, storing, protecting, and utilizing personal data. Discrepancies between policy and practice can potentially expose users to risks. This study involves an examination of the content of cookie policies across diverse companies, followed by a comparative analysis of these policies with the observed cookie practices. This approach allows us to discern any gaps or inconsistencies between stated intentions and operational realities.

2. Related Regulations

As defined by the General Data Protection Regulation (GDPR), cookies refer to small files that websites store on users' devices while users navigate through them (GDPR, 2016). First developed and deployed by Netscape in 1994, cookies have been under political scrutiny since 1998 (Jones, 2020).

Governments worldwide are increasingly focusing on privacy issues, and over 100 countries have privacy laws or regulations. Cookie-related content has emerged as a prominent topic within privacy discussions. Many regulations address cookies both directly and indirectly. For instance, the International Organization for Standardization (ISO) published its Privacy Framework on December 15, 2011. The U.S. Securities and Exchange Commission issued the Commission Statement and Guidance on Public Company Cybersecurity Disclosures on February 21, 2018. The National Institute of Standards and Technology released its cybersecurity framework on April 16, 2018. In addition, the ePrivacy Directive (EPD) was initially passed in 2002 and amended in 2009. The European Union's GDPR came into effect on May 25, 2018.

This study focuses on the principles derived from the GDPR and EPD. The GDPR, which is globally hailed as the most comprehensive and stringent privacy and security law, has garnered significant attention since its inception. While it was enacted by the European Union (EU), it is widely perceived to have a global impact (Wolford, 2019). The EPD is also closely linked to cookies, supplementing and sometimes superseding the GDPR in various areas. Notably, the EPD and GDPR outline five principles regarding cookie compliance (GDPR, 2016):

1. Receive users' consent before you use any cookies except strictly necessary cookies.
2. Provide accurate and specific information about the data each cookie tracks and its purpose in plain language before consent is received.
3. Document and store consent received from users.
4. Allow users to access your service even if they refuse to allow the use of certain cookies.
5. Make it as easy for users to withdraw their consent as it was for them to give their consent in the first place.

These five principles cover the most important topics that a company needs to consider in its cookie policies and cookie practices. While the specifics of cookie-related laws may vary across jurisdictions, these principles represent the fundamental concepts that are often found in many regulatory frameworks worldwide, not just in the EU. Therefore, we can extract variables from these principles and assess their applicability to companies.

3. Data Collection and Methodology

This section outlines the steps for data collection and analysis. Fig. 3.1 provides an overview of these methodologies.

Fig. 3.1. Overview of the Research Workflow.

First, we gathered information from Compustat on each company's website. This step begins with companies listed in Compustat on Wharton Research Data Services (WRDS) for the fiscal years 2019 and 2020. Then, we narrow down the sample to include only those companies with available "weburl" information. These companies are then categorized into micro, small, medium, and large based on their numbers of employees, following the classification standard of the Organization for Economic Co-operation and Development (OECD). Finally, we randomly select 100 companies from the sample for analysis.

Second, we define the policy content by referring to existing research and constructing some new variables based on our summary. Third, we collect the privacy and cookie policies from the companies' websites and manually label a small sample. The data are collected by December 2020. Fourth, we extract the keywords for each variable based on our labeled dataset and apply them to the larger dataset. Finally, we test the relationship between variables representing the policy content and variables from other firms' variables not related to policy. As a result, we can explain the most influential factors in a company's privacy policy.

Our data contain the list of companies, the cookie policies for these companies, and the cookie practices for these companies. The list of companies is collected using Compustat from the WRDS website. The cookie policies are derived from the official websites of each company. The cookie practices are collected manually on official websites. The website Cookiebot[1] is used as another source

[1]https://www.cookiebot.com/

for cookie practice data. Another dataset for additional tests is the list of popular websites that is collected from Cisco Umbrella Popularity List. These popular websites are frequently visited.

Our first concern is that companies of different sizes have different privacy policy disclosures. To assess this concern, we test some of the most common content on companies of different sizes. The method used to divide companies based on their size comes from OECD.[2] The company sizes are divided into four levels: micro enterprises (fewer than 10 employees), small enterprises (10–49 employees), medium-sized enterprises (50–249 employees), and large enterprises (250 or more employees).

We randomly selected 10 micro firms, 10 small firms, 10 medium firms, and 20 large firms from each group to explore their privacy policy disclosures. The results, shown in Table 3.1, indicate that large firms have significantly more complete content in their privacy policy disclosures than smaller firms.

Our analysis further confirms that large companies, as indicated by their presence on the Cisco Umbrella Popularity List,[3] attract more visitors. By contrast, small and medium companies are not informative about their policies, and their websites are not frequently visited by users. Including these companies in our study would result in data that are sparse and difficult to deal with. Therefore, we

Table 3.1. Comparison of Cookie Policy Prevalence Percentage Among Companies of Different Sizes.

Number	Privacy Policy	Micro Firm (n = 10)	Small Firm (n = 10)	Medium Firm (n = 10)	Large Firm (n = 20)
1	Disclose that the website is using cookies	40%	80%	60%	80%
2	Explain what cookies are	10%	40%	40%	75%
3	Explain how to turn off/decline cookies	30%	30%	30%	60%
4	Disclose the presence of third-party cookies on the website	10%	10%	40%	70%
5	Disclose how data are used	20%	30%	70%	100%
6	Has separate cookies policy	0	0	20%	50%

[2]https://data.oecd.org/entrepreneur/enterprises-by-business-size.html
[3]http://s3-us-west-1.amazonaws.com/umbrella-static/index.html

focus on large companies in the following exploratory analysis because large companies have complete and useful websites that help us to test their cookie practice, and their cookie policies are more informative.

4. Exploratory Analysis Results

In the five principles of cookie compliance, we note that Principle 1 is a prerequisite for Principle 5. Thus, Principle 5 will not happen without the occurrence of Principle 1. Therefore, we combine them. The new combined principle shows both the cookie consent information and its influence on website usage. Our four new principles are listed below:

1. Receive users' consent before you use any cookies except strictly necessary cookies. Allow users to access your service even if they refuse to allow the use of certain cookies.
2. Provide accurate and specific information about the data each cookie tracks and its purpose in plain language before consent is received.
3. Document and store consent received from users.
4. Make it as easy for users to withdraw their consent as it was for them to give their consent in the first place.

Since our goal is to make all variables derived from these principles easy to use in the real world, we create variables for disclosure and practice separately. For disclosure, we test whether the cookie policy discloses the consequence of users' refusal to consent, the usage of third-party cookies, cookie retention periods, and the existence of an introduction to turning off cookies. We also test if firms disclose whether and how users' consents are stored.

For the practice component of our analysis, we first test whether the consent exists. If there is consent, we test whether the website can be accessed without consenting to the usage of third-party cookies. We also test if there is an undisclosed third-party cookie and if there is an abnormal cookie retention period. Other variables include whether the cookie can be turned off easily and whether the consent is stored. A summary of variables is shown in Table 3.2. To simplify the variable names, the variables are renamed as X_n for disclosure or Y_n for practice.

From the previous analysis, it is evident that large firms typically maintain a comprehensive cookie policy. Moreover, large companies usually possess well-developed websites. We also conduct an additional test of company size on popular websites from the Cisco Umbrella Popularity List. Results show that frequently visited websites are all for large firms. Therefore, in this section, we randomly select 100 large companies for further examination to analyze the discrepancies between their stated cookie policies and actual practices.

Table 3.3 summarizes the findings from our analysis of cookie policy and cookies practice for sampled large companies. It reveals that 71% of the sample companies disclose the consequences of not consenting in their policies, while only 33% actively present consent pop-ups upon a user's initial visit to their site.

Table 3.2. Variables for Disclosure and Practice.

Disclosure	Practice
Disclose the consequence of refusing the consent (X_1)	Have consent or not Normally use the website if refuse cookies (Y_1)
Disclose third-party cookie (X_2)	Check third-party cookie usage (Y_2)
Cookie retention period (X_3)	Real cookie retention period (Y_3)
Introduction to turn off cookie (X_4)	Easy to turn off cookie (Y_4)
Disclose whether and how the consents are stored (X_5)	Check whether the disclosure of consent storage exists (Y_5)

Table 3.3. Cookie Policy and Cookies Practice for Sampled Large Companies.

	X_1	X_2	X_3	X_4	X_5	Y_1	Y_2	Y_3	Y_4	Y_5
Number	71	74	37	70	26	33	88	66	53	21
Percentage	71%	74%	37%	70%	26%	33%	88%	66%	53%	21%

Further analysis indicates that 29 out of the 71 companies that disclose the consequences of non-consent also implement consent pop-ups (40.8%). Conversely, among the 29 companies that do not disclose these consequences, only four deploy consent pop-ups (13.8%). This suggests that companies that explain the repercussions of refusing third-party cookies are more likely to introduce consent pop-ups on a user's first visit.

The study also highlights a correlation between the disclosure of third-party cookie usage and adherence to cookie policies. Specifically, 68 of the 74 companies that acknowledge the use of third-party cookies, indeed, utilize them (91.9% compliance), compared to 20 out of 26 companies that do not disclose this information yet still use third-party cookies (76.9% compliance).

Regarding data retention periods, the analysis shows a marginal difference in practices related to the disclosure of retention periods. Twelve companies have unusually long retention periods (exceeding three years or their stated terms) out of the 37 that specify their retention policies (32.4%). In addition, 22 of the 63 companies that do not disclose their retention periods engage in similar practices (34.9%), suggesting a weak correlation between disclosure and actual retention practices.

The research further examines the ease of disabling cookies. Results show that 46 of the 70 companies that provide instructions for turning off cookies make it straightforward to do so (65.7% compliance). In contrast, only 7 of the 30 companies that lack such disclosures facilitate an easy opt-out (23.3% compliance), indicating that transparency about disabling cookies positively impacts user control.

Finally, among companies that disclose consent storage and employ consent pop-ups at the first visit, 9 out of 12 companies store user consent (75% compliance). For companies that neither disclose consent storage nor use initial consent pop-ups, only 7 out of 21 store consent (33.3% compliance) although the small sample size limits the conclusiveness of this trend. Nonetheless, the findings suggest that transparency regarding consent storage is positively associated with the practice of storing user consent.

The disclosure of cookie policies positively affects companies' practices related to the consequences of refusing consent and the process of disabling cookies. Disclosing cookie policies also has a positive effect on third-party cookie use and consent storage. However, the impact on retention periods remains ambiguous.

5. Conclusion

This chapter investigates companies' cookie policies and practices. First, this study examines the relationship between company size and the disclosure of privacy policies. Large companies are generally more informative and are selected for the following exploratory analysis. Second, we analyze the correlation between the cookie policies and practices. This research offers web users insights into how their web browsing activity is utilized by company websites. The analysis indicates that companies that are transparent about third-party cookie usage and the consequences of non-consent are more likely to implement and adhere to cookie consent practices, including displaying consent pop-ups and storing user consent. In addition, there appears to be a positive correlation between the disclosure of instructions for disabling cookies and the ease of opting out. Regulators can benefit from this study by gaining a better understanding of firms' cookie policies and practices. Regulators should note that enhancing transparency requirements around cookie policies may improve compliance with consent practices and user control mechanisms.

This research is subject to certain limitations. The analysis is confined to cookies from official websites, so it overlooks potentially relevant cookies from other sources. In addition, the research is limited to a small-scale survey. Future research could explore the disclosure and practice of privacy policies within specific industries, such as healthcare, finance, or e-commerce, examining how these policies are implemented. Additionally, constructing a more extensive, large-scale survey could provide broader and more reliable insights into the effectiveness of current privacy policies and their implementation in practice.

References

General Data Protection Regulation (GDPR). (2016). *Cookies, the GDPR, and the ePrivacy directive*. https://gdpr.eu/cookies/

Jamal, K., Maier, M., & Sunder, S. (2005). Enforced standards versus evolution by general acceptance: A comparative study of e-commerce privacy disclosure and practice in the United States and the United Kingdom. *Journal of Accounting Research*, *43*(1), 73–96.

Jones, M. L. (2020). Cookies: A legacy of controversy. *Internet Histories*, *4*(1), 87–104.

Schuh, J. (2020). *Building a more private web: A path towards making third party cookies obsolete*. https://blog.chromium.org/2020/01/building-more-private-web-path-towards.html

Wolford, B. (2019). *What is GDPR, the EU's new data protection law?* https://gdpr.eu/what-is-gdpr/

Part Two

Exogenous Data from Google Trends

Chapter 4

The Search Volume Index for Business Analysis

Fangbing Xiong

Rutgers Business School, USA

Abstract

This chapter explores the increasingly pivotal role of Internet search data as an exogenous component of business analysis. Search volume index (SVI) data, often called "big data," has become an essential business asset. SVI is primarily obtained through platforms like Google Trends, and it reflects the volume of specific search terms over time. As society increasingly relies on the Internet, companies can gain insights into consumers' preferences, intentions, and behaviors using SVI. Since SVI is exogenous, objective, accessible, real-time, structured, and customizable, it makes a superior data source for analysts to explore investors' attention. This chapter explores how SVI is applied in various business research domains through a review and summary of SVI studies. By leveraging SVI, firms can better understand and address their stakeholders' needs, fostering a more efficient and effective business environment, while business analysts can incorporate SVI into their assessments, augmenting the depth and accuracy of their insights.

Keywords: Search volume index; big data analytics; consumer behavior; market analysis; digital footprints; data-driven insights; investor attention; internet search trends

Exogenous Data in Accounting and Auditing in the Rutgers Series in Accounting Information Systems, 61–70

Published under exclusive licence by Emerald Publishing Limited
doi:10.1108/978-1-83608-734-220251004

1. Introduction

In today's digital age, the Internet has become an integral part of our daily lives. From checking emails to streaming videos, from shopping online to participating in virtual meetings, our dependence on the Internet is undeniable. A day without the Internet makes many of us feel disconnected, almost as if we have been transported back to the Stone Age. However, as we navigate the huge expanse of the digital world, we leave traces of our activities, creating digital footprints that are vast and ever-growing. This continuous stream of data, often referred to as "big data," is a goldmine of information.

One of the most common activities that people engage in online is searching. Whether it is investors looking for the latest market news, consumers seeking the best deals, or simply individuals exploring trending topics for entertainment, online searches are a window into our collective consciousness. Every query entered into a search engine is meticulously recorded and aggregated, forming the basis for the SVI, which tracks and quantifies our collective searching behavior, offering detailed snapshots of public interest and trends over time.

A vivid illustration of this is seen when consumers search on Google to compare the prices of products, such as the "green hats" displayed on the Google homepage with different price tags, as shown in Fig. 4.1. While a single search for the best price of a green hat on Google may not seem significant, when thousands of similar searches occur in a short timeframe, they contribute to a recognizable increase in the SVI. In this example, fluctuations or the lack of fluctuations in the SVI indicate the practical utility of the Internet in making informed purchasing decisions. Moreover, it captures real-time consumer preferences and intentions, reflecting the real-time impact of collective search behaviors on market trends.

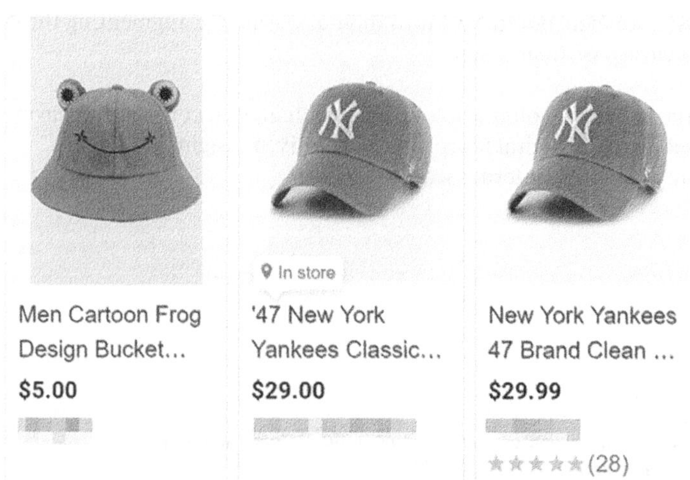

Fig. 4.1. Consumer Search on Google to Compare Prices for "green hats."
Source: Google Search, 2023.

The insights we get from SVI are about more than just numbers; they offer a real look into what people do, like, and want online. Businesses are starting to see how valuable this information is, and they are putting increasing effort into understanding it better. Analysts can spot new trends and patterns by looking closely at this data. Analyzing and diving into SVI help companies to determine what their customers are looking for and why. With this knowledge, they can make smarter choices about what to do next. Using SVI's ability to predict what might happen in the market, businesses can adjust their offerings to match what their customers want.

In addition to trend prediction and customer preference analysis, exogenous evidence from SVI can also act as a reality check for businesses. The insights from SVI can be useful for auditing purposes. By serving as an external benchmark, this data allows auditors to cross-verify a company's reported performance against observable trends in stakeholders' interests and behavior. For example, SVI can be a powerful tool for ensuring that internal records and strategies are in sync with real-world market dynamics.

2. The Back-to-school Spike: An SVI Example

Imagine a college student named Alex. As the new semester approaches, Alex realizes he needs a new backpack. Like many of us, his first instinct is to turn to Google. He types in "best backpacks for college students" and starts browsing through the results. Unbeknown to Alex, his search query is recorded by Google, not in a way that infringes on his privacy, but as an anonymous data point among billions of other searches.

Now, Alex is not the only one who has this idea. Thousands of students across the country are doing the same thing, looking for supplies, gadgets, and essentials for the upcoming academic year. As more students search for similar items, this collective behavior starts to form a pattern. Enter Google Trends. If one were to look up "best backpacks" on Google Trends during this period, they would likely notice a spike in search volume. This increase is the SVI in action. The graph would show a clear uptrend, indicating a heightened interest in this particular topic. A graph of the periodic trends in searches for "best backpacks" is shown in Fig. 4.2.

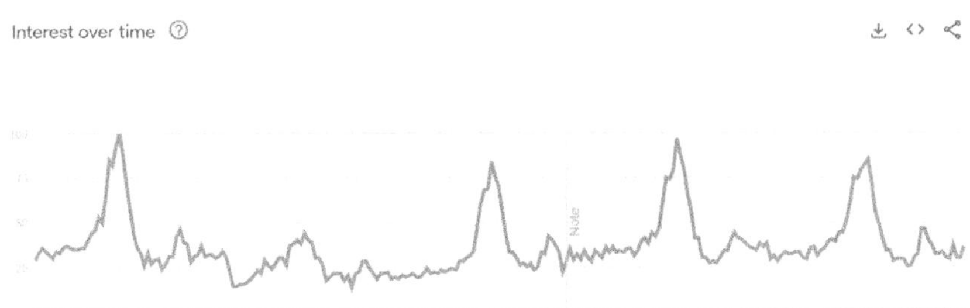

Fig. 4.2. A Periodic Peak Each August in a Google Trends Search for "best backpacks." *Source*: Google Trends, 2023.

This trend is not just a statistical result. For businesses, it is a signal. Retailers might stock up on backpacks, introduce sales, or launch targeted advertising campaigns. For analysts, it reflects consumer behavior, indicating the cyclical nature of shopping patterns that are aligned with the academic calendar.

In essence, every time Alex and his peers search for something related to their college needs, they contribute to a larger digital trend. This is a perfect example of individual actions collectively shaping the digital landscape and influencing market dynamics.

We can see from this example that SVI is a measure of how often people search for specific terms or topics over a given period. It offers a snapshot of public interest in real time, reflecting the ebb and flow of our collective curiosity.

3. A Broader Landscape of SVI

Among the various tools that provide insights into SVI, Google Trends stands out as one of the most popular. It allows users to see how frequently a term has been searched for on Google over time, visually representing its popularity. Google trends are derived from aggregating and analyzing search query data, reflecting the relative popularity or interest level for specific terms or topics. This metric is normalized and presented on a scale, allowing for comparative analysis across different terms, regions, and time frames. The process involves categorizing search queries, anonymizing user data, and aggregating results to view search trends comprehensively.

3.1. Functions of Google Trends

Google Trends is a powerful tool for anyone interested in looking into the world of search trends and understanding the digital footprint of specific terms over time. This section explores the customized functions available in Google Trends, using "Apple" as an example to demonstrate how users can customize their searches to gather insights.

Customizing search terms: When entering a term like "apple" into Google Trends, users can customize their search to distinguish among different meanings of the term. For instance, "apple" can be refined to represent the fruit or the technology company. This distinction is crucial for researchers and marketers who are interested in analyzing trends related to a specific context, as shown in Fig. 4.3.

Geographic customization: Google Trends allows users to narrow their search geographically. You can set the scope of your inquiry to be global or pinpoint a specific area, country, or region. This feature is helpful in understanding how interest in a term varies across different locations, enabling a localized analysis of trends.

Time frame adjustment: The platform offers the flexibility to change the time period of the search, ranging from as far back as 2004 to the present. This function enables users to observe how interest in a term has evolved over time, identify seasonal patterns, or assess the impact of specific events on search popularity.

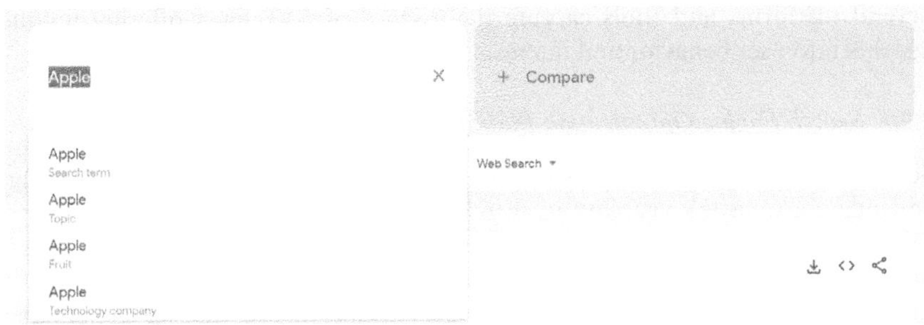

Fig. 4.3. Opportunity to Refine the Search Term "apple." *Source*: Google Trends, 2023.

Fig. 4.4. Most Popular Results for a Geographic Google Trends Search. *Source*: Google Trends, 2023.

Search type selection: Users can further refine their search by selecting the type of search they are interested in. Google Trends provides options for web search, image search, YouTube search, and more. This allows for an analysis of how a term is being explored across different Google services.

Industry categories: Google Trends categorizes searches by industry, allowing users to filter their search terms within a specific sector. This categorization helps to isolate the data relevant to a particular industry, making the insights more targeted and relevant.

Interest by subregion: Another feature of Google Trends is its ability to show interest by subregion. This function reveals the locations where your term was most popular during the specified time frame. The values are calculated on a scale from 0 to 100, where 100 represents the location with the highest popularity as a fraction of total searches in that location. A score of 50 indicates a location half as popular, and a score of 0 means there was not enough data for this term in that location. Fig. 4.4 shows the most popular results for a geographic Google Trends search.

3.2. SVI Platforms Other than Google Trends

While Google Trends is a prominent tool for gauging search interest, it is just the tip of the iceberg when it comes to understanding the broader concept of SVI.

Several platforms and tools capture the essence of SVI, each offering unique insights into user behavior and interests.

3.2.1. Search Engine Optimization Platforms

Search engine optimization (SEO) plays a pivotal role in digital marketing, enhancing a website's visibility in search engine results to attract more visitors. SEO employs SVI data to gain a better understanding of users' intent, offering valuable insights into the queries and topics that users are actively searching for. This understanding enables the strategic optimization of website content and keyword selection, enhancing a site's relevance and visibility in search results. Here are two examples of SEO platforms.

Bing keyword research tool: Much like Google, Bing offers its own keyword research tool that provides data on search volumes for specific keywords on its platform. Unlike Google Trends, which anyone can access without the need to sign in, the Bing Keyword Research Tool is designed primarily for website owners. The Bing Keyword Research tool aims to help website owners improve their website's visibility on Bing.

SEMrush: SEMrush is a comprehensive SEO toolkit that offers a wide range of features beyond keyword search volume data. It provides tools for keyword research, on-page SEO, competitor analysis, etc., making it a versatile platform for enhancing online visibility.

3.2.2. Social Media SVI

The concept of SVI is not limited to search engines. Social media platforms and topic-trending websites also employ similar metrics to gauge interest in specific topics or keywords. Here are two notable social media SVIs.

X Trends: Trending topics on X are a real-time reflection of what people are discussing on the platform. These trends can be seen as a form of SVI, indicating the most talked-about subjects at any given moment.

Instagram hashtag popularity: Instagram's popular hashtags can also be seen as a form of SVI, indicating the trending topics and interests among its user base.

Merging the data from all of these platforms gives a more complete picture of what is buzzing in the digital world. It helps business analysts to stay in tune with what people are into, spot the next big thing, and tweak their plans to fit that trend. In today's world, where digital traces are everywhere, SVI is like a roadmap, showing us the way through the ever-changing likes and wants of the online crowd.

4. Applications of SVI

4.1. Market Insights and Consumer Behavior

Businesses and marketers leverage SVI to gain insights into consumer behavior, preferences, and trends. By analyzing search volume patterns, companies can identify emerging trends, understand consumer interest in products or services, and tailor their strategies accordingly. For instance, a surge in search volume for specific products could indicate rising consumer interest, guiding businesses' inventory management, marketing campaigns, and product development. The utilization of Google Trends data as a measure of consumer "buzz" has proven effective in enhancing pre-release predictions of movie revenues, demonstrating the value of SVI in marketing and economic forecasting (France et al., 2021). Furthermore, the analysis of Google Searches related to firm products offers a novel approach to assessing revenue quality and detecting revenue management practices, highlighting SVI's role in financial assurance and fraud detection (Chiu et al., 2023). As reflected by changes in SVI, retail investors' attention significantly affects stock liquidity, enlarging the shareholder base and improving the marketability of stocks, underscoring SVI's importance in financial market analysis (Ding & Hou, 2015). In addition, applying higher frequency search query data to forecasting tourist arrivals at attractions showcases SVI's predictive power in tourism management, allowing for more accurate and timely planning decisions (Volchek et al., 2019). These examples collectively illustrate the multifaceted applications of SVI across various industries, from entertainment and finance to tourism, providing businesses with a dynamic tool for navigating the digital marketplace.

4.2. Financial Markets

SVI also has applications in the financial sector, particularly in predicting market movements and investor behavior. Studies show a significant correlation between changes in SVI and stock market activity, including trading volume and stock price volatility. For example, an increase in search volume for a company's stock is often followed by a corresponding increase in trading volume and can signal shifts in investors' attention and market sentiment. SVI has been instrumental in predicting short-term return reversals, temporary increases in volatility, and mutual fund flows, highlighting the predictive power of SVI in financial markets (Da et al., 2011, 2015). Moreover, evidence from China suggests that higher retail investor attention, as measured by SVI, is associated with a lower future stock price crash risk, indicating SVI's role in assessing market stability (Wen et al., 2019).

A study on global stock returns finds that an increase in investors' attention, as captured by SVI, leads to a significant decrease in index returns, which aligns with the investor recognition hypothesis and illustrates how SVI reflects broader market sentiments (Chen, 2017). In the realm of FX (foreign exchange) markets, investors' attention, as gauged by SVI, has been identified as a priced source of risk, further underscoring the importance of SVI in understanding market dynamics and investor behavior (Goddard et al., 2015). Finally, incorporating search queries into autoregressive models of realized volatility improves volatility forecasts, demonstrating SVI's utility in enhancing predictive models for stock market volatility (Dimpfl & Jank, 2016). These findings collectively underscore the multifaceted applications of SVI in the financial sector, offering a robust tool for analysts and investors to navigate the complexities of market movements and investor psychology.

4.3. Academic and Policy Research

Researchers utilize SVI to study various socio-economic and public health trends. By analyzing search patterns, scholars can uncover insights into public interest and awareness regarding disease outbreaks, economic changes, or political events. This data can inform policy-making, public health campaigns, and academic studies, providing a real-time pulse on societal issues. For instance, the FEARS index, derived from internet search volumes, has been used to predict market behaviors, such as short-term return reversals and mutual fund flows, reflecting broader economic sentiments that could influence economic forecasting and policy-making (Da et al., 2015). Similarly, SVI's significant relationship with oil price volatility demonstrates its potential as a tool for understanding market dynamics, offering valuable insights for policymakers in the energy sector (Campos et al., 2017). Moreover, the ability of brand-focused search traffic to forecast sales volume beyond traditional economic indicators highlights SVI's utility in economic modeling and consumer behavior analysis, suggesting its relevance for economic policy and research (Tantaopas et al., 2016). These examples collectively illustrate the multifaceted applications of SVI in providing timely insights into socio-economic and public health trends, underscoring its value to researchers, policymakers, and public health officials alike.

4.4. Challenges and Considerations

The SVI is a handy tool that offers insights into public interest and search behavior trends, that is, understanding what people are interested in by looking at their online search trends. While SVI offers valuable insights, it is not without limitations. There are a few things to keep in mind when using this tool.

First, SVI only shows us some things. It is derived from a subset of internet searches, subjected to normalization and filtering to ensure anonymity and relevance. SVI is based on many searches, but not all of them. The data has been cleaned and made anonymous, which is great for privacy, but it means that we might not get the complete picture of what people are actually searching for. So, using SVI is like getting a snapshot of interest or curiosity. SVI should be interpreted as an indicator of interest or attention, rather than a direct measure of action or opinion. For example, heightened search volumes for a product signify increased interest but do not necessarily correlate with purchase behavior.

The distinction between search interest and actual behavior underscores the importance of contextual analysis and sentiment when utilizing SVI. High search volumes may reflect curiosity or concern but do not inherently indicate a positive sentiment or engagement with the topic. This characteristic highlights the need to combine SVI data with other sources to understand consumer behavior and societal trends comprehensively. For example, many searches for a new smartphone model do not guarantee that sales will go through the roof. If the new smartphone has an obvious fault, that could lead to a vigorous online discussion but not increased sales.

SVI's value extends to serving as an exogenous data source for auditors and business analysts. Auditors can leverage SVI to verify a company's claims regarding product popularity or market trends. By comparing SVI trends with internal sales data or marketing metrics, auditors can assess the veracity of reported information, making SVI a potent tool for enhancing the accuracy and reliability of audits. However, the auditors should use SVI as support for direct evidence, rather than relying on SVI alone.

Mixing SVI with other kinds of data can maximize its effectiveness. Looking at sales data, social media trends, or customer surveys alongside SVI can give a more complete picture of what is going on. It is like putting together a puzzle – the more pieces you have, the clearer the picture becomes.

5. Conclusion

Overall, SVI is an excellent tool for presenting a valuable perspective on digital search trends, but it is important to remember its limits. By combining it with other data, business analysts can use SVI to get valuable insights into market dynamics and consumer behavior. Moreover, keep in mind that SVI shows interest rather than direct action.

References

Campos, I., Cortazar, G., & Reyes, T. (2017). Modeling and predicting oil VIX: Internet search volume versus traditional mariables. *Energy Economics*, *66*, 194–204. https://doi.org/10.1016/j.eneco.2017.06.009

Chen, T. (2017). Investor attention and global stock returns. *Journal of Behavioral Finance*, *18*(3), 358–372. https://doi.org/10.1080/15427560.2017.1331235

Chiu, P.-C., Teoh, S. H., Zhang, Y., & Huang, X. (2023). Using Google searches of firm products to detect revenue management. *Accounting, Organizations and Society*, *109*, 101457. https://doi.org/10.1016/j.aos.2023.101457

Da, Z., Engelberg, J., & Gao, P. (2011). In search of attention. *The Journal of Finance*, *66*(5), 1461–1499. https://doi.org/10.1111/j.1540-6261.2011.01679.x

Da, Z., Engelberg, J., & Gao, P. (2015). The sum of all FEARS Investor sentiment and asset prices. *Review of Financial Studies*, *28*(1), 1–32. https://doi.org/10.1093/rfs/hhu072

Dimpfl, T., & Jank, S. (2016). Can Internet search queries help to predict stock market volatility? *European Financial Management*, *22*(2), 171–192. https://doi.org/10.1111/eufm.12058

Ding, R., & Hou, W. (2015). Retail investor attention and stock liquidity. *Journal of International Financial Markets, Institutions and Money*, *37*, 12–26. https://doi.org/10.1016/j.intfin.2015.04.001

France, S. L., Shi, Y., & Kazandjian, B. (2021). Web trends: A valuable tool for business research. *Journal of Business Research*, *132*, 666–679. https://doi.org/10.1016/j.jbusres.2020.10.019

Goddard, J., Kita, A., & Wang, Q. (2015). Investor attention and FX market volatility. *Journal of International Financial Markets, Institutions and Money*, *38*, 79–96. https://doi.org/10.1016/j.intfin.2015.05.001

Tantaopas, P., Padungsaksawasdi, C., & Treepongkaruna, S. (2016). Attention effect via internet search intensity in Asia-Pacific stock markets. *Pacific-Basin Finance Journal*, *38*, 107–124. https://doi.org/10.1016/j.pacfin.2016.03.008

Volchek, K., Liu, A., Song, H., & Buhalis, D. (2019). Forecasting tourist arrivals at attractions: Search engine empowered methodologies. *Tourism Economics*, *25*(3), 425–447. https://doi.org/10.1177/1354816618811558

Wen, F., Xu, L., Ouyang, G., & Kou, G. (2019). Retail investor attention and stock price crash risk: Evidence from China. *International Review of Financial Analysis*, *65*, 101376. https://doi.org/10.1016/j.irfa.2019.101376

Chapter 5

Two Studies Using Exogenous Internet Data to Assess Investors' Attention

Maria Guangyue Zhang

Rutgers Business School, USA

Abstract

This chapter introduces two papers with the common theme of studying investors' attention using exogenous data. The first paper explores the Google Trends Search Volume (SVI) as a proxy for investors' attention and studies the change in their attention to traditional financial disclosures. The second paper uses news sources to investigate the range of topics that attract investors' attention for a new asset class: cryptocurrency. Together, these papers demonstrate the insights that can be drawn from different exogenous data sources and some analytics tools that can be used to assess unstructured data.

Keywords: Investor attention; search volume index; Google trends; cryptocurrency valuation; unstructured data; news analytics; exogenous data sources

Introduction

The two papers in this chapter study two interesting aspects of investors' attention to endogenous datasets. The first paper uses the search volume index (SVI) as a proxy for investors' attention and studies the change in investors' attention to traditional financial disclosures over time to understand the distribution of their attention between traditional financial disclosure and more real-time firm information from information intermediaries in the current information climate.

Exogenous Data in Accounting and Auditing in the Rutgers Series in Accounting Information Systems, 71–88

Published under exclusive licence by Emerald Publishing Limited
doi:10.1108/978-1-83608-734-220251005

The second paper investigates various topics of investors' attention for a new asset class – cryptocurrency – to reveal investors' areas of interest in this new asset type.

Part A – The Change in Investors' Attention to Firms' Annual Reports: Evidence from Google Trends for S&P 500 Firms from 2010 to 2020

Background

The last decade has seen an explosion in the amount of information that investors can access on firms in their portfolios. Various information channels provide all kinds of raw and processed information. Thus, the investors are no longer solely reliant on periodic firm-generated financial disclosures. Investors' information needs are growing and diversifying, such as socially responsible investors who want to see firms' sustainability efforts. Information timeliness and verifiability also matter when forming investment strategies. Entering the era of the internet and big data, investors have access to instantaneous information feeds on firms in their portfolios. This section studies whether investors' attention to firms' annual reports has changed over the past 10 years and assesses the value of traditional periodic reporting to emerging information intermediaries in real-time and exogenous information feeds to investors.

This study contributes to the research on investors' attention by providing direct empirical evidence of the change in investors' information demand through various information channels. The results have regulatory implications for reconsidering and revising the form and frequency of firms' information disclosures and standard setting to increase information usefulness. This study uses the Google Trends SVI to measure investors' attention to traditional information channels like Edgar and information intermediaries like investing.com and bloomberg.com. Investors' cumulative attention and their attention around event windows (e.g., annual report issuing date) from 2010 to 2020 are examined with a *t*-test. The significance of the change in the division of investors' attention between the traditional information channel and digital information intermediaries indicates that investors need customized, real-time, and exogenous information about reporting entities in the big data era. It is time for reporting entities to recognize and embrace the change. This section also provides thoughts on how to carry out dynamic business reporting.

Methodology

Investors' Attention Proxy and Data Collection

This study uses Google Trends SVI around the annual report publication date to proxy for investors' attention to traditional corporate disclosure. Compared to Edgar download traffic, the Google SVI has the advantage of covering more information channels that release information from annual reports. For example, information intermediaries like investing.com and bloomberg.com are major channels through which investors obtain raw or processed information disclosed in corporate annual reports. This part of investors' attention can be partially captured with SVI, which has been used to proxy for investors' information demand and has been shown to be reliable by prior research (Drake et al., 2012).

Google SVI provides the relative percentage in comparison to the date with the highest search volume in the chosen period, rather than the exact search volumes. Robotic process automation is used to collect SVI data from Google Trends. The time precision is set to a week. Due to the constraints set by Google Trends, I extract and combine data for five years at a time and use the company name as the search phrase. Google Trends provides specifications for the nature of the search phrase. Identifying the nature of the search phrase as "corporate" and avoiding confounding items, such as confusion between searches for Apple, Inc. and searches for information on fruit, improves the precision of the SVI data. The final firm-week panel shows the change in investors' attention over time. Due to the lack of precise historical search volume data, cross-sectional analysis is avoided. The empirical evidence provided in the next section is time series analysis to demonstrate the change in the relative importance of traditional financial reporting on average. The goal of this study is not to show decreasing interest in traditional financial reporting over the years. Instead, it focuses on the relative importance (i.e., the spike in search volume around the reporting release date) of periodic traditional financial reporting from firm management and real-time firm information from information intermediaries.

Event Window

Employing the Google SVI around the annual report publication date as the proxy for investors' attention to traditional corporate disclosure requires an appropriate event window around the annual report publication date in order to specify that the observed investors' attention is, indeed, on the information in corporate annual reports. Following Drake et al. (2012), this study uses an event window for earning announcements two weeks before and after the announcement date. Annual report publication dates are extracted from the Edgar company.idx files. The dates match the SVI weekly start dates, so SVIs for the two weeks before and after the matched week start are selected as the event window, and the corresponding four weekly SVIs are aggregated.

Considering the overall increasing trend of Google search usage by the general public, the trend is normalized by the yearly sum of SVIs of each firm.

Statistical Analysis of Search Trends

The statistical test used in this study is the *t*-test, which can assess the significance of the difference between investors' attention to traditional financial reporting between 2010 and 2020. Three assumptions must be made before performing the *t*-test. The first assumption is the independence of observations, meaning that the sample data has been randomly sampled from a population. The independence of observations can be assumed based on *a priori* knowledge of the data. The sample data is from S&P 500 companies, which is an independent selection of the largest companies in terms of firm value. The second assumption is the normality of data, meaning that the distribution of sample data is approximately normal, which can be tested with the Shapiro–Wilk test. The third assumption is the homogeneity of variance, meaning that the variability of the data in each group is similar, which can be tested using the Levene test. SVI data is a relative measure on a scale from 0 to 100 instead of an absolute measure, meaning that each firm in the panel has an SVI of 0 in the week with the lowest attention and an SVI of 100 representing the week with the highest attention. This relative measure proves useful in assuring the homogeneity of variance assumption.

Empirical Evidence

Sample Selection and Data Processing

The SVI data from Google Trends covers 2010–2020. The selection of firms comprises S&P 500 companies in 2010. Constrained by the availability of SVI and the operational continuity of firms, I retrieve SVI data from 2010 to 2020 for 266 firms and use Python programming language for the data analysis.

The data panels for the firm weekly SVI, the firm annual reports event window SVI, and the firm normalized annual reports event window SVI from 2010 to 2020 for the 266 firms are displayed in Figs. 5.1–5.3.

	Date	SVI	CIK
0	2019-12-22	16	1800
1	2013-03-10	36	1800
2	2013-03-17	31	1800
3	2013-03-24	35	1800
4	2013-03-31	34	1800
...	...	...	...
220899	2013-03-24	20	1474735
220900	2013-03-17	13	1474735
220901	2013-03-10	15	1474735
220902	2013-02-24	13	1474735
220903	2010-01-03	20	1474735

220904 rows × 3 columns

Fig. 5.1. Weekly SVI for Firms 2010–2020. *Source*: Google Trends SVI (2023).

	CIK	Year	index	SVI
0	1000228	2010.0	101.0	302
1	1000228	2011.0	369.0	307
2	1000228	2012.0	637.0	304
3	1000228	2013.0	905.0	320
4	1000228	2014.0	1173.0	302
...	...	...	...	...
2413	97745	2014.0	1275.0	225
2414	97745	2016.0	1543.0	179
2415	97745	2017.0	1811.0	178
2416	97745	2018.0	2079.0	193
2417	97745	2019.0	2347.0	201

2418 rows × 4 columns

Fig. 5.2. Annual Report Event Window SVI for Firms 2010–2020. *Source*: Google Trends SVI (2023).

	CIK	Year	SVI	SVI_nor
0	1000228	2010	33.082233	9.128767
1	1000228	2011	30.708413	9.997260
2	1000228	2012	29.565681	10.282192
3	1000228	2013	29.879765	10.709589
4	1000228	2014	26.580661	11.361644
...	...	...	...	...
2413	97745	2014	29.488330	7.630137
2414	97745	2016	29.738279	6.019178
2415	97745	2017	27.776828	6.408219
2416	97745	2018	29.254568	6.597260
2417	97745	2019	29.416600	6.832877

2418 rows × 4 columns

Fig. 5.3. Normalized Annual Report Event Window SVI for Firms 2010–2020. *Source*: Google Trends SVI (2023).

Empirical Results

I start by visualizing the trend of the normalized annual report event window SVI of firms and the average SVI trend from 2010 to 2020. From the displayed plot in Fig. 5.4, it is not easy to see any significant difference in trends over these 10 years in the normalized firm-week annual report event window SVI.

From the plot displayed in Fig. 5.5, the average normalized annual report event window SVI was 28.66 in 2010, slightly higher than 28.36 in 2020. To provide empirical evidence and statistical significance of the observed trend, I conduct hypothesis testing. The null hypothesis is that investors' attention to the corporate annual reports in 2020 is not significantly different from their attention in 2010.

First, I check the normality and homogeneity of the variance hypothesis before performing the t-test. The Shapiro test result (statistic = 0.612, p-value = 0) shows no significance, so the normality assumption holds. The Levene test result (statistic = 2.750, p-value = 0.0979) shows no significance, so the homogeneity of variances assumption holds.

Then, I proceed to the t-test. The result (t statistic = −0.637, p-value = 0.5242) shows no significance. Thus, I cannot reject the null hypothesis. In other words, I cannot conclude that investors' attention around the annual report publication date in 2020 is significantly different from that in 2010.

Limitations and Future Research

The insignificant test result is probably caused by this study's selection of "supercorp." The firms being analyzed belonged to the S&P 500 in 2010 and were followed for a decade after that. They are very successful and the center of

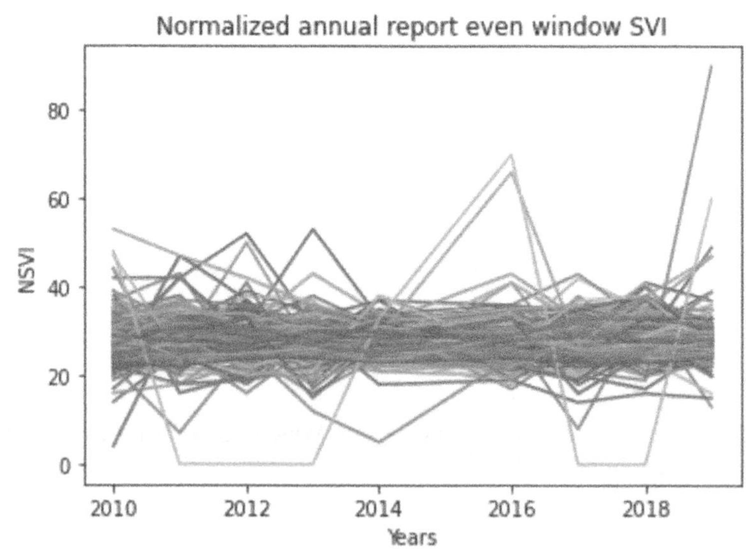

Fig. 5.4. Graph of Normalized Annual Report Event Window SVI for Firms 2010–2020. *Source*: Google Trends SVI (2023).

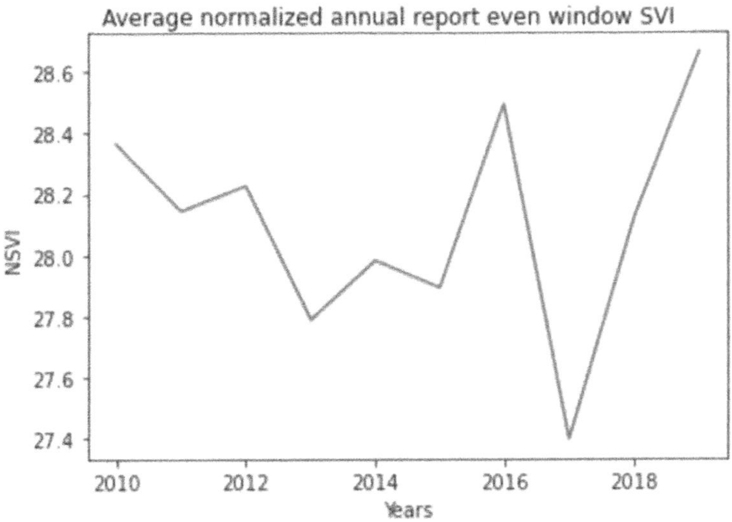

Fig. 5.5. Average Normalized Annual Report Event Window SVI for Firms 2010–2020. *Source*: Google Trends SVI (2023).

investors' attention by their nature. The test result may be different and significant if the sample firms are more diverse and include smaller firms. The current event time window is based on prior earnings announcement research.

Further research is required to study the appropriate event time window for firms' annual reports. Industry sectors may also affect the power of the search index proxy since retail sectors, for example, may suffer more noise. Different data-processing methods need to be examined, such as the normalization methods. The company name may be confused with the parent company name and its publicly traded subsidiaries when using the company name as the search phrase. Further research is needed to study the characteristics of firms with different trends of attention.

Part B – Investors' Reaction to News Information: Evidence from Cryptocurrency Valuation

Background

Problem Introduction

As a type of currency that differs significantly from fiat currencies and other financial instruments, cryptocurrencies are being traded in exchange markets. They are deeply segmented beyond the boundaries of borders and unified trading time. This means that the assets can be traded in many centralized and decentralized exchanges around the world, and there is no time limit in terms of when they can trade; these traits increase the volatility of the cryptocurrency's fiat exchange prices. The overall cryptocurrency market reaction is drastically different from that of traditional financial markets. Past study results (Shen et al., 2020) indicate that, unlike traditional financial markets, volatility in the crypto market is not associated with market downturns. When the crypto price comes down, the volatility usually does too. Studies on cryptocurrencies market price valuation and prediction explore asset pricing models (Shen et al., 2020), prediction methodology (Chen et al., 2020), and other predictive factors like social media sentiment analysis (Wolk, 2020) and socio-economic factors (Garcia et al., 2014).

News announcements are a significant way to convey relevant information, including regulations, macroeconomic events, and coin-specific incidents, to investors, which could affect investment decisions and market reaction to cryptocurrencies. For cryptocurrency valuation and future price prediction, it is important to provide empirical evidence on the topics of these announcements and their effect on the crypto market. Yet the research into news events is rare and empirical evidence of the effects of related events is limited to the exploratory paper by Coulter (2021), which provides anecdotal evidence on the effect of events in selected periods but does not study news events comprehensively because the research focus is on systematically linking Latent Dirichlet Allocation (LDA) modeling result of events to market reaction.

This section analyzes the news announcements, represents the daily announcements using LDA-based vector representation, and explores the effect of various topics on cryptocurrency market price and trading volumes. However, due to contractually limited access to data extraction, it was not possible to get sufficient data to build a price prediction model. Thus, the empirical evidence on the predictive value of news media announcements on cryptocurrency marketplace behavior remains to be explored in future studies.

For future research on cryptocurrency, it is important to build on a basic asset pricing model and add this research as an additional factor. It would also be interesting to validate the findings of this report while considering the common factor of price movement for various cryptocurrencies (e.g., the Bitwise 10 cryptocurrency portfolio). This project has valuable applications for financial trading around cryptocurrency, including cross-country arbitrage (Makarov & Schoar, 2020), cross-coin arbitrage (Figá-Talamanca et al., 2021), and ecosystem derivatives trading (Soska et al., 2021).

Research Questions

Due to the limited data sample, this study focuses on the effect of news announcements on market price and trading volume to demonstrate its potential for predicting future cryptocurrency market behavior. A potential research question for a future study could be: Does the LDA-based vector representation of news announcements increase the predictive power of existing cryptocurrency price prediction models?

This would require a more extensive literature review of the existing cryptocurrency asset pricing models with additional factors, including the role of sentiment analysis of social media and community posts, an exploration of social economic indicators, and an evaluation of the credibility of technological and consensus indicators, as well as the incorporation of comprehensive data on news announcements and cryptocurrency market price historical quotes to build new prediction model and examine the predictive power of newly proposed factors.

Dataset Description and Data Extraction

News Announcement Data Extraction

For news announcements, this study uses the NewsBank.Inc (https://infoweb-newsbank-com.proxy.libraries.rutgers.edu/apps/news/?p=AWNB) database due to its comprehensiveness, variety of advanced filtering features, and university subscription service. This website news headlines were searched for the keywords "cryptocurrency," "bitcoin," "de-fi," and "blockchain" from July 2018 to December 2018, which is a period that contains a high volume of crypto-related news. The news articles identified and downloaded all come from English language newspapers in North America to enhance credibility and reader traffic.

Cryptocurrency Market Reaction

The cryptocurrency exchange's daily trading volume and price come from the website at https://www.investing.com/crypto/bitcoin/historical-data. Daily trading volume is defined as the average trading volume for a given day, and price change is defined as the percentage change in US time-based price at the end of each 24-hour period from four major US-based exchanges (in terms of static characteristics, volumes, and market information update frequency). This study focuses on one specific active and credible cryptocurrency: Bitcoin.

Methodology and Analysis Results

Data Preparation

All data preparation and analysis use Python. The 392 news announcements identified in the search are in pdf format. They are converted to machine-readable texts using the pdfminer Python package, which achieves the best result based on several rounds of experiments. Fig. 5.6 shows the Python code to convert a pdf document into machine-readable text.

Next, a data frame is created to process the textual data. Regular expression is used to separate new announcements and parse out dates from the news announcements. Once the dates are extracted from the news announcements, they are combined with news texts of sufficient length from the same date for further analysis. This process is shown in Fig. 5.7.

At this point in the processing, the news announcements appear in combined daily texts in string format. Next, standard textual information pre-processing steps are performed. The sentences and words within those sentences are tokenized with nltk.tokenize, then pos (part-of-speech) tagged with nltk pos_tag, and each word is lemmatized according to its tag with nltk WordNetLemmatizer. After this, all non-alpha, non-English, stop words (package-defined plus self-defined) and short words are removed, and all words are changed to lowercase. Processed results are shown in Fig. 5.8. A progress map is used to track these steps.

```
from pdfminer.pdfinterp import PDFResourceManager, PDFPageInterpreter
from pdfminer.converter import TextConverter
from pdfminer.layout import LAParams
from pdfminer.pdfpage import PDFPage
from io import StringIO

def convert_pdf_to_txt(path):
    rsrcmgr = PDFResourceManager()
    retstr = StringIO()
    codec = 'utf-8'
    laparams = LAParams()
    device = TextConverter(rsrcmgr, retstr, laparams=laparams)
    fp = open(path, 'rb')
    interpreter = PDFPageInterpreter(rsrcmgr, device)
    password = ""
    maxpages = 0
    caching = True
    pagenos=set()

    for page in PDFPage.get_pages(fp, pagenos, maxpages=maxpages, password=password,cac
        interpreter.process_page(page)

    text = retstr.getvalue()

    fp.close()
    device.close()
    retstr.close()
    return text
```

```
str_text = convert_pdf_to_txt('/Users/zhangguangyue/Desktop/Articles2.pdf')
str_text
```

```
'Ohio is accepting  bitcoin for taxes\n\nNovember 27, 2018 | Columbus Dispatch, The (O
H)\nAuthor: Mark Williams; The Columbus Dispatch  Section: News  468 Words\nPage: 1B\n
OpenURL Link\n\nOhio is now accepting bitcoin to pay taxes.\n\nState Treasurer Josh Ma
ndel announced Monday the launch of OhioCrypto.com to make Ohio the first\n\nstate in
the nation to accept payments this way.\n\n"My vision is to project to the rest of the
country that Ohio is the national leader in blockchain technology\n\nand to help attra
ct talent and businesses to be part of the movement," Mandel said. Blockchain is the\n
\ntechnology used to verify bitcoin transactions.\n\nAt no time will the treasurer\'s
office hold the cryptocurrency. Payments made through OhioCrypto.com\n\nwill be immedi
ately converted into dollars before being deposited into a state account.\n\nAt this p
oint, bitcoin is the only cryptocurrency to be accepted, and it can be used to pay onl
y 23 types of\n\nbusiness taxes. Mandel\'s office would like to add other cryptocurren
cies in the future and expand it so\n\nindividuals can pay taxes with cryptocurrencies
as well.\n\nThe transactions won\'t cost the state anything.\n\nTaxpayers will pay a f
ee of 1 percent for paying with bitcoin. That\'s actually less than the 2.5 percent fe
e\n\nthey would be charged if they paid taxes with a credit card.\n\nThe state has par
tnered with BitPay, a third-party cryptocurrency payment processor, to handle the\n\np
ayments.\n\nMandel expects a slow start to OhioCrypto.com, similar to what happened wh
en he launched\n\nOhioCheckbook.com, a website where users can track spending by the s
tate and communities and\n\nschool districts that have joined. There are now more than
1 million searches on the site, he said.\n\nThe launch of the website comes as as the
```

Fig. 5.6. A Demonstration of the PDF File Converter.

LDA Topic Modeling

In this next step, a topic modeling technique is used to obtain the topics of daily announcements, and topic modeling-based vectorization is used to present these daily announcements in order to derive the correlation between these topics and changes in cryptocurrency trading price and trading volume.

To accomplish this process, the genism package and the single, bi, and gram tokenization models are imported. LDA can be conducted with bi-grams and tri-grams to make the generated topics more understandable. Given that cryptocurrency news tends to be finance-related, bi-grams and trigrams may give the topics a clearer definition. The objects for LDA genism implementation are prepared, including defining the LDA dictionary and corpus, as shown in Fig. 5.9.

```
df = pd.DataFrame(index = range(1,393),columns=['date','text','key_words','topic'])
df

    import re

    r = r'(Copyriq\sht((\s\(\sc\)\s{2})|(\,?\s))20\s18)'

    list1 = re.split(r, str_text)

    list1 = [x for x in list1 if x]
    list1 = [x for x in list1 if len(x)>1000]

    df['text'] = list1

#for extracting date
r1 = r'(January|February|March|April|May|June|July|August|September|October|November
|December)\s(\d{1,2})\,\s+(\d{4})\s\|'
for a in range(0,392):
    group = re.search(r1, df.iloc[a,1])
    df.iloc[a,0] = (group[0].translate(str.maketrans('', '', string.punctuation))).repl

    a += 1

df
```

```
In [51]: #combine articles from the same date
         df = df.groupby('date')['text'].sum().reset_index()
         df['topic'] = ''
         df['key_words'] = ''
         df
```

Out[51]:

	date	text	topic	key_words
0	August102018	[, The Hutchins on Publis hing Co., Going ...		
1	August122018	[Time s -Ne ws , The (He nde rs onville , ...		
2	August142018	[, The We natche e World, All Rig hts Re s...		
3	August152018	[, Core Me dia Group, All Rig hts Re s e rv...		
4	August162018	[, The Plain De ale r. All Rig hts Re s e r...		
...	...	...	...	...
140	September52018	[, Ne w York Pos t\n\nLearn about cryptocurr...		
141	September62018	[The Time s -Ne ws\n\nBitcoin Blackmail Sc...		
142	September72018	[, The We natche e World, All Rig hts Re s...		
143	September82018	[, Galve s ton County Daily Ne ws\n\nBitcoin...		
144	September92018	[, Wyoming Tribune -Eag le ., All rig hts r...		

145 rows × 4 columns

Fig. 5.7. Date Information Extraction from News Text.

In the next step, the number of topics is predefined after serval experiments, and the news announcements are fed into the LDA model. Nine topics are generated with token composition and ranked by weighting for all daily news announcement compilations. Each topic is defined manually. Fig. 5.10 shows the code for determining the relevance of each topic.

There are nine topics summarized by topic mining, and I can infer the topic subject from the relevant keywords. Fig. 5.11 shows the nine topics in blue in order of topic relevance, indicating how important and frequent each topic is in the news articles. Sorting from the most important and frequent topic to the least is the following: 5: government regulations on exchanges; 2: local government regulations; 0: institutional trading; 6: cryptographic/cyber security; 8: currency acceptance; 1: retail trading; 7: international events; 3: younger investor participation; 4: coin-specific.

```
In [11]: #Lemmatizing with POS tagging....Here if using upper() postag WONT work!
         import nltk
         from nltk import pos_tag
         nltk.download('averaged_perceptron_tagger')
         def pos(df):
             df['POS_tokens'] = df['tokens_sentences'].progress_map(lambda tokens_sentences: [po
         pos(df)

         [nltk_data] Downloading package averaged_perceptron_tagger to
         [nltk_data]     /Users/zhangguangyue/nltk_data...
         [nltk_data]   Package averaged_perceptron_tagger is already up-to-
         [nltk_data]       date!
         100%|██████████| 145/145 [00:19<00:00,  7.42it/s]

In [12]: from nltk.corpus import wordnet
         nltk.download('wordnet')

         def get_wordnet_pos(treebank_tag):

             if treebank_tag.startswith('J'):
                 return wordnet.ADJ
             elif treebank_tag.startswith('V'):
                 return wordnet.VERB
             elif treebank_tag.startswith('N'):
                 return wordnet.NOUN
             elif treebank_tag.startswith('R'):
                 return wordnet.ADV
             else:
                 return ''
         from nltk.stem.wordnet import WordNetLemmatizer
         lemmatizer = WordNetLemmatizer()

         def Lemmati(df):
         # Lemmatizing each word with its POS tag, in each sentence
             df['tokens_sentences_lemmatized'] = df['POS_tokens'].progress_map(
                 lambda list_tokens_POS: [
                     [
                         lemmatizer.lemmatize(el[0], get_wordnet_pos(el[1]))
                         if get_wordnet_pos(el[1]) != '' else el[0] for el in tokens_POS
                     ]
                     for tokens_POS in list_tokens_POS
                 ]
             )
         Lemmati(df)
         print(df['POS_tokens'].head(1).tolist()[0][:3])

In [9]:  #preprocessing
         import numpy as np
         from nltk.tokenize import sent_tokenize
         from tqdm import tqdm
         tqdm.pandas()

         #Tokenization
         df['text'] = df.text.progress_map(sent_tokenize)
         df['text'].head(1).tolist()[0][:3]

         100%|██████████| 145/145 [00:00<00:00, 177.30it/s]

Out[9]:  [' , The  Hutchins on Publis hing  Co.',
          'Going  a bit beyond bitcoin buzz to cash in on reality\n\nAugust 10, 2018 | China Da
         ily US Edition (USA)\nAuthor: Ullattil Manranjith  Section: News  719 Words\nPage: 14\
         nOpenURL Link\n\nTucked away amid the hustle and bustle of traffic, people and buildin
         gs in Wan Chai, Hong Kong, are\n\nsmall kiosks that hardly merit a second look.',
          'After all, in a city that sports automated teller machines and\n\ncurrency exchanges
         at virtually every nook and corner like mushrooms after a cloudburst, why would\n\nthe
         se ordinary looking terminals which do not even offer the privacy of cubicles merit an
         y attention?']

In [10]: from nltk.tokenize import word_tokenize
         def word_token(df):
             df['tokens_sentences'] = df['text'].progress_map(lambda text: [word_tokenize(x) for
             print(df['tokens_sentences'].head(1).tolist()[0][:3])
         word_token(df)

         100%|██████████| 145/145 [00:03<00:00, 44.70it/s]

         [[',', 'The', 'Hutchins', 'on', 'Publis', 'hing', 'Co', '.'], ['Going', 'a', 'bit', 'b
         eyond', 'bitcoin', 'buzz', 'to', 'cash', 'in', 'on', 'reality', 'August', '10', ',', '
         2018', '|', 'China', 'Daily', 'US', 'Edition', '(', 'USA', ')', 'Author', ':', 'Ullatt
         il', 'Manranjith', 'Section', ':', 'News', '719', 'Words', 'Page', ':', '14', 'OpenURL
         ', 'Link', 'Tucked', 'away', 'amid', 'the', 'hustle', 'and', 'bustle', 'of', 'traffic'
         , ',', 'people', 'and', 'buildings', 'in', 'Wan', 'Chai', ',', 'Hong', 'Kong', ',', 'a
         re', 'small', 'kiosks', 'that', 'hardly', 'merit', 'a', 'second', 'look', '.'], ['Afte
         r', 'all', ',', 'in', 'a', 'city', 'that', 'sports', 'automated', 'teller', 'machines'
         , 'and', 'currency', 'exchanges', 'at', 'virtually', 'every', 'nook', 'and', 'corner',
         'like', 'mushrooms', 'after', 'a', 'cloudburst', ',', 'why', 'would', 'these', 'ordina
         ry', 'looking', 'terminals', 'which', 'do', 'not', 'even', 'offer', 'the', 'privacy',
         'of', 'cubicles', 'merit', 'any', 'attention', '?']]
```

Fig. 5.8. Unstructured Textual Data Pre-processing Demonstration.

```
[[(',', ','), ('The', 'DT'), ('Hutchins', 'NNP'), ('on', 'IN'), ('Publis', 'NNP'), ('h
ing', 'VBG'), ('Co', 'NNP'), ('.', '.')], [('Going', 'VBG'), ('a', 'DT'), ('bit', 'NN'
), ('beyond', 'IN'), ('bitcoin', 'NN'), ('buzz', 'NN'), ('to', 'TO'), ('cash', 'NN'),
('in', 'IN'), ('on', 'IN'), ('reality', 'NN'), ('August', 'NNP'), ('10', 'CD'), (',',
','), ('2018', 'CD'), ('|', 'JJ'), ('China', 'NNP'), ('Daily', 'NNP'), ('US', 'NNP'),
('Edition', 'NNP'), ('(', '('), ('USA', 'NNP'), (')', ')'), ('Author', 'NN'), (':', ':
'), ('Ullattil', 'NNP'), ('Manranjith', 'NNP'), ('Section', 'NN'), (':', ':'), ('News'
, 'CC'), ('719', 'CD'), ('Words', 'NNS'), ('Page', 'NN'), (':', ':'), ('14', 'CD'), ('
OpenURL', 'NNP'), ('Link', 'NNP'), ('Tucked', 'NNP'), ('away', 'RB'), ('amid', 'IN'),
('the', 'DT'), ('hustle', 'NN'), ('and', 'CC'), ('bustle', 'NN'), ('of', 'IN'), ('traf
fic', 'NN'), (',', ','), ('people', 'NNS'), ('and', 'CC'), ('buildings', 'NNS'), ('in'
, 'IN'), ('Wan', 'NNP'), ('Chai', 'NNP'), (',', ','), ('Hong', 'NNP'), ('Kong', 'NNP')
, (',', ','), ('are', 'VBP'), ('small', 'JJ'), ('kiosks', 'NNS'), ('that', 'WDT'), ('h
ardly', 'RB'), ('merit', 'VBD'), ('a', 'DT'), ('second', 'JJ'), ('look', 'NN'), ('.',
'.')], [('After', 'IN'), ('all', 'DT'), (',', ','), ('in', 'IN'), ('a', 'DT'), ('city'
, 'NN'), ('that', 'WDT'), ('sports', 'NNS'), ('automated', 'VBD'), ('teller', 'NN'), (
'machines', 'NNS'), ('and', 'CC'), ('currency', 'NN'), ('exchanges', 'NNS'), ('at', 'I
N'), ('virtually', 'RB'), ('every', 'DT'), ('nook', 'NN'), ('and', 'CC'), ('corner', '
NN'), ('like', 'IN'), ('mushrooms', 'NNS'), ('after', 'IN'), ('a', 'DT'), ('cloudburst
', 'NN'), (',', ','), ('why', 'WRB'), ('would', 'MD'), ('these', 'DT'), ('ordinary', '
JJ'), ('looking', 'VBG'), ('terminals', 'NNS'), ('which', 'WDT'), ('do', 'VBP'), ('not
', 'RB'), ('even', 'RB'), ('offer', 'VBP'), ('the', 'DT'), ('privacy', 'NN'), ('of', '
IN'), ('cubicles', 'NNS'), ('merit', 'VBP'), ('any', 'DT'), ('attention', 'NN'), ('?',
'.')]]
```

```
In [13]: #Regrouping tokens and removing stop words
         from nltk.corpus import stopwords
         stopwords_verbs = ['say', 'get', 'go', 'know', 'may', 'need', 'like', 'make', 'see', 'w
         stopwords_other = ['one', 'mr', 'bbc', 'image', 'getty', 'de', 'en', 'caption', 'also',
         my_stopwords = stopwords.words('English') + stopwords_verbs + stopwords_other
         from itertools import chain # to flatten list of sentences of tokens into list of token
         def discartsen(df):
             df['tokens'] = df['tokens_sentences_lemmatized'].map(lambda text: list(chain.from_i
             df['tokens'] = df['tokens'].map(lambda tokens: [token.lower() for token in tokens i
                                                                  and token.lower() not in my_sto
         discartsen(df)

In [14]: df

Out[14]:
```


```
In [14]: df
Out[14]:
```


	date	text	topic	key_words	tokens_sentences	POS_tokens	tokens_sentences_lemmatized	tokens
0	August102018	[, The Hutchins on Publis hing Co., Going ...			[[,, The, Hutchins, on, Publis, hing, Co, .], ...	[[(,, ,), (The, DT), (Hutchins, NNP), (on, IN)...	[[,, The, Hutchins, on, Publis, hing, Co, .], ...	[hutchins, publis, hing, co, going, bit, beyon...
1	August122018	[Time s -Ne ws , The (He nde rs onville , ...			[[Time, s, -Ne, ws, ,, The, (, He, nde, rs, on...	[[(Time, NNP), (s, JJ), (-Ne, NNP), (ws, NN), ...	[[Time, s, -Ne, w, ,, The, (, He, nde, rs, onv...	[time, nde, rs, onville, nc, rig, hts, rve, pi...
2	August142018	[, The We natche e World, All Rig hts Re s...			[[,, The, We, natche, e, World, ,, All, Rig, h...	[[(,, ,), (The, DT), (We, PRP), (natche, VBP),...	[[,, The, We, natche, e, World, ,, All, Rig, h...	[natche, world, rig, hts, rve, cancer, treatme...
3	August152018	[, Core Me dia Group, All Rig hts Re s e rv...			[[,, Core, Me, dia, Group, ,, All, Rig, hts, R...	[[(,, ,), (Core, NNP), (Me, NNP), (dia, NNP), ...	[[,, Core, Me, dia, Group, ,, All, Rig, hts, R...	[core, dia, group, rig, hts, rve, student, acc...
4	August162018	[, The Plain De ale r. All Rig hts Re s e r...			[[,, The, Plain, De, ale, r., All, Rig, hts, R...	[[(,, ,), (The, DT), (Plain, NNP), (De, NNP), ...	[[,, The, Plain, De, ale, r., All, Rig, hts, R...	[plain, ale, rig, hts, rve, us, ne, ws, bank, ...

Fig. 5.8. Continued

LDA

```
In [15]: #Data preparation
         #Prepare bi-grams and tri-grams
         import gensim
         from gensim.models import Phrases
         def ldatoken(df):
             tokens = df['tokens'].tolist()
             bigram_model = Phrases(tokens)
             trigram_model = Phrases(bigram_model[tokens], min_count=1)
             tokens = list(trigram_model[bigram_model[tokens]])
             return tokens
         tokens1 = ldatoken(df)

In [16]: #Prepare objects for LDA gensim implementation
         from gensim import corpora

         def ldadict(tokens):
             dictionary_LDA = corpora.Dictionary(tokens)
             dictionary_LDA.filter_extremes(no_below=3)
             return dictionary_LDA

         def ldacorpus(tokens,dictionary_LDA):
             corpus = [dictionary_LDA.doc2bow(tok) for tok in tokens]
             return corpus

         dictionary_LDA1 = ldadict(tokens1)
         corpus1 = ldacorpus(tokens1,dictionary_LDA1)

In [17]: import numpy as np
         import gensim
         import gensim.models
         np.random.seed(123456)
         num_topics = 9
         %time lda_model1 = gensim.models.LdaModel(corpus1, num_topics=num_topics, \
                                                   id2word=dictionary_LDA1, \
                                                   passes=4, alpha=[0.01]*num_topics, \
                                                   eta=[0.01]*len(dictionary_LDA1.keys()))

         CPU times: user 1.96 s, sys: 15.9 ms, total: 1.98 s
         Wall time: 2 s
```

Fig. 5.9. News Topic Analysis LDA Genism Implementation.

Next, the daily news announcement textual information is converted into a 9-dimention LDA-based vectorization representation with topic weighting, as shown in Fig. 5.12.

News Announcements Topics and Cryptocurrency Market Reaction

In this phase of the analysis, the extracted market reaction data is entered into a data frame in Python and combined with the LDA-based vectorization representation of daily news announcement compilations based on date. Each daily topic vector is multiplied by the daily average trading volume and price change at the end of each 24-hour period. The results are shown in Fig. 5.13.

Finally, Fig. 5.14 shows the results when matplotlib is applied to graph the price change and trading volume against each of the nine relevant topics for the 145 trading days from July 2018 to December 2018. In the first group of trading volume plots, it is clear that Topic 3, younger investor participation, had a significant impact on Bitcoin trading volume that is distinct from other topics and could potentially be a strong predictor for changes in trading volume. The second group of plots, which focuses on changes in Bitcoin market price, indicates the typical positive and negative correlations for each topic with the changes in pricing. Topic 5, government regulations on exchanges, is the only topic with

```
In [18]: for i,topic in lda_model1.show_topics(formatted=True, num_topics=num_topics, num_words=
             print(str(i)+": "+ topic)
             print()

0: 0.008*"city" + 0.007*"bank" + 0.006*"power" + 0.005*"buy" + 0.005*"digital_currency
" + 0.004*"service" + 0.004*"issue" + 0.004*"customer" + 0.004*"investment" + 0.004*"m
uch" + 0.003*"application" + 0.003*"user" + 0.003*"purchase" + 0.003*"security" + 0.00
3*"law" + 0.003*"since" + 0.003*"online" + 0.003*"office" + 0.003*"secure" + 0.003*"pr
ocess"

1: 0.005*"investor" + 0.005*"ohio" + 0.004*"bank" + 0.004*"crypto" + 0.004*"digital_cu
rrency" + 0.003*"garza" + 0.003*"start" + 0.003*"government" + 0.003*"sentence" + 0.00
3*"good" + 0.003*"thing" + 0.003*"much" + 0.003*"price" + 0.003*"percent" + 0.003*"inv
est" + 0.002*"buy" + 0.002*"change" + 0.002*"long" + 0.002*"tell" + 0.002*"try"

2: 0.003*"us" + 0.003*"ohio" + 0.003*"bank" + 0.003*"government" + 0.003*"city" + 0.00
3*"pay" + 0.003*"even" + 0.003*"digital" + 0.003*"power" + 0.002*"future" + 0.002*"pay
ment" + 0.002*"large" + 0.002*"consumer" + 0.002*"rockcoons" + 0.002*"start" + 0.002*"
exchange" + 0.002*"process" + 0.002*"percent" + 0.002*"crypto" + 0.002*"report"

3: 0.021*"city" + 0.007*"power" + 0.005*"statement" + 0.005*"still" + 0.005*"west" + 0
.004*"rate" + 0.004*"computer" + 0.004*"pay" + 0.004*"student" + 0.004*"service" + 0.0
04*"access" + 0.004*"good" + 0.003*"operation" + 0.003*"exchange" + 0.003*"believe" +
0.003*"tower" + 0.003*"digital_currency" + 0.003*"charleston" + 0.003*"wednesday" + 0.
003*"university"

4: 0.004*"investor" + 0.004*"product" + 0.004*"garza" + 0.004*"west_hartford" + 0.004*
"site" + 0.004*"potential" + 0.004*"tech" + 0.003*"plan" + 0.003*"note" + 0.003*"inves
tment" + 0.003*"million" + 0.003*"ohio" + 0.003*"issue" + 0.003*"find" + 0.003*"securi
ty" + 0.003*"firm" + 0.003*"beyond" + 0.003*"good" + 0.003*"coin" + 0.003*"application
"

5: 0.004*"bank" + 0.003*"exchange" + 0.003*"service" + 0.003*"government" + 0.003*"pay
ment" + 0.003*"pay" + 0.003*"report" + 0.003*"still" + 0.003*"virtual_currency" + 0.00
2*"sell" + 0.002*"crypto" + 0.002*"price" + 0.002*"process" + 0.002*"back" + 0.002*"mi
llion" + 0.002*"start" + 0.002*"investor" + 0.002*"application" + 0.002*"day" + 0.002*
"add"

6: 0.005*"bank" + 0.005*"email" + 0.004*"xrp" + 0.004*"good" + 0.004*"even" + 0.004*"i
nvestor" + 0.004*"security" + 0.003*"plan" + 0.003*"build" + 0.003*"walmart" + 0.003*"
police" + 0.003*"food" + 0.003*"project" + 0.003*"pay" + 0.003*"computer" + 0.003*"pat
ent" + 0.003*"report" + 0.003*"ripple" + 0.003*"big" + 0.003*"move"

7: 0.008*"bank" + 0.007*"today" + 0.006*"issue" + 0.005*"investor" + 0.005*"ohio" + 0.
005*"price" + 0.004*"china" + 0.004*"even" + 0.004*"link" + 0.003*"network" + 0.003*"d
ecember" + 0.003*"security" + 0.003*"hold" + 0.003*"far" + 0.003*"power" + 0.003*"much
" + 0.003*"former" + 0.003*"sec" + 0.003*"payment" + 0.003*"government"

8: 0.005*"application" + 0.005*"cleveland" + 0.005*"bank" + 0.004*"service" + 0.004*"o
hio" + 0.004*"customer" + 0.004*"office" + 0.004*"payment" + 0.004*"offer" + 0.004*"co
nference" + 0.003*"look" + 0.003*"hold" + 0.003*"others" + 0.003*"right" + 0.003*"user
" + 0.003*"big" + 0.003*"exchange" + 0.003*"much" + 0.003*"area" + 0.003*"lubin"
```

Fig. 5.10. Topic Keywords with the Relevance Scores.

```
In [20]: import seaborn as sns; sns.set(rc={'figure.figsize':(10,20)})
         sns.set(rc={'figure.figsize':(10,5)})
         document_topic1.idxmax(axis=1).value_counts().plot.bar(color='lightblue')

Out[20]: <matplotlib.axes._subplots.AxesSubplot at 0x7f9a41e64550>
```

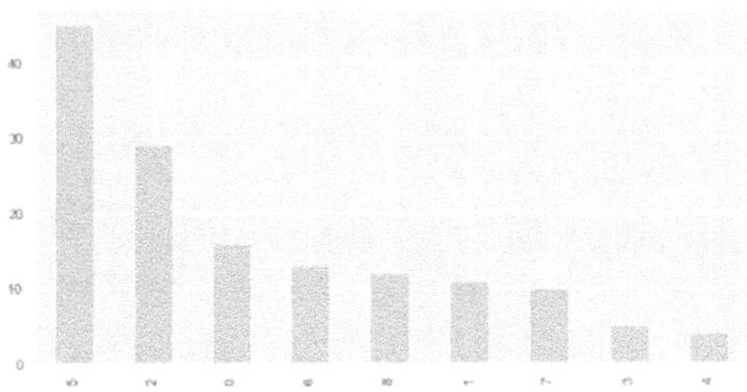

Fig. 5.11. Frequency of News Topics.

```
In [19]: def topics_document_to_dataframe(topics_document, num_topics):
             res = pd.DataFrame(columns=range(num_topics))
             for topic_weight in topics_document:
                 res.loc[0, topic_weight[0]] = topic_weight[1]
             return res

         topics1 = [lda_model1[corpus1[i]] for i in range(len(df))]
         # Like TF-IDF, create a matrix of topic weighting, with documents as rows and topics as
         document_topic1 = \
         pd.concat([topics_document_to_dataframe(topics_document, num_topics=num_topics) for top
           .reset_index(drop=True).fillna(0)
         document_topic1.head()

Out[19]:
```

	0	1	2	3	4	5	6	7	8
0	0.000000	0.0	0.592429	0.00000	0.039620	0.318270	0.0	0.039858	0.000000
1	0.697523	0.0	0.000000	0.00000	0.302321	0.000000	0.0	0.000000	0.000000
2	0.000000	0.0	0.000000	0.00000	0.000000	0.628752	0.0	0.371104	0.000000
3	0.000000	0.0	0.000000	0.11412	0.000000	0.885768	0.0	0.000000	0.000000
4	0.000000	0.0	0.000000	0.00000	0.020135	0.000000	0.0	0.000000	0.979653

Fig. 5.12. Market Information and News Information Merged Dataset.

```
In [23]: df1 = pd.read_excel('/Users/zhangguangyue/Desktop/market_reaction.xlsx')
         def convert_str_to_number(x):
             total_stars = 0
             num_map = {'K':1000, 'M':1000000, 'B':1000000000}
             if x.isdigit():
                 total_stars = int(x)
             else:
                 if len(x) > 1:
                     total_stars = float(x[:-1]) * num_map.get(x[-1].upper(), 1)
             return int(total_stars)
         df1['Vol.'] = df1['Vol.'].apply(convert_str_to_number)
         df1

In [39]: df2 = pd.merge(df1, df, on='date')
         df2

Out[39]:
```

	date	Price	Open	High	Low	Vol.	Change	text	topic	key_
0	December302018	3815.0	3708.2	3837.7	3682.5	519169	0.0292	[, Standard-Examine r\n\nStartup Showcase - ...		
1	December292018	3706.8	3861.6	3899.6	3696.0	505410	-0.0401	[The State\n\nThe bitcoin ATM has arrived ...		
2	December272018	3586.9	3793.4	3822.6	3560.8	543440	-0.0545	[The State\n\nWho Botched It Best?, Our Fa...		
3	December262018	3793.7	3762.8	3841.9	3680.3	567110	0.0083	[, The We natche e World, All Rig hts Re s...		
144	July12018	6366.8	6398.5	6445.1	6284.7	128509	-0.0050	[Tampa Bay Time s\n\nFlorida financial offi...		

Fig. 5.13. Market Information and News Information Merged Dataset.

```
In [47]: df_vol = df_vol[range(0,9)]
         df_vol.plot(subplots=True, figsize=(8, 8)); plt.legend(loc='upper right')

Out[47]: <matplotlib.legend.Legend at 0x7f9a4714b2b0>
```

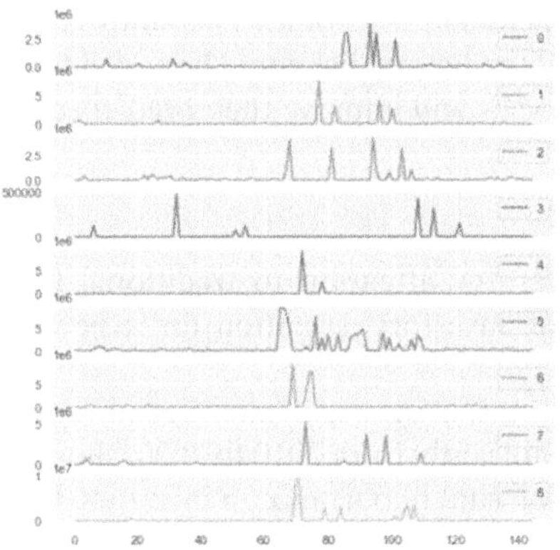

```
In [48]: df_change = df_change[range(0,9)]
         df_change.plot(subplots=True, figsize=(8, 8)); plt.legend(loc='upper right')

Out[48]: <matplotlib.legend.Legend at 0x7f9a4331b760>
```

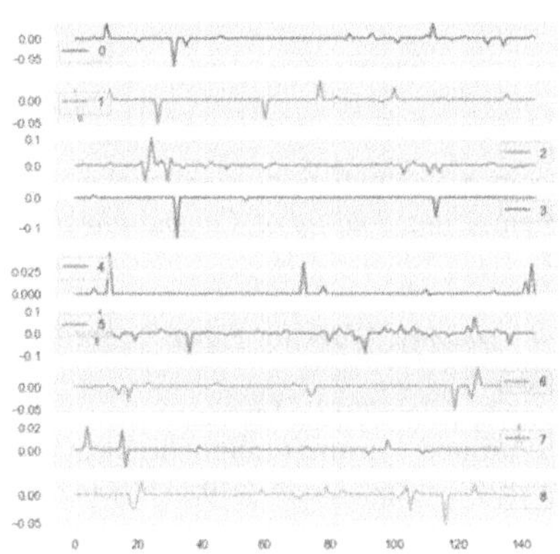

Fig. 5.14. Investors' Reaction to News Topics: Trading Volume and Market Price.

both positive and negative effects on Bitcoin market price, which is reasonable considering that such regulations could be beneficial or devastating to the adoption and application of Bitcoin and might be perceived as positive or negative by investors. Future research should better distinguish between these two effects or create more specific topics for both sides. All of the other topics show a one-sided correlation with Bitcoin pricing and could have the potential to be strong Bitcoin market predictors.

Future Research

In terms of the limited sample selection of this study, in future research with less limited data access, the wordlist for the keyword search can be expanded. In addition, the time period should be longer in order to include a wider variety of news topics. For future research, the final goal should be to construct a cryptocurrency prediction model that would be applicable to all coins and fund indexes, while taking the common market factors into account. This study is a great starting point for considering additional predictors that could be added to the existing cryptocurrency price prediction models and improve their predictive power.

Conclusion

Overall, this chapter explores investors' attention to traditional financial disclosure and the different topics of investors' attention for a new asset class: cryptocurrency.

In the first paper, I cannot conclude that investors' attention around the annual report publication has changed significantly from 2010 to 2020, showing that traditional financial disclosure is still of vital importance to investors. In the second paper, I used textual analysis for topic modeling of cryptocurrency-related news and ranked the topics according to their relevance. Building on this, I tested the correlation between each topic and Bitcoin market price. All detected topics show positive relationship, except for government regulations on exchanges.

References

Chen, Z., Li, C., & Sun, W. (2020). Bitcoin price prediction using machine learning: An approach to sample dimension engineering. *Journal of Computational and Applied Mathematics*, *365*(2020), 112395.

Coulter, K. A. (2021). *The impact of news media on cryptocurrency prices: Modelling data driven discourses in the crypto-economy*. Working Paper. University of Essex, Department of Sociology.

Drake, M. S., Roulstone, D. T., & Thornock, J. R. (2012). Investor information demand: Evidence from Google searches around earnings announcements. *Journal of Accounting Research*, *50*(4), 1001–1040. https://doi.org/10.1111/j.1475-679X.2012.00443.x

Figá-Talamanca, G., Focardi, S., & Patacca, M. (2021). Common dynamic factors for cryptocurrencies and multiple pair-trading statistical arbitrages. *Decisions in Economics and Finance*, *44*, 863–882.

Garcia, D., Tessone, C. J., Mavrodiev, P., & Perony, N. (2014). The digital traces of bubbles: Feedback cycles between socio-economic signals in the Bitcoin economy. *Journal of the Royal Society Interface*, *11*(99), 20140623.

Makarov, I., & Schoar, A. (2020). Trading and arbitrage in cryptocurrency markets. *Journal of Financial Economics*, *135*(2), 293–319.

Shen, D., Urquhart, A., & Wang, P. (2020). A three-factor pricing model for cryptocurrencies. *Finance Research Letters*, *34*(2020), 101248.

Soska, K., Dong, J. D., Khodaverdian, A., Zetlin-Jones, A., Routledge, B., & Christin, N. (2021, April). *Towards understanding cryptocurrency derivatives: A case study of BitMEX*. Proceedings of the web conference 2021.

Wolk, K. (2020). Advanced social media sentiment analysis for short-term cryptocurrency price prediction. *Expert Systems*, *37*(2), e12493.

Chapter 6

When Google Speaks: Unveiling Corporate Performance Through Google Trends

Xin Jin and Haoyun (Harry) Gao

[a]*Brazilian School of Public and Business Administration, Brazil[SJ1]*
[b]*Rutgers Business School, USA*

Abstract

Google search is commonly used in daily life but not as widely in academia. Hence, this study adopts the Google Search Volume Index (SVI) to investigate the correlation between SVI and firms' financial and environmental performance. We use Brazil's top three airlines from 2019 to 2023 as our research sample. Our findings reveal that the quarterly revenue of each company is positively associated with the SVI for the company name based on both Worldwide and Brazilian SVI in both the current quarter (i.e., revenue at time Q) and the following quarter (i.e., revenue at time Q + 1). However, we determine that the monthly revenue is significantly correlated with the Worldwide and Brazilian SVI only when the search results are compared to revenue in the same month (i.e., time M) or two months later (i.e., time M + 2). Similarly, we find that CO_2 emissions are positively correlated with SVI only when the emission data are for the current month (i.e., time M) or two months later (i.e., time M + 2). These findings highlight the relevance of considering the Google SVI when assessing firms' performance.

Keywords: Google trends; search volume index; financial performance; environmental performance; predicting revenues; aviation industry

Exogenous Data in Accounting and Auditing in the Rutgers Series in Accounting Information Systems, 89–98

doi:10.1108/978-1-83608-734-220251006

1. Introduction

The aviation industry attracted increasing attention during the COVID-19 pandemic, and many of the players became the victims of the stringent worldwide travel restrictions, with a 90% initial decrease in air travel followed by a slow recovery (OECD, 2020). In addition, the huge environmental impact of airline operations is another challenge that is yet to be resolved, with carbon emission making up 4.7% of all carbon emissions in Europe as of 2019 (European Federation for Transport and Environment, n.d.). Therefore, both industry and academia are interested in making better predictions of revenue and the environmental performance of airlines especially in this era of big data.

Google Trends has the potential to facilitate making predictions in a variety of areas (Chiu et al., 2023; Da et al., 2011a, 2011b; Teoh, 2018), which makes this data source a promising candidate for making predictions in our study. In Brazil, more than 98% of people use Google as their daily search engine (Mello, 2023), but to our knowledge, no previous papers have looked at the Google Trends SVI and its predictive power in the Brazilian aviation industry. In this chapter, we study data from Google Trends, specifically the SVI, to understand its correlation with quarterly revenue, monthly revenue, and environmental performance (CO_2 emission) of the top three Brazilian airline companies, using the SVI data points at time benchmarks (Q for quarterly data and M for monthly data). The main findings are summarized below.

We find that the quarterly revenue of each company is positively correlated with SVI for the company name based on both Worldwide and Brazilian search interest data. The relationship holds at the 5% significance level for both the current quarter (i.e., time Q) and one quarter ahead (i.e., revenue at time $Q + 1$). Similarly, we find that the monthly revenue, proxied by the monthly governmental operational data for each company, is significantly correlated with the Worldwide-SVI and Brazil-SVI only when the revenue is the same month as the search (i.e., time M) or when it is two months ahead (i.e., revenue at time $M + 2$). Finally, we observe that the CO_2 emission for each company, proxied by the airline monthly fuel consumption, is also positively correlated with SVI only when the emission data are at M and $M + 2$. This pattern is sensible and intuitive: people typically search for flights before booking them, leading to increased airline revenue as these bookings are made. Subsequently, as more flights are booked, airlines consume more fuel, resulting in higher CO_2 emissions. This sequence of events explains the observed correlations between search interest, revenue, and environmental performance.

2. Literature Review and Hypotheses

2.1. Exogenous Data

This chapter follows the thread of research that utilizes exogenous data to measure or proxy for data that we otherwise could not access. Previous research has examined exogenous datasets, such as social media (Elliott et al., 2018), social networks (Bianchi et al., 2023), and satellite images (Kang et al., 2021). These new datasets all share the characteristic of coming from sources outside of a firm. Thus, they are categorized as exogenous data (Brown-Liburd & Vasarhelyi, 2015). Examples of sources of exogenous data include locational data, weather data, and Google search data. As pointed out by Teoh (2018), these new datasets can provide economic phenomena with new insights that we otherwise could not obtain.

2.2. Google Trends Data

The Google Trends dataset, as a significant exogenous data source, has been hailed as a great source of insights in different research domains. In finance, Da et al. (2011a) find that Google Trends data, as measured by a SVI, are correlated with retail investors' timely attention compared to previous proxies and also better predict initial public offering stocks' performance. In accounting, revenue management is a pressing issue, and recent research uses Google Trends data to detect it (Chiu et al., 2023). However, we notice a research gap related to investigating the airline industry. Specifically, there has not been any research using Google Trends data to predict airline revenue and emission data.

Despite all the promises of Google Trends data, research also points out concerns about this data source in terms of accuracy, consistency, and validity. For example, the search results on Google Trends using the same queries may give different results, leading to measurement errors of approximately 5% (Cebrián & Domenech, 2023). We use the query of "ChatGPT" and "car rental" made at different times to illustrate the difference in data accuracy, as depicted in Fig. 6.1. Although we see the two lines fluctuate differently, the difference does not distort the results in a significant way, allowing for reasonable confidence in relying on a one-time query from Google Trends data.

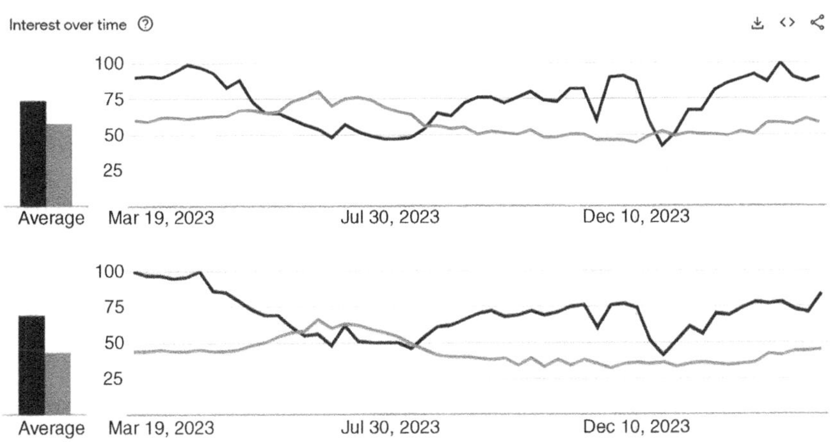

Fig. 6.1. Search Interest of ChatGPT (Blue) Versus Car Rental (Red) in the United States. *Source*: Google Trends (2023).

2.3. Operations and Environmental Concerns of the Airline Industry

The aviation sector has faced a substantial downturn during the recent global pandemic, with airlines particularly bearing the brunt in terms of business value (McKinsey & Company, 2022). To bolster resilience in varying future circumstances, it is imperative for airlines to assess passenger demand across diverse scenarios, including global pandemics.

Perhaps a blessing in disguise, Mueller et al. (2022) note a significant decline in air pollution after almost all passenger airliners were grounded during COVID-19. The aviation industry is evidently motivated not merely to regard this as a fortuitous outcome of the pandemic, but rather as an impetus to embark on the development of zero-emission technologies in alignment with the objectives of the Paris Agreement (IATA, 2021). As societal expectations continue to mount, avenues for enhanced public scrutiny warrant exploration.

Within this context, this chapter directs attention to the potential of leveraging big data sources like Google Trends to elucidate patterns indirectly in searches pertaining to fossil fuel consumption. Acknowledging the intricacies inherent in such data, we formulate the following hypotheses for our research:

> *H1.* The Google search interest in major Brazilian airlines exhibits a positive correlation with the reported revenue of these airline companies.

> *H2.* The Google search interest in major Brazilian airlines exhibits a positive correlation with the fuel consumption of these airlines.

3. Research Design

We use Brazil's top three airlines, Azul Linhas Aéreas Brasileiras S/A (Azul), Gol Linhas Aéreas S.A. (Gol), and Latam Linhas Aéreas S.A. (Latam), as our research sample. We gathered data from January 2023 to February 2024 on Brazilian airline companies' statistics, including monthly Paid Passengers, monthly Revenue Passenger Kilometers (RPK),[1] monthly Revenue Tonne Kilometers (RTK),[2] and monthly fuel consumption. We obtained the data from Agência Nacional de Aviação Civil,[3] the Brazilian civil aviation authority that is responsible for regulating and overseeing civil aviation activities, aeronautics, and aerodromes infrastructure.

Additionally, we collected SVI data from Google Trends (https://trends.google.com/trends) from January 2019 to December 2023. SVI is simply a scaled, time series of weekly search volume beginning in 2004 (Da et al., 2011b). We also gathered quarterly revenue datasets from Yahoo Finance (https://finance.yahoo.com) from January 2019 to September 2023.

[1]A passenger for whose transportation an air carrier receives commercial remuneration is called a revenue passenger. When a revenue passenger is carried one kilometer, one RPK is generated.

[2]One RTK is generated when a metric tonne of revenue load is carried one kilometer.

[3]https://www.gov.br/anac/en

4. Results

4.1. SVI and Revenue

SVI and quarterly revenue: First, we investigate the relationship between SVI and quarterly revenue from January 2019 to September 2023. We study this relationship under two circumstances: Worldwide-SVI and Brazil-SVI.

Table 6.1 presents the result for SVI and quarterly revenue. The results are positively significant at time Q ($p < 0.001$), which means that both Worldwide-SVI and Brazil-SVI are positively correlated with quarterly revenue. However, the R-squared values are not especially high, potentially indicating the necessity to incorporate other influential variables, given the absence of control variables in this analysis. In the same spirit, both Worldwide-SVI and Brazil-SVI are positively correlated with quarterly revenue at time $Q + 1$ ($p = 0.028$, Worldwide; $p = 0.046$, Brazil). Nevertheless, the significance levels decrease, and R-squared values diminish compared to those observed at time Q. Notably, at time $Q + 2$, these correlations cease to be statistically significant, suggesting that the predictive capacity of SVI for quarterly revenue is not sustained beyond one quarter. Hence, *H1* is supported.

SVI and monthly revenue: Next, we use Paid Passengers, RPK, and RTK from October 2022 to February 2024 as indirect ways to measure revenue since these variables are available at the monthly level. In addition, we research the correlation between SVI and monthly revenue in the contexts of Worldwide-SVI and Brazil-SVI.

According to Table 6.2, at time M from January 2023 to December 2023, SVI is positively associated with Paid Passengers ($p = 0.0030$, Worldwide; $p = 0.0020$, Brazil), RPK ($p = 0.0240$, Worldwide; $p = 0.0040$, Brazil), and RTK ($p = 0.0450$, Worldwide; $p = 0.0070$, Brazil), reinforcing *H1*.

At the one-month lag level, SVI is from December 2022 to December 2023, and Paid Passengers, RPK, and RTK are from January 2023 to January 2024. Table 6.3 shows that SVI is not statistically correlated with Paid Passengers ($p = 0.7930$, Worldwide; $p = 0.8120$, Brazil), RPK ($p = 0.9800$, Worldwide; $p = 0.7400$, Brazil), and RTK ($p = 0.9200$, Worldwide; $p = 0.7650$, Brazil) at time $M + 1$. Interestingly,

Table 6.1. SVI and Quarterly Revenue.

	Q		$Q + 1$		$Q + 2$	
	Worldwide	**Brazil**	**Worldwide**	**Brazil**	**Worldwide**	**Brazil**
SVI	23,398.0100	19,663.5700	13,273.59	10,326.12	1,225.5020	550.2402
P-Value	<0.001	<0.001	0.0280	0.0460	0.8490	0.9200
R^2	0.3964	0.3909	0.2365	0.2239	0.1610	0.1606
Adj-R^2	0.3622	0.3564	0.1907	0.1773	0.1075	0.107
No.	57	57	54	54	51	51

Note: No. = number of observations.

Table 6.2. SVI and Monthly Revenue (*M*).

Panel A	IV: SVI-Worldwide		
	Paid Passengers	**RPK**	**RTK**
SVI	33,181.1900	41,400,000.0000	3,377,475.0000
P-Value	0.0030	0.0240	0.0450
R^2	0.7252	0.9038	0.9218
Adj-R^2	0.6995	0.8948	0.9145
No.	36	36	36
Panel B	**IV: SVI-Brazil**		
	Paid Passengers	**RPK**	**RTK**
SVI	30,407.3100	44,900,000.0000	3,865,389.0000
P-Value	0.0020	0.0040	0.0070
R^2	0.7349	0.9131	0.9296
Adj-R^2	0.71010	0.9050	0.9230
No.	36	36	36

Note: No. = number of observations.

Table 6.3. SVI and Monthly Revenue (*M* + 1).

Panel A	IV: SVI-Worldwide		
	Paid Passengers	**RPK**	**RTK**
SVI	3,024.7700	−489,932.1000	−181,677.6000
P-Value	0.7930	0.9800	0.9200
R^2	0.6395	0.8679	0.8954
Adj-R^2	0.6086	0.8566	0.8864
No.	39	39	39
Panel B	**IV: SVI-Brazil**		
	Paid Passengers	**RPK**	**RTK**
SVI	2,405.9110	5,824,755.0000	479,143.0000
P-Value	0.8120	0.7400	0.7650
R^2	0.6394	0.8683	0.8956
Adj-R^2	0.6085	0.8570	0.8866
No.	39	39	39

Note: No. = number of observations. Fuel = fuel consumption. All dependent variables are at *M* + 1. For example, if SVI is in January 2023, paid passengers travel in February 2023.

while Brazil-SVI is positively associated with RPK and RTK, Worldwide-SVI is negatively associated with RPK and RTK. Therefore, at the one-month lag level, SVI cannot predict revenue.

At the two-month lag level, SVI is from November 2022 to December 2023, and Paid Passengers, RPK, and RTK are from January 2023 to February 2024. Surprisingly, Table 6.4 shows that SVI is statistically positively correlated with Paid Passengers (p = 0.0020, Worldwide; p = 0.0260, Brazil), RPK (p = 0.0050, Worldwide; p = 0.0270, Brazil), and RTK (p = 0.0130, Worldwide; p = 00470, Brazil) at the two-month lag level, denoting that SVI is able to predict Paid Passengers, RPK, and RTK two months in advance.

Finally, at the three-month lag level, SVI is from October 2022 to November 2023, and Paid Passengers, RPK, and RTK are from January 2023 to February 2024. Table 6.5 shows that SVI is not statistically correlated with Paid Passengers (p = 0.4030, Worldwide; p = 0.0770, Brazil), RPK (p = 0.9430, Worldwide; p = 0.4920, Brazil), and RTK (p = 0.9820, Worldwide; p = 0.5130, Brazil) at the three-month lag level, denoting that SVI loses the prediction function for revenue at time $M + 3$.

4.2. SVI and Corporate Environmental Performance

We adopt fuel consumption as the substitute for CO_2 emission in this study because the International Air Transport Association (IATA) launched a carbon

Table 6.4. SVI and Monthly Revenue ($M + 2$).

Panel A	**IV: SVI-Worldwide**		
	Paid Passengers	**RPK**	**RTK**
SVI	31,776.3000	48,600,000.0000	4,018,904.0000
P-Value	0.0020	0.0050	0.0130
R^2	0.7174	0.8985	0.916
Adj-R^2	0.6951	0.8905	0.9094
No.	42	42	42
Panel B	**IV: SVI-Brazil**		
	Paid Passengers	**RPK**	**RTK**
SVI	21,635.4500	36,000,000.0000	2,961,227.0000
P-Value	0.0260	0.0270	0.0470
R^2	0.6822	0.8905	0.9107
Adj-R^2	0.6571	0.8819	0.9037
No.	42	42	42

Note: Trend data are from Google. No. = number of observations. All dependent variables are at $M + 2$. For example, if SVI is in January 2023, paid passengers travel in March 2023.

Table 6.5. SVI and Monthly Revenue ($M + 3$).

Panel A	**IV: SVI-Worldwide**		
	Paid Passengers	**RPK**	**RTK**
SVI	−10,223.4000	1,458,470.0000	42,623.8900
P-Value	0.4030	0.9430	0.9820
R^2	0.6443	0.8752	0.9008
Adj-R^2	0.6162	0.8654	0.8930
No.	42	42	42
Panel B	**IV: SVI-Brazil**		
	Paid Passengers	**RPK**	**RTK**
SVI	−18,651.5300	−12,300,000.0000	−1,067,141.0000
P-Value	0.0770	0.4920	0.5130
R^2	0.6665	0.8767	0.9020
Adj-R^2	0.6402	0.8670	0.8942
No.	42	42	42

Note: Trend data are from Google. No. = number of observations. All dependent variables are at $M + 3$. For example, if SVI is in December 2022, paid passengers travel in March 2023.

calculation method in 2022. In addition, we research the correlation between SVI and monthly fuel consumption in two different contexts: Worldwide-SVI and Brazil-SVI. Here, SVI and monthly fuel consumption are from October 2022 to February 2024.

Table 6.6 presents the regression results between SVI and fuel consumption. SVI is statistically positively associated with monthly fuel consumption at time M ($p = 0.0710$, Worldwide; $p = 0.0080$, Brazil), and the R-squared is quite high for both Worldwide-SVI and Brazil-SVI. Thus, SVI is capable of predicting fuel consumption at time M, supporting *H2*.

However, SVI is not statistically associated with monthly fuel consumption at time $M + 1$ ($p = 0.4590$, Worldwide; $p = 0.7630$, Brazil), the coefficients for both Worldwide-SVI and Brazil-SVI are negative although the R-squared is not small for both SVIs. Thus, SVI cannot predict fuel consumption at the one-month lag level.

To our surprise, SVI is statistically positively associated with monthly fuel consumption at time $M + 2$ ($p = 0.0190$, Worldwide; $p = 0.0280$, Brazil), and the R-squared is quite high for both Worldwide-SVI and Brazil-SVI. As a result, SVI is capable of predicting fuel consumption two months ahead.

Finally, SVI is not statistically associated with monthly fuel consumption at time $M + 3$ ($p = 1.0000$, Worldwide; $p = 0.6400$, Brazil), the coefficients for both Worldwide-SVI and Brazil-SVI are negative although the R-squared is not small for both SVIs. Thus, SVI loses the prediction function at the three-month lag level.

Table 6.6. SVI and Monthly Fuel Consumption.

	Worldwide	Brazil	Worldwide	Brazil
	M		*M* + 1	
SVI	775,137.3000	966,375.5000	−353,132.0000	−127,102.4000
P-Value	0.0710	0.0080	0.4590	0.7630
R^2	0.9625	0.9668	0.9471	0.9464
Adj-R^2	0.959	0.9637	0.9426	0.9418
No.	36	36	39	39
	M + 2		*M* + 3	
SVI	991,968.4000	851,633.3000	−213.3012	−199,220.9000
P-Value	0.0190	0.0280	1.000	0.6400
R^2	0.9559	0.9552	0.9490	0.9493
Adj-R^2	0.9525	0.9516	0.9449	0.9453
No.	42	42	42	42

Note: No. = number of observations.

5. Conclusion

We adopt SVI from Google Trends, a publicly open dataset, to investigate relationships between SVI and revenue and between SVI and fuel consumption. The findings show that SVI is positively associated with quarterly revenue in *Q* and *Q* + 1, suggesting that SVI can predict quarterly revenue in current quarter and last for one more quarter. In addition, SVI is positively correlated with monthly Paid Passengers, RPK, RTK at time *M* and *M* + 2, denoting that SVI can predict revenue in the current month and two months ahead. Moreover, SVI is positively correlated with monthly fuel consumption at time *M* and *M* + 2, meaning that SVI can also predict corporate CO_2 emission in the current month and two months ahead.

However, this study is not without limitations. First, Paid Passengers, RPK, and RTK are indirect indicators for revenue, and fuel consumption is not the same as real CO_2 emissions. In addition, this study focuses only on the top three Brazilian airlines and only separates SVI into Worldwide-SVI and Brazil-SVI.

Hence, future research directions could include (1) the refinement of the revenue index and CO_2 emission; (2) the extension of sample size, for example, incorporating all Brazilian airlines and/or airlines in other countries; (3) the separation of SVI into other sub-types to identify the driving forces of the relationships between SVI and revenue and between SVI and CO_2 emission, such as SVI-Travel or SVI-News; (4) the relationship between SVI and other ESG performance measures, such as an employee-related index.

References

Bianchi, P. A., Causholli, M., Minutti-Meza, M., & Sulcaj, V. (2023). Social networks analysis in accounting and finance. *Contemporary Accounting Research*, *40*(1), 577–623. https://doi.org/10.1111/1911-3846.12826

Brown-Liburd, H., & Vasarhelyi, M. A. (2015). Big data and audit evidence. *Journal of Emerging Technologies in Accounting*, *12*(1), 1–16. https://doi.org/10.2308/jeta-10468

Cebrián, E., & Domenech, J. (2023). Is Google Trends a quality data source? *Applied Economics Letters*, *30*(6), 811–815. https://doi.org/10.1080/13504851.2021.2023088

Chiu, P.-C., Teoh, S. H., Zhang, Y., & Huang, X. (2023). Using Google searches of firm products to detect revenue management. *Accounting, Organizations and Society*, *109*(August), 101457. https://doi.org/10.1016/j.aos.2023.101457

Da, Z., Engelberg, J., & Gao, P. (2011a). In search of attention. *The Journal of Finance*, *66*(5), 1461–1499. https://doi.org/10.1111/j.1540-6261.2011.01679.x

Da, Z., Engelberg, J., & Gao, P. (2011b). *In search of fundamentals*. SSRN Scholarly Paper. Rochester, NY. https://doi.org/10.2139/ssrn.1589805

Elliott, W. B., Grant, S. M., Hodge, F. D. (2018). Negative news and investor trust: The role of $Firm and #CEO Twitter use. *Journal of Accounting Research*, *56*(5), 1483–1519. https://doi.org/10.1111/1475-679X.12217

European Federation for Transport and Environment. (n.d.). *Airplane pollution*. Transport & Environment. https://www.transportenvironment.org/challenges/planes/airplane-pollution/

IATA. (2021, October). *Net-zero carbon emissions by 2050*. IATA Press Release No. 66. https://www.iata.org/en/pressroom/pressroom-archive/2021-releases/2021-10-04-03/

Kang, J. K., Stice-Lawrence, L., & Wong, Y. T. F. (2021). The firm next door: Using satellite images to study local information advantage. *Journal of Accounting Research*, *59*(2), 713–750. https://doi.org/10.1111/1475-679X.12360

McKinsey & Company. (2022, March). *COVID-19's impact on the global aviation sector*. https://www.mckinsey.com/industries/travel-logistics-and-infrastructure/our-insights/taking-stock-of-the-pandemics-impact-on-global-aviation

Mello, P. C. (2023, May). *Google launches offensive in Brazil against fake news bill, showing emails and report*. Folha de S.Paulo. https://www1.folha.uol.com.br/internacional/en/brazil/2023/05/google-launches-offensive-in-brazil-against-fake-news-bill-showing-emails-and-report.shtml

Mueller, S. C., Hudda, N., Levy, J. I., Durant, J. L., Patil, P., Lee, N. F., Weiss, I., Tatro, T., Duhl, T., & Lane, K. (2022). Changes in ultrafine particle concentrations near a major airport following reduced transportation activity during the COVID-19 pandemic. *Environmental Science & Technology Letters*, *9*(9), 706–711. https://doi.org/10.1021/acs.estlett.2c00322

OECD. (2020). *COVID-19 and the aviation industry: Impact and policy responses*. https://www.oecd.org/coronavirus/policy-responses/covid-19-and-the-aviation-industry-impact-and-policy-responses-26d521c1/

Teoh, S. H. (2018). The promise and challenges of new datasets for accounting research. *Accounting, Organizations and Society*, *68–69*(July), 109–117. https://doi.org/10.1016/j.aos.2018.03.008

Chapter 7

Impact of the Fit for 55 Policies on the Response of Electric Vehicle Consumers in Germany: Stress Analysis in Market Trends from Google Trends

Maristela Roza, Leonardo Flach and Fabricia Silva Da Rosa

Federal University of Santa Catarina, Brazil

Abstract

The transition to electric vehicles (EVs) in Europe is driven by the European Union's Fit for 55 package, introduced in 2021. This study focuses on analyzing the behavior of active and potential EV Consumers in Germany in 2021 through 2023, addressing stress related to continuity, acquisition, battery recharging, and maintenance of EVs. Using Google Trends data, the study assesses how EU policies and the introduction of e-fuels influence mobility and contribute to a sustainable transportation future in Germany. Results indicate that during the week of the Fit for 55 announcement, there was a strong trend of continuity in EV use by active customers. On the other hand, potential customers showed a tendency to acquire EVs despite an exception that allows the sale of internal combustion vehicles that use e-fuels. However, the stress level was high in both groups, warranting further observations. Future studies should include statistical analyses of sales in the German automotive market, combined with analyses of the trends found here.

Keywords: Fit for 55; electric vehicles; stress; Google Trends; active and potential customers; e-fuel

Exogenous Data in Accounting and Auditing in the Rutgers Series in Accounting Information Systems, 99–114

doi:10.1108/978-1-83608-734-220251007

Introduction

The energy transition toward electric vehicles (EVs) in Europe has gained momentum in response to the comprehensive package of environmental and regulatory policies of the European Union (EU) in 2021, known as Fit for 55 (European Commission, 2021). This ambitious set of measures aims for a substantial reduction of greenhouse gas emissions by 2030 and sets a milestone for ending the sales of new vehicles with internal combustion engines by 2035 (European Commission, 2021). In a surprising turn, in March 2023, Germany negotiated an exception that allows the continuation of vehicles that operate with e-fuel, a type of synthetic fuel with the potential to be carbon neutral (Reuters, 2023).

This innovative juncture highlights the relevance of both active and potential consumers' emotional stress in their decisions on continuity and acquisition related to EVs, as well as services related to these vehicles. "Stress can be described as a complex and multifaceted response to certain external stimuli. It is a psychophysiological condition that arises when a person faces a considerable threat or challenge, triggering a variety of biological and behavioral reactions" (Lazarus & Folkman, 1984). It can even influence consumption trends and market dynamics, and it emerges as a key exogenous factor in this market behavior study of EVs.

In this context, the objective of this study is to identify and analyze the behavior of active and potential customers of EVs in Germany, focusing on stress related to continuity, acquisition, battery recharging, and general maintenance of EVs in scenarios of changes in the policies concerning mandatory sales of EVs and related exemptions in Germany from January 1, 2021 to December 31, 2023. Data for trend analyses are collected through Google Trends, expanding discussions of how the EU policies on the development of e-fuels are changing mobility and contributing to a sustainable transportation future in Germany.

EU Policy Context – Fit for 55

On July 14, 2021, the EU consolidated a strategic political response to the climate crisis through the legislative package known as Fit for 55 (European Commission, 2021). This ambitious policy aims for a significant reduction in greenhouse gas (GHG) emissions, cutting them by at least 55% by 2030 compared to 1990 levels (European Commission, 2021). Within this context, a central piece of legislation concerns the future of automotive mobility, specifically the planned end of sales of new cars with internal combustion engines by 2035 (EU Council, 2021). This drastic measure reflects the acute awareness that road transport is a major contributor to harmful emissions, and a shift to zero-emission vehicles is seen as crucial to achieving EU climate goals (Akshay et al., 2024).

Therefore, the target set for 2035 is more than a regulatory milestone. It represents a turning point in the automotive industry trajectory, encouraging an accelerated transition to clean propulsion technologies like EVs. This goal integrates a broader vision for energy transformation that encourages innovation, technological development, and a restructuring of the automotive value chain to align with climate priorities (EU Council, 2021).

However, after intense negotiation, Germany secured a concession in March 2023, allowing internal combustion vehicles that operate exclusively with e-fuels to continue to be sold after 2035 (EU Council, 2023). E-fuels are synthetic fuels produced from the combination of hydrogen obtained through electrolysis using renewable energy and carbon dioxide captured directly from the air (Langenmayr & Ruppert, 2023). When burned in traditional combustion engines, e-fuels release CO_2. However, if the hydrogen is produced using renewable energy and the CO_2 is captured from non-emitting sources, the process has the potential to be neutral in terms of GHG emissions.

The European Commission has developed a proposal to permit the sale of new internal combustion engine vehicles after 2035, provided that these vehicles exclusively use climate-neutral e-fuels. This plan aims to address ongoing disputes with Germany concerning the future ban on combustion engine vehicles. According to the proposal, there would be a new vehicle classification within the European Union for cars that operate solely on carbon-neutral fuels. The proposal specifies that these cars must be equipped with technology to ensure that they cannot operate on any fuels that are not carbon neutral (Reuters, 2023).

Despite being innovative, this resolution, which was incorporated into complementary legislation also approved in 2023, is not free from criticism and concerns. The technical, economic, and infrastructure challenges are immense, and the success of this transition will depend on factors that include the development of a comprehensive network of charging points for EVs, the availability and cost of raw materials necessary for batteries and other critical components, and consumer acceptance.

The impact of the e-fuels exception on meeting the EU's climate goals is also a point of debate because it raises fundamental questions about affordability, refueling infrastructure, and the lifecycle of synthetic fuels. E-fuel production is still limited and faces issues of energy efficiency and cost. Furthermore, there is an ongoing debate about the role that such technologies might play in a market dominated by the rapid rise of EVs and aggressive targets for reducing GHG emissions, which is a key aspect of the transportation decarbonization policies.

Perceptions and Behaviors of Active and Potential EV Customers

Amid the regulatory transformations of the EU aimed at electric mobility, understanding the perceptions and behavior of German consumers is important for understanding current and future outcomes concerning decisions related to the acquisition and continuity of EVs. The use of Google Trends in this study is intended to capture search trends that reflect collective interest (Kinski, 2016) in EVs and related services in Germany. Although Google Trends does not explicitly differentiate between active and potential customers, it is possible to infer consumer engagement through the frequency, continuity, and context of the searches.

Active and Potential Customers of EVs and Related Services

In the context of this study on consumers in Germany, "active customers" of EVs are people who already own or use EVs and the associated infrastructure, such as charging stations and other services necessary for the proper maintenance of such vehicles. These individuals, even if they do not realize it, are already involved with the technology and are an integral part of the current electric mobility ecosystem.

In contrast, "potential customers" are those who are considering the acquisition of an EV or show interest in such vehicles and associated services. However, they are still in the deliberation phase, researching and evaluating the feasibility and benefits of transitioning to electric mobility.

Perception and Behavior of Consumers – Google Trends

Google Trends serves as a tool to probe the curiosity and interest of these two segments, capturing the evolution of search trends related to EVs in Germany. A detailed analysis of search terms can reveal the direction of public interest and the influence of factors like regulatory changes, technological innovations, and discussions about sustainability (Kinski, 2016).

Justification

This study emerges as a timely and necessary response to recent EU policies, outlined in the Fit for 55 package, which establishes ambitious targets for reducing GHG emissions and accelerating the transition to zero-emission vehicles. With the goal of ending the sale of internal combustion cars by 2035 and reducing emissions by 55% by 2030 compared to 1990 levels, Fit for 55 represents a significant milestone in the global climate agenda.

Choosing Germany for this research is justified by its prominent position in the European automotive market, its strong automotive industry, and its leadership in technological innovation. Furthermore, the recent exemption for e-fuel vehicles in Germany, amid the ambitious EU policies for energy transition, makes this country a relevant and complex scenario for the study. Investigating the perceptions and behaviors of German consumers in relation to EVs provides valuable insights for discussions of the transition to electric mobility in Europe.

In this sense, the exception granted to Germany in March 2023, allowing the continuation of sales of vehicles that operate with e-fuels, highlights the complexity and nuances of the transition to more sustainable mobility. This exception raises important questions about the paths to achieving emission reduction goals and the role of alternative fuels in the future energy matrix.

Given that context, this study offers a detailed analysis of the role of consumer stress in the acceptance of EVs and related services. Understanding how regulatory changes and exceptions affect the perceptions and behaviors of consumers is important to anticipating the sales and adoption of EVs in Germany. Additionally, this analysis may contribute to identifying opportunities and new research trends focused on sustainable transportation.

Contextualization

Impact of Fossil Fuels on the Transportation Sector in Germany

Automobiles remain one of the main sources of CO_2 emissions in transportation in many countries, despite the growth in the number of EVs and the reduction in dependence on fossil fuels. According to research by the International Energy Agency (IEA, 2023, 2024), oil was responsible for 214 megatonnes of carbon dioxide ($MtCO_2$) in Germany in 2022, with each megatonne equivalent to a million tonnes of CO_2, representing 35.5% of total emissions.

This result is significant alongside other emissions: 36.4% from coal and 25.1% from natural gas. It is noted that there was a decline of 41%, compared to the total emission of the same fossil fuel in 2000, which reached 302 $MtCO_2$. Additionally, the transportation sector stood out negatively by contributing 23.6% of total CO_2 emissions in Germany, surpassing other sectors such as industry (14.8%) and residential (13.5%) (IEA, 2023, 2024). Data also refer to CO_2 emissions by sectors, with the transportation sector presenting a significant indicator of 23.6% of emissions. The energy, industry, and residential sectors contributed 37.4%, 14.8%, and 13.5%, respectively, while other sectors represented 3.4% (IEA, 2023, 2024).

In this concerning context, EVs sales expectations in Germany, dating back to 2021 when 360,000 battery electric vehicles (BEVs) were sold, followed by 470,000 sales of this type of vehicle, in 2022, represent a 30.5% growth in the sales sector (IEA, 2023, 2024). These data motivate this chapter's analysis of factors that influence consumer behavior and imply the need for further research to generating strategies to achieve the ideals that the scenario demands.

External Influences on the Continuity or Acquisition of Electric Vehicles – Analysis of Factors Influencing Consumer Behavior

As a sustainable alternative, EVs are prioritized over traditional gasoline and diesel cars due to their potential to reduce greenhouse gas emissions, minimize fossil fuel dependence, and enhance environmental protection (Akshay et al., 2024). Accurately forecasting EVs sales is crucial for stakeholders, such as vehicle manufacturers, policymakers, and energy providers. These projections are essential because they inform strategic decisions and policy formulations within the automotive and energy sectors (Afandizadeh et al., 2023).

Thus, factors like fuel prices, vehicle attributes, consumer preferences, and social influences affect the market share of EVs. In this sense, Shafiei et al. (2012) analyze the combination of high gasoline prices, the decrease in EVs prices, the reduction in taxes on EV, and the response to consumer concerns about recharging and conclude that these factors significantly increase the EVs market share.

This study reaffirms that the exogenous variables related to active and passive consumer stress in Germany are important components for understanding the trends of continuity or acquisition of EVs and their services, reflected in the strategies and sales projections of EVs.

Similarly, Kinski (2016) uses Google Trends data to predict consumer behavior regarding car purchase decisions from 2010 to 2014 in key countries in Europe, such as Germany and the United Kingdom, as well as the United States. The main findings indicate that search data are effective as indicators of the early stages of the purchase process and that the final purchase decision is strongly correlated with new car sales data. Thus, Kinski's research resembles this study, especially in exploring the behavior trends of vehicle customers. The coverage in Germany and the methodology used reinforce this similarity (Kinski, 2016).

A study by Afandizadeh et al. (2023) focuses on developing a hybrid predictive model to estimate the penetration of EVs in the automotive market. Using a combination of historical vehicle sales data and economic and market indicators, the proposed model is superior to conventional models based on LSTM and Conv-LSTM, presenting a lower mean absolute percentage error and higher *R*-squared values in regression analyses. This result highlights the importance of considering a wide range of economic factors, such as the Consumer Price Index and Google search trends, to effectively predict market acceptance of EVs, providing valuable insights for manufacturers and policymakers in promoting strategies that encourage the adoption of these vehicles. Therefore, this approach reinforces the research conducted here by emphasizing the importance of integrating various data sources, including web search trends. These insights into market interest and consumer behavior regarding specific vehicle models are essential to enrich the analyses and conclusions of this study.

Battery Charging for Electric Vehicles in Germany: A Sustainable Transition

BEVs emerge as a promising alternative to internal combustion vehicles, potentially reducing greenhouse gas emissions considerably. In Germany, the adoption of these vehicles is growing, motivated by incentive policies and increased environmental awareness.

Since their inception in 1823, BEVs have seen substantial efforts from both corporations and governments aimed at making them a viable option for mainstream transportation. However, widespread adoption continues to be a challenge. Persistent concerns over limited driving range, high battery costs, and an inadequate charging infrastructure are major barriers that prevent consumers from fully embracing BEVs as a mainstream transportation solution (Chakraborty et al., 2022). In this regard, the stress on the limitations that these EVs recharges require may cause uncertainties regarding the continuity or acquisition of EVs. Another important point for debate is that fast-recharging batteries are expensive and even more damaging to the environment, as is the case with lithium batteries (Chakraborty et al., 2022). In an alternative view, Victoria et al. (2020) suggest that the integration of BEV in analytical models should be treated as an exogenous parameter, not resulting from optimization processes. They state that "The costs of BEVs and their batteries are not included in the outcomes" (Victoria et al., 2020).

Thus, when considering the implementation and expansion of battery charging infrastructure for EVs, it is crucial that efforts in Germany focus not only on increasing the availability of charging points but also on ensuring that the energy provided is derived from sources with low environmental impact.

Limitations and Challenges of E-fuel Production

The study by Langenmayr and Ruppert (2023) explores the production of e-fuels in Germany under the RED II regime,[11] focusing on how the technology can be economically viable under appropriate scaling and operational conditions, especially up to 2030. The geographical location of e-fuel demand in this study is limited to national levels, addressing the impact this may have on optimizing the locations of production facilities. The term e-fuel refers to fuels produced from renewable electricity sources, such as wind and solar, used to produce hydrogen that is then converted into liquid or gaseous fuels. The main conclusion is that, despite uncertainties related to technological development and future costs, e-fuel production could result in a substantial transformation of the German energy system.

While Langenmayr and Ruppert's (2023) study does not explicitly discuss whether e-fuel production could potentially pollute more than the internal combustion of traditional vehicles, the authors focus more on the technological and policy uncertainties associated with e-fuel development, competition with other technologies that rely on electrolysis and green hydrogen, and the economic and implementation challenges related to e-fuel production in Germany and Europe. Thus, despite discussions and uncertainties about the context of e-fuel production, such as emissions related to energy derived from the combustion of lignite, coal, natural gas, or petroleum, which would not be carbon neutral, the study by Langenmayr and Ruppert (2023) did not address this in its scope.

When considering the transition to EVs and the exception for e-fuels in Germany, it is important not only to analyze technological, economic, and political factors but also to understand how stress that causes psychological pressures can affect both active and potential customers' decisions. Stress, as exogenous data resulting from environmental, economic, and political concerns, can significantly alter trends related to continuity and interest in acquisition for EVs and their relevant services, as indicated by Google Trends data. This psychosocial phenomenon is often underestimated, but it plays a key role in shaping market dynamics and corporate communication strategies.

Methodology

Research Approach

To conduct this research, an approach was adopted that combines elements of quantitative and qualitative research. This strategy was chosen to provide a comprehensive and holistic understanding of the issues under study, allowing us to explore both the quantifiable and contextual aspects related to the adoption of EVs in Germany in response to EU policies.

Quantitative Research

A quantitative approach was adopted to analyze the data collected through the Google Trends tool. This platform offers a wide range of information on the volume of searches related to key terms and uses a scoring scale from 0 to 100 to measure the interest in a term over time. A score of 100 indicates the peak maximum popularity of the term in a given period, while a low score reflects minimal interest.

This evaluation assists in understanding search trends and public interest in different topics over time, thus becoming relevant for this research.

Statistical analysis of these data enabled the identification of patterns, trends, and correlations among the variables researched, offering significant insights into public interest and fluctuations over the specified period. In this research, specific filters were established to ensure the relevance and accuracy of the results. The chosen location was Germany, with a custom period from January 1, 2021 to December 31, 2023. Additionally, the Automobiles and Vehicles category and the type of research, Web Search, were defined, contributing to obtaining relevant and reliable data.

The definition of key terms was carried out in English, due to its status as a universally considered language. This was done to ensure consistency and accuracy of the research results, allowing for a comprehensive and comparable analysis of search trends related to EVs, and the research was conducted with a focus on Germany, which ensures the relevance of the results for the German context.

Qualitative Research

In addition to quantitative analysis, qualitative data sources, such as market reports and government documents, are used to provide contextual insights into the regulatory environment and market trends related to EVs in Germany. The qualitative analysis of this information from 2021 through 2023 helps to understand the broader context of EU policies based on regulations from the European Commission and the European Council, and their implementation in Germany, as well as the perceptions and attitudes of consumers toward EVs and government policies.

Postulates

This investigation is guided by two postulates dealing with specific formulations that establish relationships between variables and predict outcomes. By testing them, we aim to understand how mandatory and exemption policies for EVs in Germany may influence consumer attitudes and behaviors toward continuity, acquisition, and services of EVs.

Postulate 1: Active customers in Germany face doubts regarding the continuity and services related to EVs due to perceived uncertainty about governmental policies of mandatory adoption and exemption, and, consequently, are expected to experience higher levels of stress. This stress may influence their tendency to consider switching to vehicles with internal combustion engines. On the other hand, they may feel secure and confident regarding the continuity and services offered

Postulate 2: Potential customers in Germany will demonstrate greater hesitation in acquiring EVs and obtaining related services due to perceived uncertainty about governmental policies of mandatory adoption and exemptions. This hesitation may be influenced by feelings of stress among these consumers, especially during periods of significant changes in these policies.

Data Analysis

Statistical Analysis of Google Trends Data to Identify Patterns, Trends, and Correlations Among the Variables Researched

First, it is important to understand the current landscape of active and potential consumers' interests and concerns, especially when it comes to emerging technologies and issues relevant to society. An important tool for exploring this dynamic is Google Trends, which offers insights into online search trends and is adopted in this study.

Five key terms are used to analyze and identify patterns of behavior and predominant areas of interest among users: "Stress, Electric Vehicles, Electric Vehicle Charging, Continuity of Electric Vehicles, and Mechanical Services". The insights offered by the key terms and how they can influence business strategies and decision-making are than explored in more detail.

Status 1 – Active Customers

Key Terms: Stress, Electric Vehicles, Electric Vehicle Charging, Continuity of Electric Vehicles, Mechanical Services

Fig. 7.1 presents the overall Google Trends search data for active customers from 2021 to 2023, highlighting "Stress," "Electric Vehicles," "Electric Vehicle Charging," "Continuity of Electric Vehicles," and "Mechanical Services." It shows interest patterns over time.

Explanation of the Analysis of Active Customers with Results Similar to Potential Customers in Lower Saxony

There is a convergence in the data for active and potential customers, who exhibit highly similar search patterns from 2021 to 2023 for the terms "Stress and Electric Vehicles". This uniformity suggests a homogeneous market response that warrants a detailed analysis.

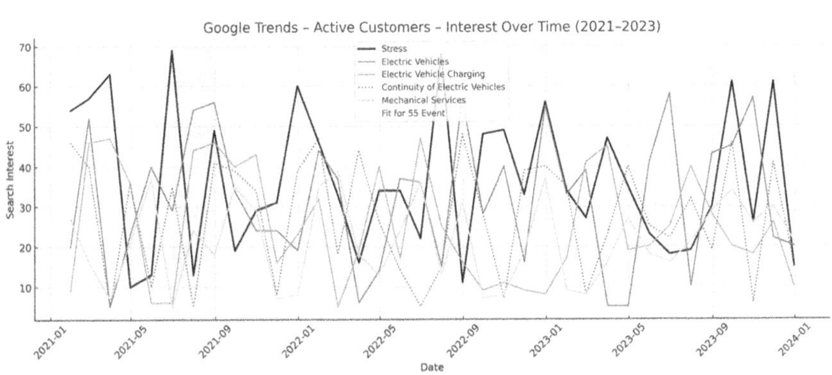

Fig. 7.1. Google Trends – Active Customers – Overview. *Source*: Google Trends, 2024.

Active customers, who are typically already engaged with the EVs market, exhibited response patterns similar to those of potential customers. This similarity in response could indicate that both segments are equally influenced by significant external factors, such as regulatory changes, technological innovations in the electric vehicle sector, or regional economic events that impact all demographic layers.

Both active and potential customers appear to be responding similar to major changes. This might include reactions to regulatory adjustments, advancements in EVs technology, or broader economic shifts that affect the entire population. Such a uniform response across different segments of the market suggests a widespread impact of these factors.

The similar outcomes could also reflect the effects of specific events or policies that have received extensive media coverage and public attention. For instance, stricter environmental laws or government subsidies for EVs purchases might have triggered a simultaneous spike in interest among both existing and potential consumers.

Given that Lower Saxony is a significant automotive hub, trends observed there might be particularly sensitive to shifts within the automotive industry. Active customers, who already own or use EVs, may closely monitor these trends to make informed decisions about technological upgrades, maintenance, or new purchases. This behavior may align with the concerns and interests of potential customers.

The analysis underscores the need for marketing strategies and product development that recognize the uniformity of interest trends. Businesses can utilize this convergence to enhance or tailor their marketing campaigns by focusing on messages that resonate uniformly across both customer segments.

Key Terms: Stress, Continuity of Electric Vehicles

Fig. 7.2 illustrates active customers' Fit for 55 Google Trends search results for EVs, with an emphasis on the status of "Stress" and "Continuity of Electric Vehicles" in Germany from 2021 to 2023.

Analysis of Interest Trends in Stress and Continuity of Electric Vehicles Among Active Customers, August 8–14, 2021

During the week of August 8–14, 2021, "Google Trends" data show that active customers recorded high interest levels in the terms "Stress" (77 searches) and "Continuity of Electric Vehicles" (73 searches). These results occur in the context of the recent introduction by the European Union of the Fit for 55 package in July 2021, which sets ambitious goals to reduce greenhouse gas emissions and promote sustainable technologies, including EVs.

The high interest in "Stress" may reflect consumers' concerns about how rapid regulatory changes will affect their investments and future choices in EVs, as well as possible challenges in adapting to new infrastructure and technology requirements.

The high interest in "Continuity of Electric Vehicles" suggests an optimistic view and a belief in the continuation of efforts to promote EVs. This interest

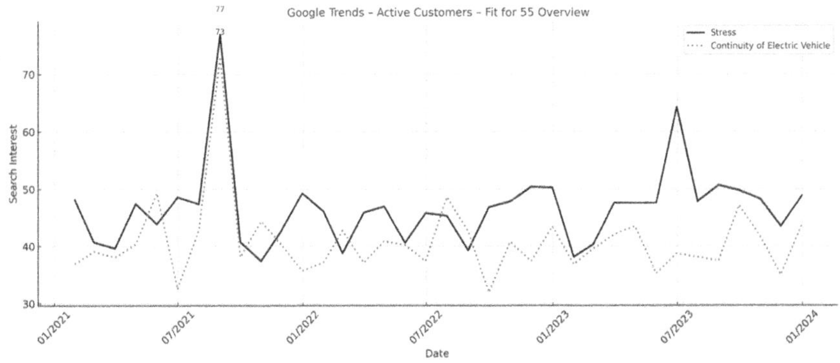

Fig. 7.2. Google Trends – Active Customers – Fit for 55 Overview.
Source: Google Trends, 2024.

indicates that, despite concerns, there is a positive expectation that support for EVs will persist and expand, especially in response to proactive policies like those outlined in the Fit for 55 package.

The analysis shows a mix of concern and optimism among active consumers. The concern is evidenced by the high interest in "Stress", while optimism is captured by the robust interest in "Continuity of Electric Vehicles". This reflects a complex dynamic in which consumers are attentive to changes but also hopeful and confident about the ongoing development and support for EVs technology.

These insights are important for vehicle manufacturers, policymakers, and stakeholders in the energy sector. They point to the need for clear communication not only about imminent changes but also about the assurances of ongoing support for EVs. Moreover, strategies should emphasize building a robust infrastructure and providing incentives that alleviate consumers' concerns and strengthen their confidence in the EVs market.

Status 1 – Potential Customers

Key Terms: Stress, Electric Vehicles, Electric Vehicle Charging, Buying of Electric Vehicles, Mechanical Services

Fig. 7.3 presents the overall Google Trends search trends for potential customers from 2021 to 2023, highlighting "Stress," "Electric Vehicles," "Electric Vehicle Charging," "Buying of Electric Vehicle," and "Mechanical Services." It reveals interest patterns over time.

Analysis of Interest Trend in Stress and Electric Vehicles in Lower Saxony from 2021 to 2023

During the period from 2021 to 2023, Google Trends data for Lower Saxony reveal a consistent interest trend in the key terms "Stress" (71 searches) and "Electric Vehicles" (29 searches). These data indicate trends of specific dynamics and local market reactions in the face of global and European economic and technological transformations.

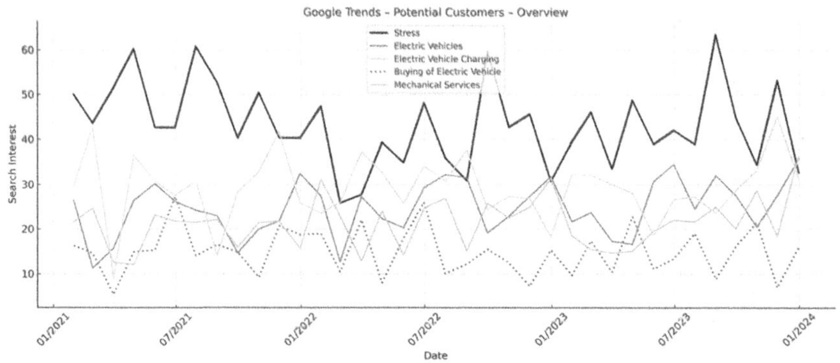

Fig. 7.3. Google Trends – Potential Customers – Overview. *Source*: Google Trends, 2024.

Factors Contributing to the Observed Trends

Lower Saxony is a significant hub for the automotive industry, hosting major manufacturers like Volkswagen in Wolfsburg. The transition to EVs, spurred by stricter environmental regulations in Germany and the European Union, may have increased Stress due to concerns about industrial restructuring, employment, and adaptation of local supply chains.

Despite the growth in interest for "Electric Vehicles", the relatively lower number of searches might reflect limitations in infrastructure, such as a lack of charging stations or less attractive government incentives compared to other regions. This could slow down the adoption of EVs by local consumers.

The trends may also be influenced by local and national policies, such as subsidies for EVs and the promotion of clean energy alternatives. The variation in interest might reflect the effectiveness of these policies in alleviating "Stress" related to economic changes and in promoting the acceptance of new technologies.

The analysis suggests that news about e-fuel legislation in Germany may have played a key role in shaping search trends. This is relevant to understanding not only market dynamics but also consumer behavior in the context of rapid regulatory and technological changes. This insight is relevant for policymakers, investors, and stakeholders in the automotive sector because it highlights the market's sensitivity to regulatory changes and their immediate consequences on public perception.

Status 2 – Potential Customers

Key Terms Highlighted: Stress, Electric Vehicles

Fig. 7.4 shows the Google Trends search trends related to the e-fuel exemption for potential customers during the week of April 16–22, 2023. During this week, there was a significant peak in interest for the keywords "Stress" and "Electric Vehicles."

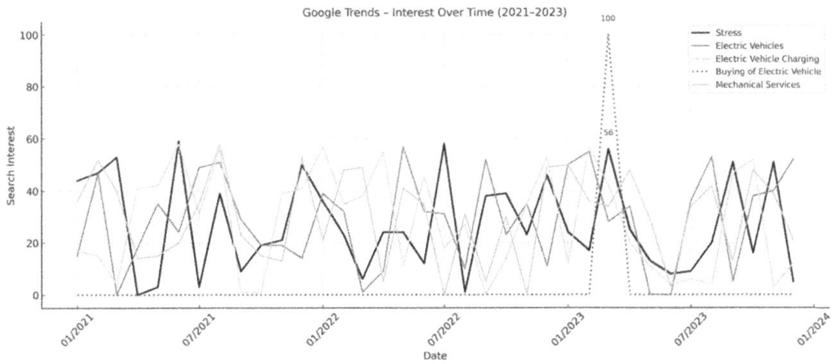

Fig. 7.4. Google Trends – Potential Customers – E-fuels Exception Overview. *Source*: Google Trends, 2024.

Analysis of Interest Trends in Stress and Electric Vehicles: April 16, 2023

During the week of April 16–22, 2023, the analysis of Google Trends data reveals a significant peak in the level of interest for the keyword "Stress", which reached the maximum of 100 searches. Simultaneously, interest in the keyword "Electric Vehicles" registered a score of 56 searches. These results indicate a notable variation in users' search behavior, potentially associated with specific external events.

In March 2023, news was released in Germany regarding a legal exception for e-fuels, a decision that may have affected perceptions and behaviors in the automotive market regarding EVs. This legislation, which differentiates cars that use e-fuels from EVs, may have caused uncertainties or confusions among consumers, reflected in an increase in searches related to Stress.

The correlation between these peaks of interest can be interpreted from the perspective of consumer anxiety about the implications of rapid changes in automotive regulations. The peak in interest for "Stress" may indicate a direct response to concerns about the affordability, viability, and long-term sustainability of EVs compared to e-fuel vehicles, an emerging technology viewed as a potentially more flexible alternative to stringent environmental restrictions.

The analysis suggests that the news about e-fuel legislation in Germany could have played a role in shaping search trends. This helps to understand not only market dynamics but also consumer behavior in the context of rapid regulatory and technological changes. This insight is also relevant for policymakers, investors, and stakeholders in the automotive sector because it highlights the market's sensitivity to normative changes and their immediate consequences on public perception.

Status 3 – Potential Customers

Key Terms Highlighted: Stress, Buying of Electric Vehicles

Fig. 7.5 highlights Google Trends search trends concerning the e-fuel exception for potential customers during the week of July 9–15, 2023. During this period,

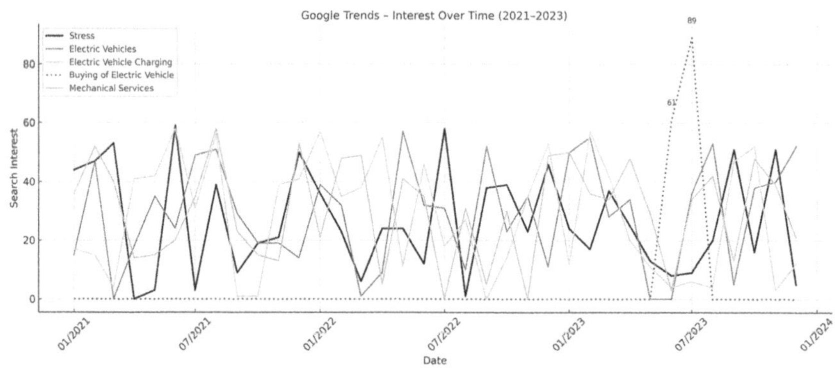

Fig. 7.5. Google Trends – Potential Customers – E-fuel Exception View. *Source*: Google Trends, 2024.

there was a significant peak in interest for the keywords "Stress" and "Buying of Electric Vehicles."

Analysis of Interest Trends in Stress and Buying of Electric Vehicles Among Potential Customers: July 9–15, 2023

During the week of July 9–15, 2023, Google Trends data for potential customers show significant interest in the term "Stress" (61 searches) and "Buying of Electric Vehicles" (89 searches). This period is particularly noteworthy because it follows the exemption granted by the European Union to Germany regarding restrictions on e-fuels, announced in March 2023.

The peak of 89 searches for "Buying of Electric Vehicles" indicates a strong tendency among potential consumers to explore the acquisition of EVs. This surge in interest can be interpreted as a reaction to existing incentives for EVs since consumers may be looking to capitalize on these advantages before a possible shift in regulatory and market focus to e-fuels.

On the other hand, the interest of 61 searches for Stress may reflect the concerns of these potential consumers regarding the rapid changes in the regulatory landscape and their possible implications for the long-term viability of EVs compared to e-fuels. The correlation of these data suggests that regulatory announcements have a direct impact on the behavior and concerns of potential consumers, affecting their research and purchase decisions.

This analysis highlights the sensitivity of potential consumers to political and regulatory changes in the automotive sector. Understanding these trends may help sector stakeholders, including policymakers and automotive companies, as they plan strategies that align technological developments with consumer needs and expectations.

Conclusion

The analyses in this study respond to the issue of whether stress affects the trend of continuity and acquisition of EVs and related services for active and potential customers when mandatory and exemption policies concerning EVs sales change in Germany.

The week when the Fit for 55 package was introduced was a positive event for active customers who own EVs, but it caused high stress even with a strong likelihood that these active customers would continue to use EVs. Attention should be paid to this high stress that can lead to the discontinuity of EVs if the event is negative for active customers. These results support Postulate 1. By contrast, Postulate 2 is not confirmed since potential customers tend to buy EVs even in the weeks after the announcement of the exception for the sale of e-fuels in Germany. However, the stress shown by these consumers was also high and should continue to be observed because high stress may change the behavior of this type of consumer and lead them to forego future acquisitions and services related to EVs.

The convergence of active and potential customers' interests during a period of substantial regulatory change offers an opportunity for vehicle manufacturers, policymakers, and investors to understand consumers' concerns. Effective strategies should address these customers' stresses through clear communication about the future of EVs, including supportive policies and plans for investments in infrastructure that would facilitate a smoother and less stressful energy transition for consumers. Future studies should include statistical analyses of automotive market sales and trends in Germany.

References

Afandizadeh, S., Sharifi, D., Kalantari, N., & Mirzahossein, H. (2023). Using machine learning methods to predict electric vehicles penetration in the automotive market. *Scientific Reports*, *13*, 8345. https://doi.org/10.1038/s41598-023-35366-3

Akshay, K. C., Grace, G. H., Gunasekaran, K., & Samikannu, R. (2024). Power consumption prediction for electric vehicle charging stations and forecasting income. *Scientific Reports*, *14*, 6497. https://doi.org/10.1038/s41598-024-56507-2

Chakraborty, P., Parker, R., Hoque, T., Cruz, J., Du, L., Wang, S., & Bhunia, S. (2022). Addressing the range anxiety of battery electric vehicles with charging en route. *Scientific Reports*, *12*, 5588. https://doi.org/10.1038/s41598-022-08942-2

Council of the European Union. (2023). *Regulation (EU) 2023/851 of the European Parliament and of the Council*. http://data.europa.eu/eli/reg/2023/851/oj

European Commission. (2021). *Transport*. https://www.consilium.europa.eu/pt/topics/transport/

European Commission. European Council. (2024). *Make transport greener*. https://ec.europa.eu/commission/presscorner/detail/en/fs_21_3665

Google Trends. (2024). *Explore what the world is searching*. https://trends.google.com/trends/

International Energy Agency (IEA). (2023). *Explore and download the full data behind the Global EV Outlook*. https://www.iea.org/data-and-statistics/data-tools/global-ev-data-explorer

International Energy Agency (IEA). (2024). *Emissões de CO2 provenientes da combustão de combustível na Alemanha*. https://www.iea.org/countries/germany/emissions#what-are-the-main-sources-of-co2-emissions-in-germany

Kinski, A. (2016). *Tendências do Google como ferramenta complementar para previsão de vendas de carros novos: uma comparação entre países ao longo da jornada do cliente* [Tese de Mestrado, Universidade de Twente].

Langenmayr, U., & Ruppert, M. (2023). *Renewable origin, additionality, temporal and geographical correlation – eFuels production in Germany under the RED II regime*. Institute for Industrial Production, Karlsruhe Institute of Technology, Karlsruhe, Germany. Energy Policy. https://doi.org/10.1016/j.enpol.2023.113830

Lazarus, R. S., & Folkman, S. (1984). *Stress, appraisal, and coping*. Springer Publishing Company.

Reuters. (2023, March 21). *Exclusive: EU drafts plan to allow e-fuel combustion engine cars*. Reuters. https://www.reuters.com/business/autos-transportation/eu-proposes-exception-e-fuel-combustion-engines-2035-2023-03-21/

Shafiei, E., Thorkelsson, H., Ásgeirsson, E. I., Davidsdottir, B., Raberto, M., & Stefansson, H. (2012). An agent-based modeling approach to predict the evolution of market share of electric vehicles: A case study from Iceland. *Technological Forecasting and Social Change*, *79*(9), 1638–1653.

Victoria, M., Zhu, K., Brown, T., Andresen, G. B., & Greiner, M. (2020). Early decarbonisation of the European energy system pays off. *Nature Communications*, *11*, 6223. https://doi.org/10.1038/s41467-020-20015-4

Part Three

Exogenous Data from Social Media

Chapter 8

Beyond the Facade: Misinformation on the Internet and Identification of Paid Posters on Social Media

Shaoyu (Shawn) Liu

Rutgers Business School, USA

Abstract

In today's digitized business landscape, online opinions significantly influence a company's value and perception. Empirical studies highlight the profound impact of online opinions on consumer behaviors, business fundamentals, and stock returns. However, the proliferation of the digital platform has also introduced challenges such as misinformation and the rise of compensated postings. This research delves into the complexities of online misinformation, examining numeric ratings, textual reviews, and the psychological mechanisms amplifying the impact of paid posters on social media. By emphasizing the necessity for robust detection methodologies, the study underscores the urgent need to differentiate genuine opinion from manipulated content. As the boundary between honest advocacy and compensated postings becomes increasingly ambiguous, the establishment of authenticity and accountability in the online realm emerges as crucial for safeguarding the integrity of the digital business environment.

Keywords: Misinformation; social media; electronic word-of-mouth; minority influence theory; paid posters; internet water army

Exogenous Data in Accounting and Auditing in the Rutgers Series in Accounting Information Systems, 117–132

Published under exclusive licence by Emerald Publishing Limited
doi:10.1108/978-1-83608-734-220251008

1. Introduction

In the modern business environment, online opinion has emerged as an essential exogenous variable, wielding the power both to uplift and challenge a business's standing. From product ratings on e-commerce platforms to commentary threads on social media channels, a wealth of empirical literature has showcased the undeniable impact that online opinions can have. This influence spans from swaying consumer decision-making processes to shaping perceptions, which subsequently affect business fundamentals and stock returns (Baik et al., 2016; Chen et al., 2014; Hales et al., 2018; Huang, 2018; Tang, 2018).

However, with the rapid rise of the digital landscape and the ubiquity of online interactions, there also emerges a darker underbelly. Concerns have escalated regarding the potential for misuse and manipulation of online opinions. Social media, while a boon for businesses aiming to reach wider audiences, has also given rise to an environment where misinformation can thrive. Such misleading content, generated with malicious motives, holds the potential to severely skew business measurements and mislead consumers. Adding fuel to this fire is the proliferation of paid posters – individuals who, often masked behind anonymity, get compensated for their posts to either unduly promote or maliciously detract from certain products or firms.

Thus, the significance of differentiating genuine opinions from misinformation and paid posts becomes paramount. This chapter unravels multifaceted dimensions of misinformation online, from numeric ratings to textual reviews and proper detection models based on a variety of features of misinformation. Considering the massive influence of social media, this chapter then shifts exploration to the concept of paid posters on social media and the underlying psychological theories, such as minority influence, that potentially amplify their impact. Delving into detection methodologies, this chapter emphasizes the urgent need for robust and scalable solutions to discerning the real from the fake.

In a world where the lines between genuine advocacy and influenced endorsements are increasingly blurred, equipping businesses, consumers, and stakeholders with knowledge and tools to discern truth from fiction is not just beneficial – it is absolutely vital for the integrity of the digital ecosystem.

2. Online Opinion and Misinformation

2.1. E-commerce and eWord-of-Mouth

As the contemporary digital landscape continues to evolve and expand, e-commerce has experienced rapid development in the past decades. Especially during the Covid-19 pandemic, people purchase groceries and other consumer goods online because they could not or would choose not to step out due to lockdown policy and social distancing requirements. It is estimated that e-commerce sales grew to $870 Billion and represented 13.1% of all retail sales in the United States during the pandemic (Forbes, 2022). As consumers enjoy the convenience brought by digitalization, one disadvantage of digitalized shopping appears. Without additional information but the merchant's description, the customers cannot know the quality of the products or services they purchased ex-ante until the moment they receive those products or services. However, product descriptions alone cannot improve consumers' purchase intentions (Mou et al., 2020). Thus, people need additional information to help make purchase decisions in the e-commerce scenario.

The Internet provides a common space where consumers can share and communicate opinions (Goldsmith & Horowitz, 2006). This communication process, known as electronic word of mouth (eWOM), provides consumers with additional sources of information to learn about products or services offered online. Online opinions and eWOM substantially impact consumers' purchase decisions (Hennig-Thurau et al., 2004). Furthermore, consumer opinion is also a key exogenous variable that can be used to measure business value (Chen et al., 2012) because it contains vital information about firm fundamentals and stock prices (Huang, 2018).

However, one concern raised with the use of online opinion is the existence of fake information or misinformation. When saying misinformation, this chapter means untruthful ratings, reviews, or posts on social media related to products and services made by malicious users either to undermine the commodity or to promote a particular commodity. Research has demonstrated the vulnerability of the social rating system in that malicious users can attack the system to manipulate the rating and then either selfishly promote or maliciously demote certain items (Feng et al., 2012; Yao et al., 2012).

2.2. Reputation System

Reputation system is a common practice used to mitigate the influence of misinformation. A reputation system evaluates the trustworthiness or credibility of individuals, organizations, or entities based on their past behavior and interactions. It is a way to establish and maintain trust in a community or marketplace where participants are often unknown to one another (Feng et al., 2012). Reputation systems can be based on various factors, such as ratings, reviews, feedback, endorsements, and other types of social proof. These systems are used in many contexts, including e-commerce, online marketplaces, social networks, and online communities. A reputation system can help buyers to make informed decisions about purchasing from a particular seller based on their feedback and ratings from previous transactions. Reputation systems have been used widely in e-commerce marketplaces, such as eBay and Amazon, and online review communities, such as Yelp.com and BizRate. In the e-market, customers can rate on scales specified by the marketplace, e.g., a rating from 1 to 5 stars on Amazon. Users can also leave textual feedback for specific products or sellers. In online review communities, users can also give ratings and feedback for a business. For example, a user can rate a restaurant or body shop he visits on Yelp.com. Other users will consult previous users' ratings and feedback to decide whether to choose a specific store.

Reputation systems are essential because they provide a mechanism for establishing trust where traditional forms of trust, such as personal relationships or social cues in face-to-face interactions, may be absent. By providing a means for evaluating the behavior and reputation of others, reputation systems can help to build trust and promote service quality (Dellarocas, 2010). Thus, a reputation system can reduce uncertainty and risk (Jøsang et al., 2007) and promote positive interactions and customer loyalty (Dellarocas, 2010).

However, reputation systems are not impeccable. Anecdotal evidence indicates that the usefulness of online reputation information is questionable. Academic researchers find that users may provide inaccurate ratings and feedback to influence the party being rated negatively (Alnemr & Meinel, 2011). Attackers also exploit the reputation system to selfishly promote or maliciously demote certain items or businesses (Feng et al., 2012). Academics and industry have established techniques to fight against unfaithful ratings and feedback. The underlying technique and physiology to distinguish fake numerical ratings and textual feedback reviews differ. It is vital to comprehensively understand various misleading information detection techniques for reputation systems from the perspective of content being detected.

3. Misinformation Detection Methods

3.1. Numeric Product Ratings

Product ratings are the numerical rating the buyers give to purchased products or sellers they transact with on the electric marketplace. It is critical to establish trust among buyers, sellers, and e-marketplaces. The literature reviewed is summarized in Table 8.1. Considering the numerical characteristics of rating that users give, many detection models focus on the rating itself to detect potential malicious ratings that differ from normal ratings based on mathematical features of the rating. Several studies explore rating-based features for detection (Bhaumik et al., 2006; Feng et al., 2012; Kolhar, 2018; Wang et al., 2011, 2014). Other studies exploit the user-based attributes to discover how attackers' rating patterns differ from that of normal users to find malicious users (Burke et al., 2006; Chirita et al., 2005; Chung et al., 2013; Liu & Sun, 2010; Mehta, 2007; Mehta et al., 2007; Mehta & Nejdl, 2009). Other scholars combine rating- and user-based features to develop more accurate detection models (Jnanamurthy et al., 2013; Jnanamurthy & Singh, 2013; Mobasher et al., 2007).

As for detection methods, early researchers tried to use statistical methods. For example, Chirita et al. (2005) use statistical methods to examine user-based features, such as the standard deviation in users' ratings or the degree of agreement with other users, to identify malicious users. Bhaumik et al. (2006) also use statistical methods to analyze rating-based metrics, such as the distribution, mean, confidence interval, and time interval of ratings, to identify anomalous ratings. Then scholars started to exploit machine-learning techniques to perform the detection task. Burke et al. (2006) construct classification models based on attributes of normal users and well-known attack models. Mobasher et al. (2007) combine user-based, item-based, and knowledge-based attributes and enhance them with semantics to construct a classification model. Since classification methods require a large amount of training data but yield low precision, Mehta et al. (2007) develop a clustering model based on similarity with most users, deviation from

Table 8.1. Product Ratings Detection.

Metrics	Method	Literature
User-based	Statistical method	Chirita et al. (2005)
Rating-based	Statistical anomaly detection	Bhaumik et al. (2006)
User-based	Classification	Burke et al. (2006)
Dual-based	Classification	Mobasher et al. (2007)
User-based	Clustering	Mehta et al. (2007)
User-based	Clustering	Mehta (2007)
User-based	Clustering	Mehta and Nejdl (2009)
User-based	TAUCA	Liu and Sun (2010)
Rating-based	Cumulative sum (CUSUM) method and Pearson correlation coefficient	Wang et al. (2011)
Rating-based	Systemically review and mathematical analysis	Feng et al. (2012)
Dual-based	QRA	Jnanamurthy and Singh (2013)
Dual-based	MBACS	Jnanamurthy et al. (2013)
User-based	Beta-protection anomaly detection	Chung et al. (2013)
Rating-based	CUSUM control chart and Pearson correlation coefficient	Wang et al. (2014)
Rating-based	Cumulative sum (CUSUM) method	Kolhar (2018)

mean vote value, and deviation from the mean for the attacked item. Mehta (2007) and Mehta and Nejdl (2009) use principal component analysis to reduce the dimensions of features and construct more accurate clustering models.

Later, scholars started to explore other detection methods that aim to improve performance and cope with the scarcity of data. Liu and Sun (2010) exploit temporal and user correlation analysis (TAUCA) to identify the products under attack, the time the attack happened, and malicious users who inserted dishonest ratings. Feng et al. (2012) review different attack models and mathematically analyzes defense methods. Jnanamurthy and Singh (2013) use a quality repository approach (QRA) to collect feedback and analyze user behavior. Jnanamurthy et al. (2013) perform mean bisector analysis and cosine similarity (MBACS) to analyze ratings and user behavior, identify malicious and fake ratings, and provide trustful ratings. Wang et al. (2011), Wang et al. (2014), and Kolhar (2018) explore the cumulative sum method and person correlation coefficient to detect malicious ratings and adjust ratings. Chung et al. (2013) exploit the beta distribution to detect and remove malicious user profiles. This method does not need known attacks as training data or prior knowledge of the rating distribution of each item.

3.2. Textual Product Reviews

In addition to numerical ratings, buyers can also choose to give textual reviews to the items purchased, or sellers transacted with. Most studies use machine-learning methods (supervised, semi-supervised, or unsupervised) based on the textual content attributes or user behavior patterns to detect fake reviews. Some scholars utilize network analysis to construct graphic representations of user networks to identify malicious users. The literature is summarized in Table 8.2.

As the pioneers in malicious review detection, Jindal and Liu (2007) use logistic regression based on the review content attributes. Building on their previous work, Jindal and Liu (2008) constructed a classification model based on content and user behavior features such as ratings written after the first good reviews. Ott et al. (2011) use part of speech and Linguistic Inquiry and Word Count to process review content and extract linguistic features that are used in the classification model. Mukherjee et al. (2013) find that pure linguistic features are insufficient to detect fake reviews in real-life contexts using the Yelp.com dataset.

Table 8.2. Product Reviews Detection.

Metrics	Method	Literature
Content-based	Distribution	Feng et al. (2012)
Content-based	Supervised	Jindal and Liu (2007)
Behavior-based	Supervised	Jindal and Liu (2008)
Content-based	Supervised	Ott et al. (2011)
Content-based	Supervised	Mukherjee et al. (2013)
Content-based	Supervised	Li et al. (2016)
Behavior-based	Supervised	Zhang et al. (2016)
Content-based	Supervised	Yao et al. (2017)
Multi-dimension	Supervised	Barbado et al. (2019)
Graph based	Network analysis	Wang et al. (2011)
Graph based	Network analysis	Wang et al. (2012)
Graph based	Network analysis	Akoglu et al. (2013)
Multi-dimension	Network analysis	Lu et al. (2013)
Multi-dimension	Network analysis	Rayana and Akoglu (2015)
Graph based	Network analysis	Fayazi et al. (2015)
Content-based	Semi-supervised	Fusilier et al. (2015)
Content-based	Semi-supervised	Zhang et al. (2017)
Multi-dimension	Semi-supervised	Wu et al. (2015)
Content-based	Unsupervised	Dong et al. (2018)
Behavior-based	Unsupervised	Liu and Pang (2018)

Feng et al. (2012) try to use content-based feature distribution to detect fake reviews. Li et al. (2016) add new features such as review density, semantics, and emotion to the classification model. Zhang et al. (2016) add behavioral features, such as friend count, follower count, average post rate, and use of photos, into the classification model to improve performance. Yao et al. (2017) identify a new attack model that utilizes deep learning, which is hard to be detected by previous detection models. Yao et al. (2017) exploit the lossy transformation introduced by the deep learning model and develop a new defense model. Barbado et al. (2019) use real-life data from Yelp.com and combine content and behavior features in the classification model.

Due to the scarcity of labeled data, scholars also explore semi-supervised and unsupervised methods to detect fake reviews. Fusilier et al. (2015) and Zhang et al. (2017) propose the PU-learning method based on positive unlabeled instances in review contents. Dong et al. (2018) develop an unsupervised topic-sentiment joint probabilistic model (UTSJ) based on Latent Dirichlet Allocation (LDA) model on the word, sentiment, topic, and document levels. Liu and Pang (2018) also exploit unsupervised models to detect abnormity signals.

In addition to machine-learning techniques, a group of scholars performs network analysis based on user relationships. Wang et al. (2011) and Wang et al. (2012) analyze the relationship among reviewers, reviews, and stores without involving any text feature. Akoglu et al. (2013) examine the network between reviewers and products using an unsupervised method with no labeled data. Lu et al. (2013) propose a review factor graph incorporating multidimensional features, including content, behavior, and graphs, to explore the relationship between reviews and reviewers. Rayana and Akoglu (2015) include both relational data (i.e., review network) and meta-data (i.e., text, timestamps, and ratings). Fayazi et al. (2015) try to construct a reviewer–reviewer graph with a clustering method to identify groups of similar reviewers.

4. Social Media – New Platform and New Challenge

4.1. Social Media – A Powerful Platform

Social media platforms obtain increasing influence by connecting people, disseminating information, and creating "wisdom of the crowd" from users. Social media allows firms to promote products to customers as well as letting customers share opinions about products (Mangold & Faulds, 2009). Employing social media platforms in marketing strategy to promote products, build brand awareness and stimulate sales is known as social media marketing. Social media plays a vital role in today's e-commerce environment because it brings numerous benefits to businesses. The sentiment expressed by users toward a brand or product on social media has a more substantial impact on firms' stock returns than traditional media (Yu et al., 2013). In addition to stimulating the performance of the stock market, social media can generate real impacts on firms' sales and return on investment (Kumar et al., 2013), as well as increase customer consumption of a variety of products, such as alcohol, digital information goods, and music (Alhabash et al., 2015; Dewan & Ramaprasad, 2014; Hoffman et al., 2014; Hong, 2012).

4.2. Paid Poster Concerns

However, social media does not come at no cost. There are many concerns related to the abuse of social media. Anecdotal evidence suggests widespread concern that malicious users could exploit social media to achieve selfish purposes. Some users are compensated for posting or sharing content on social media platforms like Twitter to undermine competitors maliciously or sugarcoat negative information. This user group is usually called paid posters or "Internet Water Army" in China (Fan, 2018; Yang, 2018). Moreover, the existence of paid posters is not only speculation but a fact that exists in today's Internet environment. There is a commercial website where people can get 100 tweet comments posted for only $38. And it is not only for Twitter. People can buy comments, likes, and followers on Tiktok, Facebook, and Instagram.

While the use of paid posters to spread misinformation for political purposes is well documented in the literature (e.g., Anspach & Carlson 2020), little research focuses on marketing and consumer reaction (Domenico et al., 2021), and there is limited evidence on the capital market. Whether paid posters exist in corporate information dissemination and how paid posters impact the capital market reaction still need to be answered.

Drawing from minority influence theory, a minority group, through a consistent and confident expression of their opinions, can influence the majority to adopt their viewpoint on a given event (Moscovici et al., 1969). Paid posters may not outnumber the whole population of normal users when expressing opinions on a given event. However, paid posters can alter the population's attitude by expressing consistent and confident statements.

4.3. Minority Influence Theory

Social psychology literature focused on the majority influence until the 1970s, that is, how majority groups influence the attitude or opinion of the population (e.g., Allen, 1965). Moscovici et al. (1969) first shed light on how a minority group can influence the majority's opinion through the famous blue-green experiment and theorize the minority influence theory. A minority is defined as a numerically smaller group or group with less power (Moscovici, 1976). Considering the context that social media paid posters are usually not influencers individually, this study adopts the small number definition.

Moscovici et al. (1969) conducted a blue-green color recognition experiment. In the experiment, a group of participants is asked to identify whether the color of the slides is blue. With no manipulation, the group of participants can reach a consensus on the correct color of the slides. However, when a numerical minority within the group gives pre-agreed responses (i.e., call the slides green), the whole group replies green as the answer. Moscovici et al. (1969) find that a minority group constantly calling the slides green will increase the number of times the naïve group also calls the slides green.

Moscovici (1976) theorizes the minority influence theory by developing a genetic model of minority social influence. Moscovici (1976) proposes that minority groups can make themselves visible by consistently disrupting the established social norms and procedures. Furthermore, minority groups can amplify their visibility by incorporating certainty, confidence, and commitment (Moscovici, 1976). When minority groups express their standpoint that they will not compromise, the only solution to reinstate social stability is for the majority to shift toward the minority (Moscovici, 1976). Moscovici et al. (1969) and Moscovici (1976) recognize the two most essential mechanisms of how a minority group can alter the majority group's opinion by expressing the same or similar opinion consistently and confidently.

Drawing from the minority influence theory, this study argues that paid posters, even though they might be a numerically smaller group compared to the normal user, can still influence normal users' opinions toward certain events by consistently expressing similar opinions confidently.

4.4. Social Media and Business Measurement

Since the SEC approved Facebook and Twitter as the formal corporate disclosure outlets in 2013, an increasing number of firms and executives have used social media platforms to highlight firm operations, communicate and interact with investors, and disseminate the firm's earning information (Lei et al., 2019). Scholars find that firms' use of social media is associated with lower abnormal returns (Blankespoor et al., 2014; Lee et al., 2015). Scholars also find that investors develop trust when they interact with the CEO's personal social media account (Elliott et al., 2017). In addition to firm-generated information on social media, studies also examine user-generated social media information and its impact on capital market and operating outcomes. Scholars find that user-generated social medial information has strong predictive power for a firm's stock return and operating performance (Baik et al., 2016; Bartov et al., 2018; Chen et al., 2014; Hales et al., 2018; Tang, 2018; Yu et al., 2013).

Despite the well-examined upside of using social media, there are widespread concerns about social media in the capital market. The SEC keeps publishing investor alerts about fraudulent investment schemes using social media (e.g., SEC 2014, 2015a, 2015b, 2017, 2018, 2022). Experimental evidence also suggests that firms may use social media strategically to distract investors' attention from negative events (Cade, 2018). Social media is becoming a fertile ground for rumors and opinion spamming because of its complex information environment (Lei et al., 2019). Unlike reviews on online marketplaces, where only buyers who conducted transactions can write reviews, the content on social media is user-generated with few limitations on users' identity. It leaves chances for unethical firms and malicious users to promote or maliciously demote certain items or businesses. Understanding the techniques available to detect paid postings on social media is essential.

5. Paid Poster Detection

Posts on social media platforms are similar to product reviews on e-marketplaces, given their textual characteristics. Furthermore, social media comments may

Table 8.3. Social Media Opinion Detection.

Metrics	Method	Literature
Behavior-based	Binary N-gram	Peng et al. (2016)
Content-based	Classification	Chen et al. (2013)
Behavior-based	Classification	Lee et al. (2015)
Behavior-based	Classification	Tacchini et al. (2017)
Multi-dimension	Classification	Ko et al. (2017)
Content-based	Classification	Aldwairi and Alwahedi (2018)
Content-based	Clustering	Jiang and Wilson (2018)
Multi-dimension	Classification	Lian et al. (2019)
Content-based	Classification	Selvaraj et al. (2020)
Multi-dimension	Classification	Xiao and Qiu (2020)
Multi-dimension	Network analysis	Tam et al. (2019)
Content-based	Tf-IDF and LDA	Xu et al. (2019)
Behavior-based	Deep learning	Sahoo and Gupta (2021)
Multi-dimension	BCMM-GRU	Luo et al. (2021)

contain factually incorrect information (Anspach & Carlson, 2020). Building upon previous literature on detecting malicious textual product reviews on an e-marketplace, many researchers explore machine-learning methods to detect fake information on social media. Like fake review detection, scholars construct a detection model based on post content, poster behavior, or a combination of both. Table 8.3 summarizes the literature in this field.

Content-based features are common because social media posts are textual messages that researchers in the fake review detection area have explored. Chen et al. (2013) analyze social media comments regarding famous events and develop a classification model to detect fake information. Aldwairi and Alwahedi (2018) use a logistic classifier based on the features of the title and post. Jiang and Wilson (2018) extract linguistic signals from user comments on social media. Selvaraj et al. (2020) combine a random forest algorithm with natural language processing to analyze social media posts' words, phrases, and sentences.

Paid poster detection is a significant application in detecting misinformation on social media. Since paid posters usually do not act alone, the user behavior features are essential in developing the detection model. Lee et al. (2015) analyze the characteristics of paid Twitter workers who get compensation by posting comments or tweets in favor of or maliciously undermining specific organizations or products. Peng et al. (2016) use the binary *n*-gram method to identify authorship that appears to be the same person leading the opinion. Tacchini et al. (2017) propose using a classification model to detect fake news on social media based on how users interact with others. Ko et al. (2017) extract paid posters' content and behavior features based on the authors' observations and develop a classification model to detect paid posters. Based on supernetwork theory, Lian et al. (2019) develop an internet water army (i.e., paid poster) detection model by constructing a four-layer supernetwork that considers the personal information of users, the dissemination process of information, the transformation process of different psychologies, the similarity between different keywords, and the connections between different subnetworks are considered in the model. Sahoo and Gupta (2021) explore the use of deep learning to analyze the account's behavior.

As attack models become sophisticated, it is difficult to distinguish paid posters from normal users solely based on content features or users' behavior features. Tam et al. (2019) exploit a graph-based scan approach to analyze the relationships among users, posts, and hashtags on social platforms. Xiao and Qiu (2020) incorporate the psycholinguistic styles of opinion spam and explore their behavior patterns and network structure into a classification model. Luo et al. (2021) exploit post content, the topology network of posts, and metadata extracted from post datasets and develop a post-based representation approach. This post-based representation approach can process post content of rumor events in the early stages of their dissemination backward compression mapping mechanism (BCMM) (Luo et al., 2021). The authors also combine BCMM with a gated recurrent unit (GRU) to spike the model performance (Luo et al., 2021).

6. Conclusion

The digital realm has cast a new light on how businesses are perceived and evaluated. The power of online opinions, as manifested through product ratings, reviews, and social media interactions, has a profound effect on a business's standing in the market and its financial outcomes. The empirical research unequivocally links online opinion with consequential shifts in consumer behavior, business fundamentals, and stock returns. However, the blessing of digital interactivity comes with the curse of misinformation and the proliferation of paid posters, whose actions can distort the genuine public perception of products and firms.

The exploration of misinformation in numeric ratings and textual reviews unveils a complex landscape where malicious actors operate with significant anonymity and reach. The utilization of detection models based on a variety of features has shown promise in identifying and mitigating the impact of misinformation. Similarly, the investigation into the realm of paid posters on social media sheds light on the psychological mechanisms, such as minority influence, which could potentially amplify their deceptive impact.

The need for robust, scalable solutions to tackle the challenges of misinformation and paid posting is not only imperative but also exigent. Businesses, consumers, and stakeholders at large are navigating through a digital ecosystem that is increasingly being muddied by dishonest narratives. The endeavor to discern the real from the fake, to differentiate genuine advocacy from influenced endorsements, is central to reinstating trust and integrity in the digital milieu. Furthermore, as the digital landscape continues to evolve, staying ahead of the malicious actors by continually improving and adapting the detection methodologies is vital.

This chapter underscores the necessity to equip the digital community with the knowledge, tools, and frameworks to combat misinformation and ensure a fair and transparent online business environment. As we forge ahead into a future where digital interactions will continue to dominate the business–consumer relationship, fostering a culture of authenticity and accountability is paramount for the sustenance and growth of a healthy digital ecosystem.

References

Akoglu, L., Chandy, R., & Faloutsos, C. (2013). *Opinion fraud detection in online reviews by network effects*. Proceedings of the international AAAI conference on web and social media.

Aldwairi, M., & Alwahedi, A. (2018). Detecting fake news in social media networks. *Procedia Computer Science*, *141*, 215–222. https://doi.org/10.1016/j.procs.2018.10.171

Alhabash, S., McAlister, A. R., Quilliam, E. T., Richards, J. I., & Lou, C. (2015). Alcohol's getting a bit more social: When alcohol marketing messages on Facebook increase young adults' intentions to imbibe. *Mass Communication and Society*, *18*(3), 350–375.

Allen, V. L. (1965). Situational factors in conformity. *Advances in Experimental Social Psychology*, *2*, 133–175.

Alnemr, R., & Meinel, C. (2011, June 29–July 1). *From reputation models and systems to reputation ontologies*. Trust Management V: 5th IFIP WG 11.11 international conference, IFIPTM 2011, Copenhagen, Denmark.

Anspach, N. M., & Carlson, T. N. (2020). What to believe? Social media commentary and belief in misinformation. *Political Behavior*, *42*(3), 697–718. https://doi.org/10.1007/s11109-018-9515-z

Baik, B., Cao, Q., Choi, S., & Kim, J.-M. (2016). *Local Twitter activity and stock returns*. SSRN 2783670.

Barbado, R., Araque, O., & Iglesias, C. A. (2019). A framework for fake review detection in online consumer electronics retailers. *Information Processing & Management*, *56*(4), 1234–1244. https://doi.org/10.1016/j.ipm.2019.03.002

Bartov, E., Faurel, L., & Mohanram, P. S. (2018). Can Twitter help predict firm-level earnings and stock returns? *The Accounting Review*, *93*(3), 25–57.

Bhaumik, R., Williams, C., Mobasher, B., & Burke, R. (2006). *Securing collaborative filtering against malicious attacks through anomaly detection*. Proceedings of the 4th workshop on intelligent techniques for web personalization (ITWP'06), Boston, MA.

Blankespoor, E., Miller, G. S., & White, H. D. (2014). The role of dissemination in market liquidity: Evidence from firms' use of Twitter™. *The Accounting Review*, *89*(1), 79–112.

Burke, R., Mobasher, B., Williams, C., & Bhaumik, R. (2006). *Classification features for attack detection in collaborative recommender systems*. Proceedings of the 12th ACM SIGKDD international conference on knowledge discovery and data mining.

Cade, N. L. (2018). Corporate social media: How two-way disclosure channels influence investors. *Accounting, Organizations and Society*, *68*, 63–79.

Chen, C., Wu, K., Srinivasan, V., & Zhang, X. (2013). *Battling the internet water army: Detection of hidden paid posters*. Proceedings of the 2013 IEEE/ACM international conference on advances in social networks analysis and mining.

Chen, H., De, P., Hu, Y., & Hwang, B.-H. (2014). Wisdom of crowds: The value of stock opinions transmitted through social media. *The Review of Financial Studies*, *27*(5), 1367–1403. https://doi.org/10.1093/rfs/hhu001

Chen, Y., Liu, Y., & Zhang, J. (2012). When do third-party product reviews affect firm value and what can firms do? The case of media critics and professional movie reviews. *Journal of Marketing*, *76*(2), 116–134.

Chirita, P.-A., Nejdl, W., & Zamfir, C. (2005). *Preventing shilling attacks in online recommender systems*. Proceedings of the 7th annual ACM international workshop on web information and data management.

Chung, C.-Y., Hsu, P.-Y., & Huang, S.-H. (2013). ⊠P: A novel approach to filter out malicious rating profiles from recommender systems. *Decision Support Systems*, *55*(1), 314–325. https://doi.org/10.1016/j.dss.2013.01.020

Dellarocas, C. (2010). Online reputation systems: How to design one that does what you need. *MIT Sloan Management Review*, *51*(3), 33.

Dewan, S., & Ramaprasad, J. (2014). Social media, traditional media, and music sales. *MIS Quarterly*, *38*(1), 101–122. https://www.jstor.org/stable/26554870

Domenico, G. D., Sit, J., Ishizaka, A., & Nunan, D. (2021). Fake news, social media and marketing: A systematic review. *Journal of Business Research*, *124*, 329–341. https://doi.org/10.1016/j.jbusres.2020.11.037

Dong, L.-Y., Ji, C.-J., Zhang, C.-J., Zhang, Q., Chiu, D. W., Qiu, L.-Q., & Li, D. (2018). An unsupervised topic-sentiment joint probabilistic model for detecting deceptive reviews. *Expert Systems with Applications*, *114*(30), 210–223.

Elliott, W., Gale, B., & Grant, S. (2017). *Navigating through the crowd: How do features of social media platforms influence investor judgments*. SSRN https://ssrn.com/abstract=2945657 or http://dx.doi.org/10.2139/ssrn.2945657

Fan, K. (2018). China's government cracks down on paid internet posts, while employing its own. *Los Angeles Times*. https://www.latimes.com/world/asia/la-fg-china-water-army-20180512-story.html

Fayazi, A., Lee, K., Caverlee, J., & Squicciarini, A. (2015). *Uncovering crowdsourced manipulation of online reviews*. Proceedings of the 38th international ACM SIGIR conference on research and development in information retrieval.

Feng, Q., Liu, L., & Dai, Y. (2012). Vulnerabilities and countermeasures in context-aware social rating services. *ACM Transactions on Internet Technology (TOIT)*, *11*(3), 1–27.

Feng, S., Xing, L., Gogar, A., & Choi, Y. (2012). *Distributional footprints of deceptive product reviews*. Proceedings of the international AAAI conference on web and social media.

Forbes. (2022). *E-commerce sales grew 50% to $870 billion during the pandemic*. https://www.forbes.com/sites/jasongoldberg/2022/02/18/e-commerce-sales-grew-50-to-870-billion-during-the-pandemic/?sh=3aba42594e83

Fusilier, D. H., Montes-y-Gómez, M., Rosso, P., & Cabrera, R. G. (2015). Detecting positive and negative deceptive opinions using PU-learning. *Information Processing & Management*, *51*(4), 433–443.

Goldsmith, R. E., & Horowitz, D. (2006). Measuring motivations for online opinion seeking. *Journal of Interactive Advertising*, *6*(2), 2–14. https://doi.org/10.1080/15252019.2006.10722114

Hales, J., Moon, J. R. Jr., & Swenson, L. A. (2018). A new era of voluntary disclosure? Empirical evidence on how employee postings on social media relate to future corporate disclosures. *Accounting, Organizations and Society*, *68*, 88–108.

Hennig-Thurau, T., Gwinner, K. P., Walsh, G., & Gremler, D. D. (2004). Electronic word-of-mouth via consumer-opinion platforms: What motivates consumers to articulate themselves on the internet? *Journal of Interactive Marketing*, *18*(1), 38–52.

Hoffman, E. W., Pinkleton, B. E., Weintraub Austin, E., & Reyes-Velázquez, W. (2014). Exploring college students' use of general and alcohol-related social media and their associations with alcohol-related behaviors. *Journal of American College Health, 62*(5), 328–335. https://doi.org/10.1080/07448481.2014.902837

Hong, S. (2012). Online news on Twitter: Newspapers' social media adoption and their online readership. *Information Economics and Policy, 24*(1), 69–74. https://doi.org/10.1016/j.infoecopol.2012.01.004

Huang, J. (2018). The customer knows best: The investment value of consumer opinions. *Journal of Financial Economics, 128*(1), 164–182. https://doi.org/10.1016/j.jfineco.2018.02.001

Jiang, S., & Wilson, C. (2018). Linguistic signals under misinformation and fact-checking. *Proceedings of the ACM on Human-Computer Interaction, 2*(CSCW), 1–23. https://doi.org/10.1145/3274351

Jindal, N., & Liu, B. (2007). *Review spam detection*. Proceedings of the 16th international conference on World Wide Web.

Jindal, N., & Liu, B. (2008). *Opinion spam and analysis*. Proceedings of the 2008 international conference on web search and data mining.

Jnanamurthy, H., & Singh, S. (2013). *Detection and filtering of collaborative malicious users in reputation system using quality repository approach*. 2013 International conference on advances in computing, communications and informatics (ICACCI).

Jnanamurthy, H., Warty, C., & Singh, S. (2013). *Threat analysis and malicious user detection in reputation systems using mean bisector analysis and cosine similarity (MBACS)*. 2013 Annual IEEE India conference (INDICON).

Jøsang, A., Ismail, R., & Boyd, C. (2007). A survey of trust and reputation systems for online service provision. *Decision Support Systems, 43*(2), 618–644. https://doi.org/10.1016/j.dss.2005.05.019

Ko, M.-C., Huang, H.-H., & Chen, H.-H. (2017). *Paid review and paid writer detection*. Proceedings of the international conference on web intelligence.

Kolhar, M. (2018). E-commerce review system to detect false reviews. *Science and Engineering Ethics, 24*(5), 1577–1588. https://doi.org/10.1007/s11948-017-9959-2

Kumar, V., Bhaskaran, V., Mirchandani, R., & Shah, M. (2013). Creating a measurable social media marketing strategy: Increasing the value and ROI of intangibles and tangibles for hokey pokey. *Marketing Science, 32*(2), 194–212. http://www.jstor.org.proxy.libraries.rutgers.edu/stable/24544940

Lee, K., Webb, S., & Ge, H. (2015). Characterizing and automatically detecting crowdturfing in Fiverr and Twitter. *Social Network Analysis and Mining, 5*(1), 2. https://doi.org/10.1007/s13278-014-0241-1

Lei, L., Li, Y., & Luo, Y. (2019). Production and dissemination of corporate information in social media: A review. *Journal of Accounting Literature, 42*(1), 29–43.

Lee, L. F., Hutton, A. P., & Shu, S. (2015). The role of social media in the capital market: Evidence from consumer product recalls. *Journal of Accounting Research, 53*(2), 367–404.

Li, Y., Feng, X., & Zhang, S. (2016). *Detecting fake reviews utilizing semantic and emotion model*. 2016 3rd International conference on information science and control engineering (ICISCE).

Lian, Y., Dong, X., Chi, Y., Tang, X., & Liu, Y. (2019). An internet water army detection supernetwork model. *IEEE Access, 7*, 55108–55120. https://doi.org/10.1109/ACCESS.2019.2913005

Liu, Y., & Pang, B. (2018). A unified framework for detecting author spamicity by modeling review deviation. *Expert Systems with Applications, 112*, 148–155.

Liu, Y., & Sun, Y. (2010). *Anomaly detection in feedback-based reputation systems through temporal and correlation analysis*. 2010 IEEE second international conference on social computing.

Lu, Y., Zhang, L., Xiao, Y., & Li, Y. (2013). *Simultaneously detecting fake reviews and review spammers using factor graph model*. Proceedings of the 5th annual ACM web science conference.

Luo, Y., Ma, J., & Yeo, C. K. (2021). BCMM: A novel post-based augmentation representation for early rumour detection on social media. *Pattern Recognition*, *113*, 107818. https://doi.org/10.1016/j.patcog.2021.107818

Mangold, W. G., & Faulds, D. J. (2009). Social media: The new hybrid element of the promotion mix. *Business Horizons*, *52*(4), 357–365. https://doi.org/10.1016/j.bushor.20:9.03.002

Mehta, B. (2007). *Unsupervised shilling detection for collaborative filtering*. Proceedings of the twenty-second AAAI conference on artificial intelligence, July 22–26, 2007, Vancouver, British Columbia, Canada.

Mehta, B., Hofmann, T., & Fankhauser, P. (2007). *Lies and propaganda: Detecting spam users in collaborative filtering*. Proceedings of the 12th international conference on intelligent user interfaces.

Mehta, B., & Nejdl, W. (2009). Unsupervised strategies for shilling detection and robust collaborative filtering. *User Modeling and User-Adapted Interaction*, *19*(1), 65–97. https://doi.org/10.1007/s11257-008-9050-4

Mobasher, B., Burke, R., Bhaumik, R., & Williams, C. (2007). Toward trustworthy recommender systems: An analysis of attack models and algorithm robustness. *ACM Transactions on Internet Technology (TOIT)*, *7*(4), 23.

Moscovici, S. (1976). *Social influence and social change* (Vol. 10). Academic Press.

Moscovici, S., Lage, E., & Naffrechoux, M. (1969). Influence of a consistent minority on the responses of a majority in a color perception task. *Sociometry*, *32*(4), 365–380.

Mou, J., Zhu, W., & Benyoucef, M. (2020). Impact of product description and involvement on purchase intention in cross-border e-commerce. *Industrial Management & Data Systems*, *120*(3), 567–586. https://doi.org/10.1108/IMDS-05-2019-0280

Mukherjee, A., Venkataraman, V., Liu, B., & Glance, N. (2013). *What Yelp fake review filter might be doing?* Proceedings of the international AAAI conference on web and social media.

Ott, M., Choi, Y., Cardie, C., & Hancock, J. T. (2011). *Finding deceptive opinion spam by any stretch of the imagination*. arXiv:1107.4557.

Peng, J., Choo, R. K.-K., & Ashman, H. (2016). *Astroturfing detection in social media: Using binary n-gram analysis for authorship attribution*. 2016 IEEE Trustcom/BigDataSE/ISPA.

Rayana, S., & Akoglu, L. (2015). *Collective opinion spam detection: Bridging review networks and metadata*. Proceedings of the 21th ACM SIGKDD international conference on knowledge discovery and data mining.

Sahoo, S. R., & Gupta, B. B. (2021). Multiple features based approach for automatic fake news detection on social networks using deep learning. *Applied Soft Computing*, *100*, 106983. https://doi.org/10.1016/j.asoc.2020.106983

SEC. (2014). *Updated investor alert: Social media and investing – Avoiding fraud*. www.sec.gov/oiea/investor-alerts-bulletins/ia_socialmediafraud.html

SEC. (2015a). *Investor alerts: Social media and investing – Stock rumors*. www.sec.gov/oiea/investor-alerts-bulletins/ia_rumors.html

SEC. (2015b). *SEC investor bulletin: 15 investment tips for 2015*. www.sec.gov/oiea/investor-alerts-bulletins/ib_tips2015.html

SEC. (2017). *Investor alert: Beware of stock recommendations on investment research websites*. https://www.investor.gov/additional-resources/news-alerts/alerts-bulletins/investor-alert-beware-stock-recommendations

SEC. (2018). *Elon Musk charged with securities fraud for misleading Tweets*. https://www.sec.gov/news/press-release/2018-219

SEC. (2022). *Social media and investment fraud – Investor alert*. https://www.sec.gov/oiea/investor-alerts-and-bulletins/social-media-and-investment-fraud-investor-alert.

Selvaraj, A. V. J., Haffishthullah, A. B., & Nehru, J. A. (2020). A dynamic approach for detecting the fake news using random forest classifier and NLP. *Computational methods and data engineering: Proceedings of ICMDE 2020* (Vol. 2, pp. 331–341). Springer.

Tacchini, E., Ballarin, G., Della Vedova, M. L., Moret, S., & De Alfaro, L. (2017). *Some like it hoax: Automated fake news detection in social networks*. arXiv:1704.07506.

Tam, N. T., Weidlich, M., Zheng, B., Yin, H., Hung, N. Q. V., Stantic, B. (2019). From anomaly detection to rumour detection using data streams of social platforms. *Proceedings of the VLDB Endowment, 12*(9), 1016–1029.

Tang, V. W. (2018). Wisdom of crowds: Cross-sectional variation in the informativeness of third-party-generated product information on Twitter. *Journal of Accounting Research, 56*(3), 989–1034.

Wang, G., Xie, S., Liu, B., & Philip, S. Y. (2011). *Review graph based online store review spammer detection*. 2011 IEEE 11th international conference on data mining.

Wang, G., Xie, S., Liu, B., & Yu, P. S. (2012). Identify online store review spammers via social review graph. *ACM Transactions on Intelligent Systems and Technology (TIST), 3*(4), 1–21.

Wang, S., Zheng, Z., Sun, Q., Zou, H., & Yang, F. (2011). *Evaluating feedback ratings for measuring reputation of web services*. 2011 IEEE international conference on services computing.

Wang, S., Zheng, Z., Wu, Z., Lyu, M. R., & Yang, F. (2014). Reputation measurement and malicious feedback rating prevention in web service recommendation systems. *IEEE Transactions on Services Computing, 8*(5), 755–767.

Wu, Z., Wang, Y., Wang, Y., Wu, J., Cao, J., & Zhang, L. (2015). *Spammers detection from product reviews: A hybrid model*. 2015 IEEE international conference on data mining.

Xiao, Y., & Qiu, J. (2020). *Exploring and detecting opinion spam on social media*. 2020 Chinese Automation Congress (CAC).

Xu, K., Wang, F., Wang, H., & Yang, B. (2019). Detecting fake news over online social media via domain reputations and content understanding. *Tsinghua Science and Technology, 25*(1), 20–27.

Yang, Y. (2018). China's battle with the "internet water army". *Financial Times*. https://www.ft.com/content/b4f27934-944a-11e8-b67b-b8205561c3fe

Yao, Y., Ruohomaa, S., & Xu, F. (2012). Addressing common vulnerabilities of reputation systems for electronic commerce. *Journal of Theoretical and Applied Electronic Commerce Research, 7*(1), 20. https://doi.org/10.4067/S0718-18762012000100002

Yao, Y., Viswanath, B., Cryan, J., Zheng, H., & Zhao, B. Y. (2017). *Automated crowdturfing attacks and defenses in online review systems*. Proceedings of the 2017 ACM SIGSAC conference on computer and communications security.

Yu, Y., Duan, W., & Cao, Q. (2013). The impact of social and conventional media on firm equity value: A sentiment analysis approach. *Decision Support Systems, 55*(4), 919–926.

Zhang, D., Zhou, L., Kehoe, J. L., & Kilic, I. Y. (2016). What online reviewer behaviors really matter? Effects of verbal and nonverbal behaviors on detection of fake online reviews. *Journal of Management Information Systems, 33*(2), 456–481.

Zhang, L., Wu, Z., & Cao, J. (2017). Detecting spammer groups from product reviews: A partially supervised learning model. *IEEE Access, 6*, 2559–2568.

Chapter 9

Exogenous Data in Governmental Accounting: Expanding Auditing Practices

Huaxia Li

Rutgers Business School, USA

Abstract

This chapter explores the transformative role of exogenous data in governmental accounting and auditing. Exogenous data, originating outside traditional governmental systems, includes environmental, social, and governance (ESG) data, public sentiment, and data from intergovernmental organizations, all of which provide deep insights into public sector performance. The chapter highlights the applications of this data in improving government operations, such as budget planning, predictive modeling, payroll system auditing, and real-time reporting. Through case studies on social media and governmental data utilization, the chapter demonstrates how exogenous data enhances audit accuracy and efficiency. Ethical concerns, including data privacy, security, transparency, and the need for regulatory guidelines, are also discussed. Ultimately, this chapter emphasizes the potential of exogenous data to revolutionize governmental accounting by improving audit processes, enhancing accountability, and ensuring more efficient service delivery.

Keywords: Exogenous data; governmental accounting; government auditing; ESG data; public sentiment analysis; predictive modeling; real-time reporting; data privacy and security; cross-checking audits; digital transformation in government

Exogenous Data in Accounting and Auditing in the Rutgers Series in Accounting Information Systems, 133–142

doi:10.1108/978-1-83608-734-220251009

1. Introduction

This chapter discusses the utilization of exogenous data in the context of governmental accounting and auditing. Exogenous data, as defined in governmental accounting information systems studies (Brown-Liburd et al., 2019; Cheong et al., 2022; Li et al., 2024), refers to data that originates outside of the governmental system but provides substantial insights into public sector performance and operations. In an era of ubiquitous digitalization, exogenous data is a potential game-changer in governmental accounting and auditing practice.

The chapter first elucidates the different types of exogenous data pertinent to governmental accounting, including public data and indices, ESG data, public sentiment data, foot traffic data, and geopolitical and geo-economic data. Then, this chapter explicates how such data can be utilized in various aspects of governmental operations from budget planning and predictive modeling to payroll system auditing and real-time reporting, and more.

Specific case studies focusing on the utilization of social media information, such as Twitter (X) data (Duan et al., 2023), and Official Gazettes (Li et al., 2024) in government accounting and auditing are highlighted, demonstrating the versatility and potential of exogenous data in evaluating government services and auditing payroll systems. Similarly, the role of data from other governmental organizations is explored in relation to their use in cross-checking during audits. The chapter also delves into the ethical implications and challenges inherent in the use of exogenous data, including data privacy and security concerns, transparency issues, and the need for regulatory guidelines.

Overall, this chapter aims to broaden our understanding of the transformative potential of exogenous data in governmental accounting, emphasizing its role in improving audit processes, ensuring efficient service delivery and infrastructure maintenance, and enhancing overall accountability.

2. The Rise of Exogenous Data

Numerous studies have explored the burgeoning role of exogenous data within the sphere of governmental accounting and auditing (Bora et al., 2021; Brown-Liburd et al., 2019; Duan et al., 2023; Li et al., 2024; Wang, 2023), spotlighting its transformative impact in an age characterized by rapid digital evolution. Exogenous data is a critical enhancement to the relevance and accuracy of governmental reporting and auditing (Bora et al., 2021; Li et al., 2024). It allows for full population assessments and the application of sophisticated data analytics, thus elevating the quality of reporting (Duan et al., 2023; Wang, 2023).

The momentum to harness exogenous data is intensifying across both the public and nonprofit sectors. Academia and industry professionals are delving into the utilization of these datasets, highlighting their capacity to amplify the effectiveness and efficiency of the accounting and audit functions within the public domain (Wang, 2023). Among the driving factors, digitalization and the development of data analytics are pivotal contributors. The richness of online structured and unstructured information (Li et al., 2025) and all kind of information from

IoT (Internet of Things) devices (Gu et al., 2023), as well as a gamut of progressive tools, such as machine learning (Zhang et al., 2022), text mining (Li et al., 2023), and process mining (Jans et al., 2014), play an instrumental role in the integration of exogenous data, thus enhancing the quality of governmental reporting and auditing.

Among these studies, unstructured textual data like social media posts are acknowledged as the most primary source of exogenous data. Employing text mining and machine-learning techniques on such data yields significant insights, such as public sentiment from Twitter posts, thereby offering a better gauge of governmental performance and public service perception (Duan et al., 2023; Li et al., 2022). It is anticipated that governmental accounting systems will increasingly amalgamate extensive exogenous textual data with traditional accounting records. For instance, online citizen comments and social surveys could be leveraged to evaluate the fiscal health and service level of local governmental units. This integration will encapsulate not only the financial dimension but also infrastructure, service delivery, ESG, and cybersecurity metrics, providing a comprehensive view of government operations (Bora et al., 2021). Contemporary research is also investigating pioneering measurement approaches that apply exogenous data for economic monitoring, such as intangible asset (Dardani et al., 2024). These approaches can also be applied in the governmental context and are poised to fundamentally reform governmental accounting and auditing practices.

3. Types of Exogenous Data Relevant to Governmental Accounting

Exogenous data is information that originates outside of governmental systems. Various types of exogenous data pertain to governmental accounting, each bearing distinct characteristics and potential applications. However, note that there are more types of exogenous data that may be relevant to governmental accounting in addition to the ones introduced in this section. The first group in this study is the public data and indices published by organizations outside of the current government itself (Li et al., 2024). Some examples include departmental performance reports, crime rates, and transportation data. This type of data usually includes demographic statistics, economic indicators, and public service performance metrics that are instrumental in gauging public sector performance and operations.

Another category is ESG data, which encompasses information relating to environmental impact, social responsibility, and governance practices of governmental entities (Gu et al., 2023). Typical exogenous governmental ESG data includes the carbon emissions of public sector facilities detected by IoT devices, diversity statistics from local governmental websites, and compliance with international human rights standards. By analyzing ESG data, stakeholders can glean insights into the sustainable and ethical facets of governmental operations, thereby enhancing accountability and transparency.

Public sentiment data, often harvested from social media platforms, online forums, or surveys, represents a critical category of exogenous data within the governmental domain (Duan et al., 2023). This data reflects the public's perceptions and attitudes toward government policies, initiatives, and the quality of services provided. By employing sophisticated sentiment analysis tools that utilize natural language processing and machine-learning algorithms, or more recent large language model (LLM) (Li et al., 2024), governmental authorities can decipher the nuances of public sentiment. This analysis can reveal the mood of citizens regarding specific issues, such as new legislation, infrastructure projects, or public health interventions (e.g., pandemic-related policies).

Foot traffic data is another innovative and important data source from mobile devices, Wi-Fi analytics, Bluetooth Beacons, or other tracking technologies. It is a powerful tool for urban planners and government officials to understand and improve public space utilization. It offers critical insights into daily movement patterns, enabling data-driven decisions about urban planning and infrastructure development and maintenance. By analyzing these patterns, authorities can optimize public transportation schedules, enhance emergency services deployment, and evaluate the use of facilities like parks and public areas. It can also be leveraged to avoid significant public safety events, such as the Seoul Halloween crowd crush (Wikipedia, 2022). Additionally, in public health, this data aids in monitoring the effectiveness of social distancing policies during health crises. However, the careful, ethical management of this data is essential to protect individual privacy while harnessing its benefits for societal advancement.

Geopolitical and geo-economic data, which includes detailed analyses of political stability, economic trends, trade policies, and international relations, is pivotal for government entities to comprehend the broader context within which they operate. Such data can influence governmental budget planning and financial management because it encapsulates potential risks and opportunities arising from the international arena. For instance, changes in foreign policy or global market fluctuations can directly affect domestic economic projections and necessitate adjustments in fiscal policies (Olanipekun et al., 2019). By closely monitoring these indicators, governments can anticipate and mitigate the adverse impacts of geopolitical events, such as sanctions, trade disputes, or shifting alliances, ensuring more resilient and adaptive economic strategies. This foresight is vital for maintaining economic stability and securing the nation or government's strategic interests in an interconnected world.

4. Application of Exogenous Data in Governmental Operations

This section offers several examples of how various types of exogenous data can refine government functions, leading to greater efficiency, transparency, and accountability.

Budget planning: Exogenous data can be used for budget planning, offering insights into economic trends, public needs, and other key variables. By leveraging indicators, such as market trends, population demographics, and sentiment analysis, governments can tailor budget allocations to better meet the actual requirements of their constituents, ensuring that funds are directed where they are most needed.

Predictive modeling: Exogenous data is invaluable for predictive modeling, empowering governments to forecast future trends and identify potential issues before they arise. By analyzing patterns in Google search queries, mobility data, and financial transactions through banks, predictive models can help authorities respond proactively to the evolving needs of the public and optimize resource distribution.

Real-time reporting: Digital technologies have enabled real-time reporting, a process greatly enhanced by the use of exogenous data. Instantaneous insights from digital platforms like social media or 311 (non-emergency) phone systems can provide up-to-the-minute feedback on the public's reception of services and policies, allowing for quick adjustments and more responsive governance.

Operational evaluation: The assessment of governmental effectiveness and efficiency is significantly improved by exogenous data. External data sources enable a comprehensive evaluation of policy impacts and service delivery, revealing strengths to build upon and weaknesses to address, thereby streamlining operations and improving public service outcomes.

Cross-checking during audits: The availability of databases from other governmental organizations and exogenous data from various sources facilitates a more robust and comprehensive audit process. Cross-referencing internal data with exogenous data can unveil discrepancies, validate findings, and ensure a higher level of accuracy and transparency in audits (Li et al., 2024).

Enhanced public engagement: Exogenous data, especially public sentiment data, provides a window into the public's perceptions and experiences. By engaging with this data, governmental entities can foster a more open and interactive relationship with the public, thereby promoting transparency, accountability, and public trust.

5. Case Study

5.1. Utilization of Social Media Information

Social media platforms like Twitter have become instrumental in gauging public sentiment and obtaining real-time feedback on governmental performance. The first research case by Duan et al. (2023) primarily focuses on developing an alternative metric for assessing street cleanliness in New York City (NYC) using exogenous data and presenting a methodological blend of text mining and machine learning to analyze and classify Twitter data relevant to the city's street cleanliness.

The methodology employed in the study involves the collection, cleaning, and processing of Twitter data, followed by the application of various machine-learning models (Naïve Bayes, Random Forest, and XGBoost) to classify tweets pertaining to street cleanliness accurately. Moreover, sentiment analysis is performed to capture and quantify public opinion regarding the issue at hand. Notably, the analysis reveals a predominantly negative sentiment toward street cleanliness in NYC, contradicting the official cleanliness ratings provided by the city's Scorecard inspection program, a strength that exogenous data offers. Fig. 9.1 shows the dashboard proposed by Duan et al. (2023) to reveal the social media sentiment.

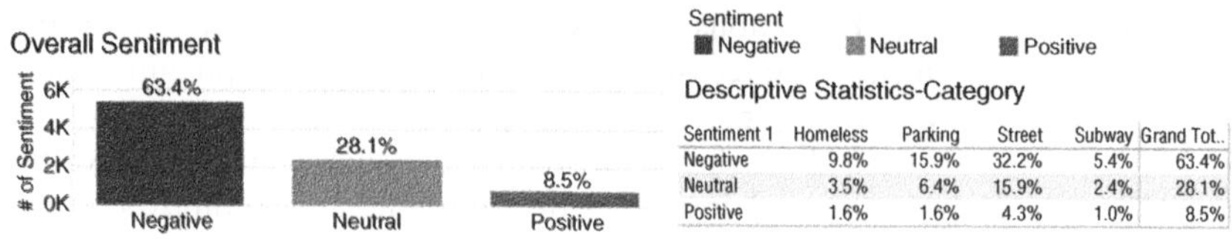

Fig. 9.1. Twitter Sentiment Dashboard. *Source*: Adapted from Duan et al. (2023).

The findings from this study underscore the value of social media information in enhancing governmental decision-making and public service evaluation. Particularly, the superior performance of the machine-learning model in classifying relevant tweets illustrates the practical applicability of advanced techniques in processing and extracting valuable insights from large-scale exogenous data. Furthermore, an extended analysis involving Facebook data indicates that Twitter is a more valuable information source for this specific context, suggesting that the nature of content shared across different platforms can significantly influence their utility in governmental assessments.

5.2. Enhanced Continuous Auditing of Payroll System with Official Gazettes

The second case by Li et al. (2024) proposes a framework to enhance government auditing through the use of exogenous data and LLMs. This framework leverages external, unstructured textual data from Official Gazettes to enhance the efficiency and accuracy of audits, particularly within complex environments like governmental payroll systems. At the core of this framework are three primary stages: (1) continuous acquisition of external textual data, (2) conversion and preprocessing of this data to ensure its relevance, and (3) the use of LLMs to extract audit variables from the vast amounts of unstructured data.

Before leveraging LLM to extract the variables, the study involves data retrieval and preparation using text mining to identify related descriptions from exogenous data. Then, the study designs prompt engineering techniques to allow ChatGPT to parse audit-relevant details from the Official Gazettes as audit evidence. This information is further used to cross-verify internal records from the payroll system. Figs. 9.2 and 9.3 illustrate Li et al.'s (2024) framework. The study demonstrates the framework using internal auditors from a Brazilian governmental unit. The feedback loop from auditors indicates that the framework plays a vital role in refining and enhancing the cross-verification process, further improving the framework's effectiveness and resolving the auditors' existing difficulties in performing similar tasks. The demonstration results indicate that implementing LLMs led to a remarkable 96% accuracy rate, coupled with an 83% reduction in the time costs associated with traditional, manual auditing processes. These findings underscore the potential for leveraging exogenous data with advanced tools like LLMs to enhance audit efficiency significantly in the government domain.

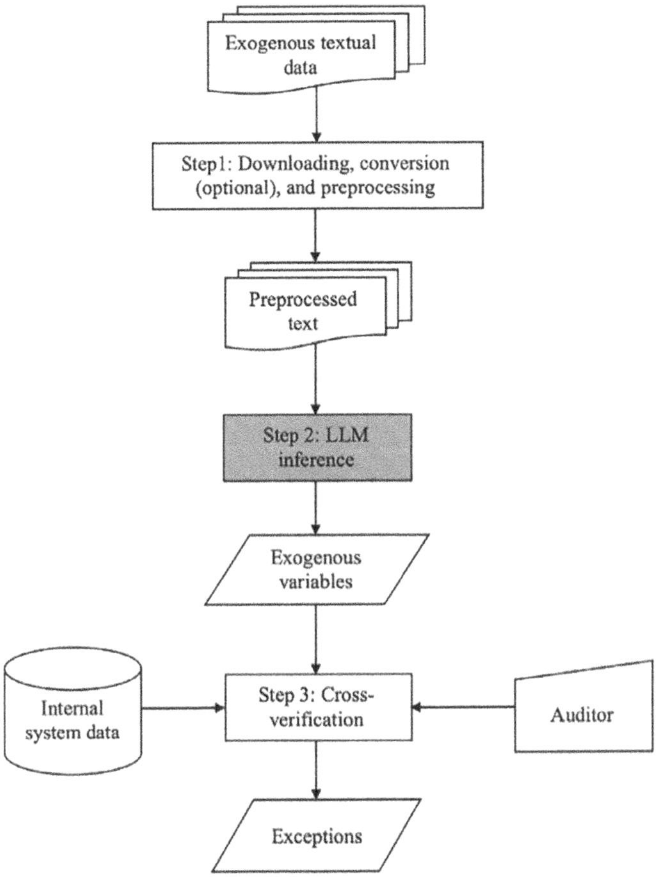

Fig. 9.2. Illustration of the Framework (Li et al., 2024).

6. Ethical Implications and Challenges

Although exogenous data has many benefits when applied in the government accounting and auditing area, its utilization also entails ethical implications and challenges. Since the data originates outside of the governmental system, issues concerning data privacy, security, transparency, and regulatory compliance become paramount. This section discusses these ethical quandaries, providing an understanding of the challenges and proposing potential pathways to navigate them.

Data privacy and security are the primary concerns. As governmental entities leverage exogenous data, ensuring the privacy and security of the data is crucial. This includes encrypting sensitive information and adhering to data protection laws to maintain public trust and confidence. Any format for requesting and

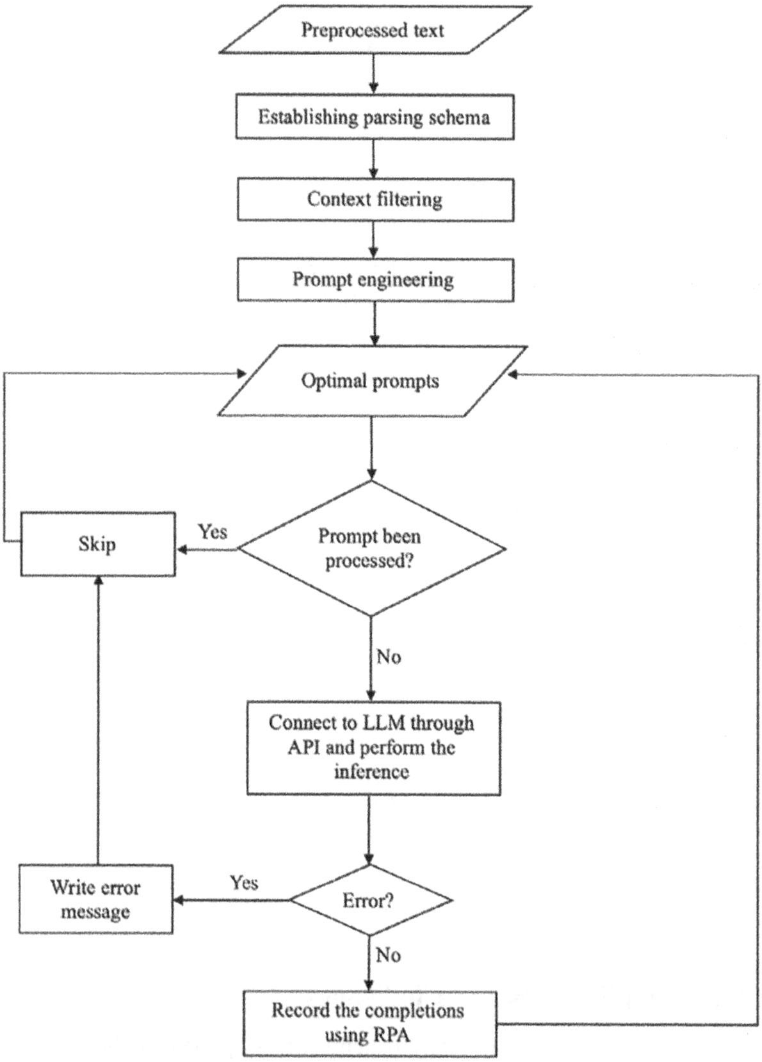

Fig. 9.3. Illustration of the LLM Inference Process (Li et al., 2024).

sharing data should go through a series of security procedures. During the usage stage, transparency is a cornerstone of ethical governmental operations. The use of exogenous data should be conducted in a transparent manner, ensuring that the data collection, analysis, and usage processes are clear and open to scrutiny. It is also essential to obtain proper consent from individuals or entities whose data is being used and to respect the ownership rights pertaining to that data. If objections are raised in any form, the government should take steps to ensure the individual's data is no longer collected or analyzed.

In addition, the regulatory landscape governing the use of exogenous data in governmental accounting and auditing needs to be robust. Compliance with existing laws and regulations is essential, and the development of new regulatory frameworks may be necessary to address the unique challenges posed by exogenous data. The government should also consider that building the capacity of governmental entities to handle exogenous data ethically is imperative. This includes training personnel, developing ethical guidelines, and establishing mechanisms for oversight and accountability.

Next, when using exogenous data, it is important to resolve any biases and maintain the representativity of the data since exogenous data may carry inherent biases or may not be representative of the broader population. Public engagement is essential to resolve this concern. Engaging with the public and other stakeholders in discussions surrounding the collection and use of exogenous data can foster a more informed and inclusive approach to leveraging this data. Addressing these issues is crucial to ensure that the insights derived from the data are accurate and equitable.

The ethical considerations surrounding the use of exogenous data are complex and multifaceted. Navigating these challenges requires a concerted effort from governmental entities, regulatory bodies, and the broader community. Establishing clear ethical guidelines and regulatory frameworks, coupled with public engagement and capacity-building, can significantly contribute to the responsible and effective use of exogenous data in governmental accounting and auditing.

7. Conclusion

The exploration of exogenous data within the governmental accounting and auditing realms presents a compelling narrative of transformation and innovation. This chapter underscores the significant potential that exogenous data holds in enhancing governmental operations from budget planning and predictive modeling to operational evaluation and beyond. Through detailed case studies and an examination of various types of exogenous data, the chapter illuminates ways that such data can serve as a catalyst for improved efficiency, transparency, and accountability in government functions.

However, as the journey toward integrating exogenous data progresses, the ethical implications and challenges highlighted in the discussion serve as a crucial reminder of the responsibility that comes with this innovation. The privacy and security of data, along with the transparency of its use and adherence to regulatory standards, are paramount considerations that must guide the ethical use of exogenous data in governmental practices. Moving forward, the commitment to navigating these ethical challenges, alongside the continuous refinement of methodologies for data utilization, will be key to unlocking the full potential of exogenous data.

References

Bora, I., Duan, H. K., Vasarhelyi, M. A., Zhang, C. A., & Dai, J. (2021). The transformation of government accountability and reporting. *Journal of Emerging Technologies in Accounting*, *18*(2), 1–21.

Brown-Liburd, H., Cheong, A., Vasarhelyi, M. A., & Wang, X. (2019). Measuring with exogenous data (MED), and government economic monitoring (GEM). *Journal of Emerging Technologies in Accounting*, *16*(1), 1–19.

Cheong, A., Duan, H. K., Huang, Q., Vasarhelyi, M. A., & Zhang, C. A. (2022). The rise of accounting: Making accounting information relevant again with exogenous data. *Journal of Emerging Technologies in Accounting*, *19*(1), 1–20.

Dardani, M. A., Gu, Y., Hu, H., Medinets, A. F., Palmon, D., & Vasarhelyi, M. A. (2024). Rethinking the standard-setting process: The role of intangibles. *Journal of Emerging Technologies in Accounting*, *20*(2), 1–20.

Duan, H. K., Vasarhelyi, M. A., Codesso, M., & Alzamil, Z. (2023). Enhancing the government accounting information systems using social media information: An application of text mining and machine learning. *International Journal of Accounting Information Systems*, *48*, 100600.

Gu, Y., Dai, J., & Vasarhelyi, M. A. (2023). Audit 4.0-based ESG assurance: An example of using satellite images on GHG emissions. *International Journal of Accounting Information Systems*, *50*, 100625.

Jans, M., Alles, M. G., & Vasarhelyi, M. A. (2014). A field study on the use of process mining of event logs as an analytical procedure in auditing. *The Accounting Review*, *89*(5), 1751–1773.

Li, H., de Freitas, M. M., Lee, H., & Vasarhelyi, M. (2024). Enhancing continuous auditing with large language models: AI-assisted real-time accounting information cross-verification. https://ssrn.com/abstract=4163242

Li, H., Gao, H. (Harry), Wu, C., & Vasarhelyi, M. A. (2025). *Extracting financial data from unstructured* sources: Leveraging large language models. *Journal of Information Systems*, *39*(1), 135–156.

Li, H., Wang, X., & Issa, H. (2022). *Exploring Mayors' disclosure patterns on social media: Evidence from Twitter (X) expressions.* https://ssrn.com/abstract=4163242

Li, H., Wei, D. K., Moffitt, K., & Vasarhelyi, M. A. (2023). *Addressing the last mile problem in open government data: Using AIS technologies to enhance governmental financial reporting.* https://ssrn.com/abstract=4385883

Olanipekun, I. O., Olasehinde-Williams, G., & Güngör, H. (2019). Impact of economic policy uncertainty on exchange market pressure. *SAGE Open*, *9*(3), 2158244019876275.

Wang, X. (2023). *Three essays on applying analytics and exogenous data to government and nonprofit accounting*. Rutgers The State University of New Jersey, Graduate School – Newark.

Wikipedia. (2022). *Seoul Halloween crowd crush.* https://en.wikipedia.org/w/index.php?title=Seoul_Halloween_crowd_crush&oldid=1210994681

Zhang, G., Atasoy, H., & Vasarhelyi, M. A. (2022). Continuous monitoring with machine learning and interactive data visualization: An application to a healthcare payroll process. *International Journal of Accounting Information Systems*, *46*, 100570.

Chapter 10

An Exogenous Leading Indicator of Box Office Revenue: Piracy as a Consumer Proxy

Steven Katz

Rutgers Business School, USA

Abstract

Modern movies often represent a significant investment of time and resources, with some costing tens or hundreds of millions of dollars to create over years of planning and production time. However, not all movies manage to recoup their expenses, and even those that do may not make enough to justify their risk. While it is relatively straightforward to calculate box office revenue in retrospect, many studies (e.g., Song & Han, 2013; Wang et al., 2020; Zhang et al., 2009) have attempted to predict box office revenue. Doing so would inform investors, managers, and accountants while providing exogenous evidence to support retrospective revenue reporting. So far, leading indicators of box office revenue have looked at either movie traits (e.g., lead actor, genre, release date) or social media responses, but both proxies are incomplete. This paper presents alternative sources of leading exogenous information: torrenting statistics and piracy-based social media chatter. Piratical downloads represent an alternative but potentially representative impression of how many people in the population are interested in seeing a movie. Similarly, piracy-based social media can be mined for users' requests for access or impressions of a given film, and they have the added benefit of being relatively free of corporate public relations that may skew aggregated impressions. Challenges and opportunities are discussed, and future research avenues are outlined.

Keywords: Exogenous data; social media; predicting revenue; movies; media piracy; torrents; leading indicators

Exogenous Data in Accounting and Auditing in the Rutgers Series in Accounting Information Systems, 143–150

doi:10.1108/978-1-83608-734-220251010

1. Introduction

Exogenous data can be described as information that is both external to a system and relevant to that system's outcomes. Often, exogenous factors' distance from a system allows them to offer perspectives that are difficult to discern using internal data alone. This perspective can come from something as direct as a third-party review. Third parties' separation from the product or company they are reviewing allows for the presumption of relative objectivity. By acting independently of each other and any corporate system, third parties can provide exogenous information that can support or discredit endogenous claims.

Firms that produce films have expectations about how films will be received. These expectations have generally been studied in the context of data endogenous to the films themselves. This chapter explores the value of including exogenous data in predictions about film profitability. Specifically, the predictive value of media piracy is considered a potential proxy for box office revenue. Piracy implications and potential implementations of piracy as an exogenous predictor are considered.

2. Predicting Box Office Revenue

Modern movie theater offerings generally represent significant financial investments, frequently budgeting tens or hundreds of millions of dollars (Movie Budgets, 2023). While detailed information about a movie's performance is relatively easy to access in retrospect (Box Office Revenues, 2023), leading indicators are less accessible, but more valuable. They can suggest to management and stakeholders what to expect from a firm's future performance, facilitating decision-making and setting market expectations. They can also be used for auxiliary audit evidence to assure reported earnings.

Past research has investigated the predictive power of a variety of factors related to films themselves, including film budget, whether it is a sequel, critics' reviews, actor/director profit history, genre, ESRB rating, release date, and various interaction variables (Antipov & Pokryshevskaya, 2017; Lash & Zhao, 2016; Simonoff & Sparrow, 2000). However, these tend to be traits attributable to movies themselves, and not reflections of consumer behaviors. Rather than measure what consumers are doing now to form a leading indication of box office revenue, trait-based indicators rely on trends set by the performance of movies past. This approach is vulnerable to systemic changes, whether introduced slowly over time (e.g., a cultural shift away from certain movie genres) or an abrupt disruption (e.g., a scandal involving a once-respected director). A complementary avenue of research has tapped social media as a source of non-trait-based exogenous data to draw conclusions about movie performance.

3. Alternative Leading Indicators

Social media has provided a rich source of exogenous data for research and income predictions, with multiple studies exploring whether the volume or valence of feedback on various social media outlets (e.g., microblogging, IMDB reviews, forums) could predict consumer behavior (Baek et al., 2017; Chintagunta et al., 2010; Lee et al., 2019; Lehrer & Xie, 2017; Liu et al., 2016; Song et al., 2019; Yoon et al., 2017). However, collecting and processing social media data can be onerous and expensive. In addition, the lack of structure inherent in text-based posts, as well as biases in the sorts of opinions expressed by consumers, may complicate drawing conclusions from social media (Geva et al., 2013).

As predictors of box-office earnings, trait-based or social media-based predictors have complementary benefits and detriments. Traits are relatively accessible and objective, but they are only indirect indicators of audience preferences. Social media posts are diffuse and subjective, but they directly access audience opinions and behaviors. An accessible, objective, direct measure of audience behavior could be a valuable tool for predicting box office revenue, but one has yet to present itself.

However, there may be an unorthodox alternative – a leading indicator of audience behavior that is simultaneously accessible, objective, and a direct measurement of collective viewing intent: piracy.

4. Piracy in Practice

Piracy is the widespread practice of illegally using someone's creation in ways that violate copyright protections, and it has become particularly associated with sharing software and multimedia on the internet ("Piracy," 2023). It has been, and remains, an enormously popular way to access content and software for free (Hill, 2007; Spajic, 2023). A majority of movie piracy takes the form of visiting illegal streaming sites that host copyrighted content in a manner not dissimilar to legal platforms (e.g., YouTube), or by downloading content directly from a file hosting website (e.g., Megaupload) (Online Piracy in Numbers, 2023). This method of piracy is difficult to measure for parties without access to website or hosting statistics. Downloading via peer-to-peer (P2P) file sharing, commonly referred to as "torrenting," is another popular method for circumventing copyright protections. Torrent activity is, by design, visible to anyone accessing the torrent, and it is often accessible using torrent tracking hubs that compile and list torrented files and their associated popularity (e.g., The Pirate Bay). Torrents permit users to download (leech) files from an uploading user's device. Once the download is complete, the leecher can also make their copy of the file available (seed) for other users to download. In this way, a file can be leeched and seeded among hundreds or thousands of users.

Intuitively, piracy activity is an appropriate proxy for viewership interest since it represents users actively seeking out media in the same way that someone might go see a movie at a theater. Encouragingly, research on the consequences of piracy has found that an increase in piratical downloads is related to an increase in media sales, represented via placement of music tracks on the Billboard popularity rankings (Koenigstein et al., 2009). Notably, while Billboard rankings are retrospective in a manner similar to theaters' retrospective summaries of viewership and revenue, torrenting statistics are publicly available in real time. If torrenting statistics can predict Billboard rankings for music, it may be that they can also predict box-office revenues.

In addition to public torrenting statistics, there are multiple piracy-based websites that feature forums as their own social media. These forums can vary in use and scope but often relate to inquiries for specific media. In the same way that activity on other social media platforms (e.g., Twitter) has been mined for textual data on user opinions, smaller, piracy-based forums may provide a window into pirates' interest in a given movie, whether through requests for access to a movie, demands for more seeding users, inquiries into higher quality versions of movies, or discussing a film's qualities (before or after release).

Taken together, it is possible that the popularity of a movie file among pirates (as measured by downloads, uploads, or various types of forum activity) may act as an exogenous leading indicator of box office revenue. Moreover, torrenting statistics offer a numerical value that represents user interest in both receiving (leeching) and sharing (seeding) a given film. Relatively objective statistics, like the volume of actions taken, can be more straightforward to interpret than subjective measures like the valence of social media postings (Kim et al., 2019).

This chapter outlines relevant past research on piracy behavior and its uses as a leading indicator and then concludes with prospects for future research in this area.

5. A Review of Piracy's Corollaries

According to a review of research on piracy conducted by Herjanto et al. (2014), there is strong focus in the piracy literature on its negative consequences (e.g., income lost or jobs eliminated). Painting a profile of demographics or morals to describe the average pirate is also a frequent focus. However, the negative relationship between pirates and the products they procure is not universal. Some research portrays the consequences of piracy as being more complex. Herjanto et al. (2014) group piracy consequences recorded in research into broad categories. Increased product diffusion makes users more aware of a product and can spread positive word of mouth. Network externalities generate opportunities for higher pricing, particularly when legitimate customers are persuaded to purchase a product because of its piracy-driven ubiquity. Companies are driven to innovate when faced with the prospect of allowing an easily accessible pirated version of their product to circulate, and they may update or improve their product to a newer version in response. In particular, studies focused on movie or generalized piracy find that piracy increases innovativeness (Rayna, 2004), increases demand (Bounie et al., 2006), and improves customer welfare (Cremer & Pestieau, 2009).

There is further evidence to support the claim that piracy is related to media sales in general and box office revenue specifically. Peukert et al. (2017) study whether the closing of a popular direct download (i.e., non-torrent based) website affects box office revenue. The closing of the website acts as an exogenous shock to pirates in that it makes piracy less attractive whether because it is more difficult to rely on an unfamiliar website for downloads or because the publicity of the host's shutdown made the act of copyright infringement less appealing. Comparing box office revenue before and after the website was shut down shows a significant change, but whether the effect of the shutdown is positive or negative on box office revenue depends on how prominent the films are to begin with. Relatively unknown films lose revenue, likely because piracy generates word of mouth that can motivate others to see movies legally, or it demonstrates to pirates the merits of watching a movie legally, even after they have already watched it illegally. More popular movies gain revenue after a piracy website goes down, presumably because some pirates start watching movies legally, and any loss of free advertising from pirates means little to movies that are already well-known. This concurs with other findings that suggest that piracy is not wholly harmful and may have positive effects via product diffusion (Givon et al., 1995; Herjanto et al., 2014; Prasad & Mahajan, 2003).

Piracy being related to box office revenues does not necessarily imply that measuring it can act as a leading indicator. Fortunately, a study by Koenigstein et al. (2009) suggests that piracy is potentially a powerful leading indicator, albeit in a different media arena. Koenigstein et al. extract from the internet the number of times that specific songs are shared via P2P networks. They find that increased P2P torrenting of music files predicts placement in the Billboard popularity rankings weeks later. Pirates act as a representative, immediately observable sample of the larger customer base. Because torrent statistics are available in real time, while Billboard rankings are periodic, piracy statistics can serve as a leading indicator for popularity, which is strongly indicative of revenue. It stands to reason that a similar phenomenon may manifest when extrapolating movie popularity, and therefore revenue, from pirates' behavior.

Piracy is not a practice pursued proportionately in the population. Perpetrators tend to be young and male, and believe that, compared to physical theft, piracy is both an inoffensive offense and unlikely to result in any punishment (Hill, 2007). Piracy is often done socially, where active pirates provide content for others in their social circles (Loh, 2019). Despite this social component, there is a significant emphasis on in-group status in piracy subcultures. Interviews with members of a private pirate community reveal that adherence to a code of conduct is not just necessary for continued membership, but a matter of personal pride (Beekhuyzen et al., 2011).

The sociality of piracy is potentially valuable; while some communities are highly insular, there are many public forums (e.g., Reddit) that aggregate updated information on the most reliable and effective piracy websites, list best practices for new pirates, and offer a community setting where members can make posts or comments for questions, complaints, and other social interactions. Whereas P2P torrent tracking websites only offer information on a single kind of piracy (torrenting), piracy forums can feature discussions about any kind of piracy (direct download, streaming, etc.), potentially offering a wider view of pirate behaviors. Because social media forums have been used as a source of exogenous data to predict automotive sales (Geva et al., 2013), it bears investigating whether activity on pirate forums may serve as an additional exogenous leading predictor of movie sales.

6. Opportunities for Future Research

Future studies may extend research relating torrent statistics to Billboard rankings (Koenigstein et al., 2009) by measuring leeching activity for a variety of films and comparing the results to the films' eventual box office revenue. At any given time, there may be many torrent streams for different uploads of the same movie. Upload source, quality, format, and language can all vary across these streams, and they each have their own seed/leech statistics. Counting the number of leeching users is analogous to counting attendees at a movie although future research may also examine whether the number of seeding users (potentially analogous to recommending a movie) offers independent insight into box office revenue. As a preliminary attempt at utilizing this data source, the single most popular version of a movie's torrent or the aggregate value of all torrent streams featuring the same film could be used as the benchmark for popularity. Web scraping Python packages, such as Selenium, or Robotic Process Automation bots, can input a movie title into a search bar and extract the relevant seed/leech information for the top torrent on the results page automatically.

Piracy forum activity may also offer a complementary source of data for social media analysis. Reddit is a popular forum platform that houses numerous subforums, each oriented around a unifying concept (e.g., horror movies, Bollywood movies, Marvel movies), including multiple forums related to different kinds of piracy. After compiling a list of either general piracy or movie-specific forums, web scrapers can search for and extract the number of threads relating to a specific movie, the number of comments on each thread, or the valence of discussion surrounding a movie.

Any analysis of the usefulness of piracy data or piracy forums in predicting box office revenues should focus on their contributions after removing the variance explained by trait-based predictors. Therefore, future research would ideally include control variables like genre, budget, and release month, all of which are somewhat predictive of box office revenue (Simonoff & Sparrow, 2000).

There is a tremendous amount of data being generated naturally from users' behaviors every day. These data are raw and may be difficult to interpret, but they hold significant value (Santesteban & Longpre, 2020). By drawing from unfamiliar venues, researchers can alchemize exogenous data into actionable information. In this case, piracy can be thought of as a second theater, one that mirrors the box office without being directly tied to it, like an exogenous microcosm of movie enjoyment. If we want to know how many people are going to see a movie in the real theater, looking into the statistics and public opinions of people who are seeing the same movie in this more transparent parallel theater can only enhance our understanding.

7. Conclusion

It is relatively rare to find a proxy for a behavior that so closely mirrors the behavior itself. There are conceptual, behavioral, and demographic differences worthy of exploration. Archivists may download films with no intention of watching them. The relatively lowered barrier of entry (effort vs the price of a theater ticket) may make viewing a less costly and, therefore, less comparable decision for pirates than legal movie-goers. Watching a movie at home may be a different enough experience from traveling to a theater to watch the same film in a crowd that they appeal to entirely different populations. Pirates as a whole may be too demographically distinct to fairly represent the larger movie-watching population. All proxies are compromises. Despite these challenges, piracy as a proxy for seeing a film in theaters still involves making the conscious decision to acquire access to, and presumably watch, the same movie. No other predictor, endogenous or exogenous, can say the same.

It is also relatively rare to find an exogenous variable that lends itself to prediction. Many exogenous variables are retrospective or concerned with exogenously verifying current events. The potential for piracy to predict box office outcomes makes it an especially useful, intriguing exogenous variable.

References

Antipov, E. A., & Pokryshevskaya, E. B. (2017). Are box office revenues equally unpredictable for all movies? Evidence from a random forest-based model. *Journal of Revenue and Pricing Management*, *16*(3), 295–307. https://doi.org/10.1057/s41272-016-0072-y

Baek, H., Oh, S., Yang, H.-D., & Ahn, J. (2017). Electronic word-of-mouth, box office revenue and social media. *Electronic Commerce Research and Applications*, *22*, 13–23. https://doi.org/10.1016/j.elerap.2017.02.001

Beekhuyzen, J., von Hellens, L., & Nielsen, S. (2011). Underground online music communities: Exploring rules for membership. *Online Information Review*, *35*(5), 699–715. https://doi.org/10.1108/14684521111176453

Box Office Revenues. (2023). *Box Office Mojo*. https://www.boxofficemojo.com/

Bounie, D., Waelbroeck, P., & Bourreau, M. (2006). Piracy and the demand for films: Analysis of piracy behavior in French universities. *Review of Economic Research on Copyright Issues*, *3*(2), 15–27. https://papers.ssrn.com/abstract=1144313

Chintagunta, P. K., Gopinath, S., & Venkataraman, S. (2010). The effects of online user reviews on movie box office performance: Accounting for sequential rollout and aggregation across local markets. *Marketing Science*, *29*(5), 944–957.

Cremer, H., & Pestieau, P. (2009). Piracy prevention and the pricing of information goods. *Information Economics and Policy*, *21*(1), 34–42.

Geva, T., Oestreicher-Singer, G., Efron, N., & Shimshoni, Y. (2013). *Do customers speak their minds? Using forums and search for predicting sales* (Vol. 2). International conference on information systems (ICIS 2013): Reshaping society through information systems design.

Givon, M., Mahajan, V., & Muller, E. (1995). Software piracy: Estimation of lost sales and the impact on software diffusion. *Journal of Marketing*, *59*(1), 29–37. https://doi.org/10.1177/002224299505900103

Herjanto, H., Gaur, S., Saransomrurtai, C., & Quik, W. H. (2014). Allowing digital piracy for strategic benefits to businesses. *Journal of Information, Communication and Ethics in Society*, *12*(4), 314–322. https://doi.org/10.1108/JICES-12-2013-0056

Hill, C. W. L. (2007). Digital piracy: Causes, consequences, and strategic responses. *Asia Pacific Journal of Management*, *24*(1), 9–25. https://doi.org/10.1007/s10490-006-9025-0

Kim, K., Yoon, S., & Choi, Y. K. (2019). The effects of eWOM volume and valence on product sales – An empirical examination of the movie industry. *International Journal of Advertising*, *38*(3), 471–488. https://doi.org/10.1080/02650487.2018.1535225

Koenigstein, N., Shavitt, Y., & Zilberman, N. (2009). *Predicting billboard success using data-mining in P2P networks* (pp. 465–470). 2009 11th IEEE International symposium on multimedia. https://doi.org/10.1109/ISM.2009.73

Lash, M. T., & Zhao, K. (2016). Early predictions of movie success: The who, what, and when of profitability. *Journal of Management Information Systems, 33*(3), 874–903. https://doi.org/10.1080/07421222.2016.1243969

Lee, C., Xu, X., & Lin, C.-C. (2019). Using online user-generated reviews to predict offline box-office sales and online DVD store sales in the O2O era. *Journal of Theoretical and Applied Electronic Commerce Research, 14*(1), 68–83. https://doi.org/10.4067/S0718-18762019000100106

Lehrer, S., & Xie, T. (2017). Box office buzz: Does social media data steal the show from model uncertainty when forecasting for Hollywood? *The Review of Economics and Statistics, 99*(5), 749–755. https://doi.org/10.1162/REST_a_00671

Liu, T., Ding, X., Chen, Y., Chen, H., & Guo, M. (2016). Predicting movie box-office revenues by exploiting large-scale social media content. *Multimedia Tools and Applications, 75*(3), 1509–1528. https://doi.org/10.1007/s11042-014-2270-1

Loh, B. Y. H. (2019). "Do you have a link?": The effects of piracy and online streaming services on the sharing practices of television content. *SEARCH Journal of Media and Communication Research, 11*(2), 41–55.

Movie Budgets. (2023). *The numbers*. https://www.the-numbers.com/movie/budgets/all

Online Piracy in Numbers. (2023). *Go-Globe*. https://www.go-globe.com/online-piracy-in-numbers-facts-and-statistics-infographic/

Peukert, C., Claussen, J., & Kretschmer, T. (2017). Piracy and box office movie revenues: Evidence from Megaupload. *International Journal of Industrial Organization, 52*, 188–215. https://doi.org/10.1016/j.ijindorg.2016.12.006

Piracy. (2023). *In Merriam-Webster*. https://www.merriam-webster.com/dictionary/piracy

Prasad, A., & Mahajan, V. (2003). How many pirates should a software firm tolerate?: An analysis of piracy protection on the diffusion of software. *International Journal of Research in Marketing, 20*(4), 337–353.

Rayna, T. (2004, May). *Piracy and innovation: Does piracy restore competition*. DRUID Summer Conference.

Santesteban, C., & Longpre, S. (2020). How Big Data confers market power to Big Tech: Leveraging the perspective of data science. *The Antitrust Bulletin, 65*(3), 459–485. https://doi.org/10.1177/0003603X20934212

Simonoff, J. S., & Sparrow, I. R. (2000). Predicting movie grosses: Winners and losers, blockbusters and sleepers. *Chance, 13*(3), 15–24. https://doi.org/10.1080/09332480.2000.10542216

Song, J., & Han, S. (2013). Predicting gross box office revenue for domestic films. *Communications for Statistical Applications and Methods, 20*(4), 301–309.

Song, T., Huang, J., Tan, Y., & Yu, Y. (2019). Using user- and marketer-generated content for box office revenue prediction: Differences between microblogging and third-party platforms. *Information Systems Research, 30*(1), 191–203. https://doi.org/10.1287/isre.2018.0797

Spajic, D. (2023, April 10). *Piracy is back: Piracy statistics for 2023*. https://dataprot.net/statistics/piracy-statistics/

Wang, Z., Zhang, J., Ji, S., Meng, C., Li, T., & Zheng, Y. (2020). Predicting and ranking box office revenue of movies based on big data. *Information Fusion, 60*, 25–40.

Yoon, Y., Polpanumas, C., & Park, Y. J. (2017). The impact of word of mouth via Twitter on moviegoers' decisions and film revenues: Revisiting prospect theory: How WOM about movies drives loss-aversion and reference-dependence behaviors. *Journal of Advertising Research, 57*(2), 144–158. https://doi.org/10.2501/JAR-2017-022

Zhang, L., Luo, J., & Yang, S. (2009). Forecasting box office revenue of movies with BP neural network. *Expert Systems with Applications, 36*(3), 6580–6587.

Chapter 11

A Conceptual Model for Mining Customer Reviews

Talha Afzal

Rutgers Business School, USA

Abstract

Online reviews have become a critical factor in consumers' buying decisions, with Trustpilot reporting that 93% of consumers rely on reviews before making purchases. However, traditional methods of collecting customer feedback, such as surveys and questionnaires, fall short in capturing the full breadth of customer opinions. This chapter introduces a conceptual model for mining unstructured textual reviews, which combines topic modeling and sentiment analysis to uncover diverse customer perspectives. By applying Latent Dirichlet Allocation (LDA) to Amazon reviews from the Toy category, spanning January to December 2015, the model extracts topics and links them to star ratings. The results reveal a broader range of customer concerns than those typically captured by traditional methods. By associating star ratings with topics and using the total number of reviews as a proxy for product sales, this method provides insights into which topics have the most significant impact on purchase decisions. The proposed model offers businesses a practical tool to evaluate customer feedback and gauge its influence on sales outcomes, contributing to the field of big data analysis in customer sentiment mining.

Keywords: Online reviews; customer sentiment analysis; topic modeling; Latent Dirichlet Allocation; big data analysis; unstructured data mining; consumer decision-making

Exogenous Data in Accounting and Auditing in the Rutgers Series in Accounting Information Systems, 151–155

doi:10.1108/978-1-83608-734-220251011

1. Introduction

Trustpilot reports that 93% of consumers base their buying decisions on online reviews, which underscores the importance of these reviews. Traditionally, businesses have relied mainly on customer feedback through formal channels. The key challenge with evaluating customer feedback through traditional channels is that it relies on traditional data collection and analysis techniques like questionnaires and surveys. The closed-ended nature of such techniques renders them inappropriate for sourcing a wider variety of customer opinions. It also fails to capture the ever-changing, dynamic nature of customers' tastes and preferences. Techniques that actually look at customers' reviews primarily focus on basic metrics, such as the total number of reviews, star ratings, reviewer credibility, upvotes on reviews, word count, and the presence of positive or negative language. This chapter introduces a conceptual model to mine unstructured textual reviews in order to extract broad topics. The technique combines topics with the associated sentiments (using star count) to uncover a variety of customer opinions that go beyond formal feedback. The chapter provides a conceptual walkthrough of how to decompose customer reviews into topics and then associate each topic with its star count. Furthermore, it shows how to link the star count for each topic to product sales in order to identify customer opinions that influence purchase decisions. This method equips business managers with a practical tool to deconstruct reviews into broad topics, evaluate their favorability from the customer perspective, and gauge their impact on outcomes like product sales.

To validate the conceptual model's effectiveness, the model is applied to customer reviews from Amazon's Toy category between January and December 2015, containing approximately four million reviews. The large number of reviews puts it in the big data space. Therefore, this method contributes to the demand for big data models.

The results provide insights into customer satisfaction across a wide range of customer concerns. The test run reveals that the breadth of topics unveiled by this technique go beyond the limited dimensions typically covered by feedback questions, such as communication, pricing, punctuality, and item descriptions.

2. Data Collection and Preparation

Reviews can be obtained from the Stanford Library (https://snap.stanford.edu/data/web-Amazon.html) and come in various file formats like JSON. For the purpose of this walkthrough, the reviews are in TSV format. Along with reviews, there are other data, such as product ID, review headline, date of review, review ID, product parent, product title, star ratings, helpful votes, and verified purchase. The data do not include quantity of products sold because this information is only available to sellers. To proxy for quantity of products sold, the number of total reviews for each product is used. This proxy is grounded in theory and has been used in academic studies (e.g., Öğüt, H., & Onur Taş, 2012).

Python is used in this walkthrough to demonstrate how topics can be modeled, linked with the star ratings, and eventually associated with products sold, proxied by the number of reviews. The first step is to import and read the data file and store it in computer memory as a Python object. Data files can come in several formats such as CSV, TSV, or JSON. Files that are larger than your computer's memory cannot be read at once. They will need to be chunked or sliced. There are several packages available to do that. For each chunk, take the review, clean it up, a technique known as pre-processing in natural language processing (NLP), and store it with the remaining columns in a database. Assign a primary key to each entry. For this demonstration, we use SQLite database.

Once the data have been collected, it is submitted to a series of pre-processing steps. Pre-processing includes tokenization, elimination of stop words, and stemming. Tokenization is a straightforward procedure that takes unprocessed information and transforms it into a useful sequence of data. In the realm of NLP, tokenization is employed to dissect paragraphs and sentences into smaller segments, which aids in the assignment of meaning. Initiating the NLP process involves procuring the data, usually in the form of a sentence, and segmenting it into comprehensible elements, typically words. For instance, consider the data string: "How is the weather today?" For a machine to comprehend this sentence, tokenization is executed on the string to fragment it into discrete constituents. Through tokenization, the outcome might resemble: "how" "is" "the" "weather" "today." While this might appear straightforward, segmenting a sentence into its constituent parts empowers a machine to grasp both the individual elements and the entirety of the sentence. Stop words encompass a collection of frequently employed terms within a language. Instances of stop words in English include words like "a," "the," "is," "are," and the like. In the domain of Text Mining, stop words are frequently employed to filter out words that possess minimal meaningful information due to their widespread usage. For instance, imagine a search system where your query is "What is a financial statement?" In this scenario, the objective is to prioritize documents discussing the concept of "financial statement" rather than documents addressing the phrase "what is a." Stemming is aimed at condensing words to their core or fundamental structure. Through the conversion of words into their stems, NLP models can treat diverse variations of the same word as a singular entity, thus simplifying the intricacies of textual data. As an example, stemming would condense words like "faster," and "fastest" to their stem form "fast." This allows the NLP model to grasp the shared concept among these words even though their forms may differ.

3. Corpus Vectorization

This step aims to convert the previously processed data into feature vectors that can subsequently be fed into the LDA machine-learning algorithm. The transformation seeks to establish a mathematical illustration for the entire corpus, effectively placing each document as a point within a vector space. For this purpose, create a connection to the database and read each processed review from the table. If the reviews are stored as strings, parse each string and evaluate it as a Python expression. Then map these words into a dictionary, which is simply a vehicle for referencing words. The mathematical principle that underlies this step involves a mapping process that changes unstructured documents to a bag-of-words representation. It operates on the fundamental concept of transforming each document into a vector that contains the words specific to that document and their respective frequencies. The dictionary can be stored to disk as binary files for future retrieval.

4. Topic Modeling

Next, the LDA) algorithm is used to create a topic model. LDA is a widely utilized statistical technique for topic modeling. Within the framework of LDA, documents are portrayed as a mix of topics, where a topic is a cluster of words. These topics exist in an underlying stratum, often referred to as the latent layer. LDA functions by analyzing a document to ascertain a collection of topics that are probable sources of the contained words. Consequently, if a document employs particular words that align with a specific topic, it is safe to deduce that the document revolves around that topic. However, the composition of a topic is not characterized by equal likelihoods among its constituent words. To illustrate, consider the topic "pets," which might exhibit a likelihood distribution of 40% for "dog," 40% for "cat," and 20% for "hamster." The LDA method is composed of two essential components: the words encompassed within a document and the probability of words being associated with a particular topic. The algorithm attempts to determine, for a given document, the count of words related to a specific topic. Furthermore, it attempts to learn how many documents align with a specific topic due to the presence of a specific word.

Based on domain knowledge, the first step is to decide on the number of topics. For the test run, T is set to 40 to obtain the 40 most discussed topics. This choice enables us to obtain an abstract overview of customer reviews. The topics obtained are a mix of broad and specific topics. The broad topics in our case were product design and assembly, product photo versus actual, color, price and deals, value for money, packaging, appearance and fit, age group, durability and sturdiness, ordering process, shipment and arrival, and product impression in days that follow. Remaining topics were narrow and specific to toys. Examples of narrow topics include plush toys, toy buttons, Lego pieces, bubble wand and bottle, guns and darts, dolls and outfits, bands and bracelets, pack of cards and dice, helicopters and remote-controlled planes, coloring books and stickers, cars and train tracks, and batteries and replacement.

A review can have multiple topics, each with a different share of the review. To choose the most dominant topic, an algorithm is written to select the topic with the highest probability assignment. The highest probability topic for each review is then stored in a new table in the same database. A primary key is assigned to each entry. This table is then joined with the previous table using an SQL query with the primary keys of each table as the common denominator.

The table is then loaded to Python as a DataFrame. Next, you average star ratings on a product level for each topic separately. For example, if a product had three reviews talking about the topic "shipment and delivery" and the stars for each review were 4, 2, and 1, the mean rating would be 2.3 stars. On a product

Table 11.1. Sample Python DataFrame.

Product1	Date1	Avg rating	Count
Product2	Date1	Avg rating	Count
Product3	Date1	Avg rating	Count
Product1	Date2	Avg rating	Count
Product2	Date2	Avg rating	Count
Product3	Date2	Avg rating	Count

level, total reviews serve as the proxy for the amount of each product sold, and total reviews are calculated by counting the total number of reviews.

Next, you regress review count (the proxy for products sold) on average star rating for each topic. This is done on a product level, that is, one observation equals the review count and average star rating for one product. This gives a correlation between star ratings for each topic and product sales (proxied using total reviews).

As a future consideration, causality and directionality can also be established. The star ratings for each topic can be linked temporally to the reviews obtained in the next period. With the help of Python DataFrames, this can be done by grouping reviews by product, date, average rating, and then count. As an example, Table 11.1 shows how the DataFrame would look.

The assumption here is that the effect of star ratings on one day reflects in product sales the next day. If this is not true, no link will be observed. Therefore, it is important to choose the right time window.

5. Conclusion

The technique presented here is in contrast to traditional methods of administering customer satisfaction surveys in which customer opinions are gathered across limited dimensions that are predetermined. This technique provides a methodological way to discover common topics among customer reviews. It also offers a way to determine which topic has the most impact on quantities sold. Although no causal inference has been made in this study, future research can develop this methodology to study further which customer review topics have the most impact on sales quantities.

References

Öğüt, H., & Onur Taş, B. K. (2012). The influence of internet customer reviews on the online sales and prices in hotel industry. *Service Industries Journal*, *32*(2), 197–214. https://doi.org/10.1080/02642069.2010.529436

Chapter 12

A Review of the Use of LinkedIn in Accounting Studies

Lanxin Jiang

Rutgers Business School, USA

Abstract

LinkedIn has emerged as a valuable data source for researchers in the accounting and financial fields. This chapter provides a comprehensive overview of studies that utilize LinkedIn data to investigate various aspects related to accounting and financial analysis. It summarizes the key findings of each study and discusses improvements that LinkedIn data has brought to these research endeavors. The review covers research on the use of LinkedIn profile photos (Li et al., 2020; Peng et al., 2022), connections (Li et al., 2023), individual characteristics, such as educational background, work experience, gender, and competency (e.g., Lang et al., 2024; Lee et al., 2022; Renschler et al., 2023), survey recruitment for accounting studies (Eulerich et al., 2022; Libby & Rennekamp, 2016), and other usage (Belnap, 2023; Chen et al., 2021). The insights provided by this review underscore the importance of LinkedIn as a valuable data source in the accounting domain, promising further advancements and illuminating key phenomena within the industry.

Keywords: Social media; LinkedIn; professional connections, experience, and skills; ESG reporting; machine learning; natural language processing

1. Introduction

LinkedIn, a prominent professional networking platform, has gained significant attention as a valuable data source in accounting and finance research. This chapter

Exogenous Data in Accounting and Auditing in the Rutgers Series in Accounting Information Systems, 157–162

Published under exclusive licence by Emerald Publishing Limited
doi:10.1108/978-1-83608-734-220251012

provides a comprehensive overview of research that employs LinkedIn data to investigate various aspects of the field. The review highlights key findings and improvements brought about by the integration of LinkedIn data into accounting research. The covered topics include the analysis of LinkedIn profile photos to measure personal traits, the utilization of LinkedIn connections as an indicator of social competencies, and the exploration of individual demographic characteristics, such as educational background and work experience. Additionally, the review encompasses research on survey recruitment, and other applications of LinkedIn data in accounting studies.

2. LinkedIn Profile Photos

Several studies explore the use of LinkedIn profile photos to measure individual characteristics in the accounting and financial domains. For instance, Peng et al. (2022) apply machine-learning techniques to gauge impressions about sell-side analysts using their LinkedIn photos. The findings indicate that impressions of trustworthiness and dominance positively affect forecast accuracy, especially after recent in-person meetings between analysts and firm managers. The attractiveness of analysts' photos influences accuracy only for new analysts or firms with new CEOs or CFOs. Similarly, Li et al. (2020) investigate how gender and attractiveness influence the likelihood of being voted an All-Star financial analyst in the United States and China. LinkedIn photos were utilized for U.S. analysts, while New Fortune Magazine provided the photos for Chinese analysts. The research reveals that female analysts are more likely to be voted All-Stars in the United States, but attractiveness works against them. In contrast, female analysts in China experience a positive relationship between attractiveness and All-Star votes.

More recently, Jiang (2025) collect a variety of variables from LinkedIn, including facial attractiveness based on profile photos, social connections, experience, educational background, and demographic information, and use explainable AI to understand how audit partners are matched with client companies.

3. LinkedIn Connections as a Measure of Social Skills

In a unique approach, Li et al. (2023) utilize the number of LinkedIn connections as a proxy for social skills to investigate the effect of financial analysts' social skills on their performance. This investigation provides robust, large-scale evidence underscoring the pivotal role that social skills play in enhancing the effectiveness of professionals within the financial analysis sector.

4. LinkedIn Profiles on Background and Work Experience

LinkedIn has evolved into an indispensable resource for researchers seeking to gather data on individuals' backgrounds and professional experiences across a range of studies within the accounting field. This platform provides a rich repository of information, enabling scholars to access detailed profiles that offer insights into professionals' educational qualifications, work history, and skill sets. This wealth of data has proven to be particularly useful in accounting research, where understanding the nuances of individuals' expertise and career trajectories can significantly enhance the quality and depth of analysis.

Fang and Hope (2021) find that teamwork has a positive impact on sell-side analysts' performance. They document that forecast accuracy positively relates to team diversity based on LinkedIn data, including sell-side analysts' experience, educational background, and gender. This study highlights the crucial role of teamwork and diversity in understanding sell-side analysts' performance. Do and Zhang (2022) study individual differences among reviewers by collecting data from LinkedIn. They find that reviewers with active LinkedIn accounts differ from reviewers without them in terms of leadership positions, salaries, gender, and accounting expertise. Chen et al. (2021) examine the association between tax departments and tax planning outcomes using data on corporate tax employees from S&P 1500 firms. The study hand-collects LinkedIn information to identify tax employees' specialization and establish a trade-off between tax avoidance and tax risk. Lee et al. (2022) investigate whether the audit quality of Big 4 audit firms is influenced by an audit office's proximity to target universities for recruiting staff auditors. Using LinkedIn data, they identify target universities and find that audit offices closer to these universities exhibit higher audit quality. Aslan (2022) links sell-side equity analysts to their deed records and LinkedIn profiles to study the impact of personal wealth shocks on analysts' forecasts and stock recommendations. Hendricks et al. (2022) explore the hiring of former PCAOB employees by audit firms and its effect on audit quality. The study uses a premium LinkedIn account to compile a sample of former PCAOB employees hired by large audit firms. Guo et al. (2022) use the PCAOB's Form AP data matched with Big 4 audit partner's LinkedIn profiles to investigate auditors' exposure to Arthur Andersen's collapse and its impact on audit quality.

Klein et al. (2020) use LinkedIn to search for information on buy and sell recommendations, upgrades, and the behavior of analysts. Bogdani et al. (2022) study the effects of voluntary assurance on capital formation in equity crowdfunding companies using LinkedIn data. Do and Zhang (2022) investigate whether individual securities regulators exhibit personal styles in their work using SEC comment letters and LinkedIn data. Cadman et al. (2014) examine the determinants of including earnout provisions in acquisition agreements using hand-collected data on top-level executives of target firms from LexisNexis and LinkedIn. Merkley et al. (2020) explore the impact of cultural differences among analysts on the quality of consensus earnings forecasts using LinkedIn data on analysts' gender and unique university majors. Lang et al. (2024) analyze the effects of the 2014 Markets in Financial Instruments Directive (MiFID II) using LinkedIn data on analysts' movements. Amiram et al. (2020) use LinkedIn and Bloomberg data to study the benefits and costs of reporting financial misconduct. Campbell et al. (2019) investigate the effects of cognitive constraints and biases on the processing and interpretation of soft information in private lending using LinkedIn data on loan officers' backgrounds. Fang and Hope (2021) reiterate the findings that teamwork and diversity affect sell-side analysts' performance based on hand-collected analyst research reports and LinkedIn data. Pisano et al. (2017) explore the relationship between ownership concentration and human capital disclosure released via LinkedIn. Renschler et al. (2023) overcome data limitations in research on the internal audit function by using LinkedIn data on employees' resumes. Stewart (2023) examines the influence of acquirer-provided incentives on target managers' disclosures by tracking their career paths through LinkedIn data. Using analysts' prior employment background data obtained from LinkedIn, Bradley et al. (2017) explore analysts' industry expertise, and Bradley et al. (2017) examine whether analysts' industry expertise influences their ability to serve as effective external firm monitors.

Overall, the use of LinkedIn data in accounting studies enriches our understanding of various accounting-related phenomena, such as the impact of teamwork on analysts' performance, the association between tax departments and tax outcomes, audit quality, equity crowdfunding companies' success, and the influence of individual characteristics on regulatory decisions. Researchers have successfully utilized LinkedIn to gather valuable information on analysts, auditors, regulators, and executives, leading to significant advancements in the field of accounting.

5. LinkedIn for Survey Recruitment

Researchers have increasingly turned to LinkedIn Groups as a strategic tool for recruiting participants for survey-based studies. In a notable application of this method, Libby and Rennekamp (2016) conduct a survey targeting experienced managers. Their research focuses on exploring the phenomenon of self-serving attribution bias within the context of management's practice of issuing earnings forecasts. This approach allows them to gather insights from individuals with direct experience in the field, enriching the validity and relevance of their findings. Similarly, Eulerich et al. (2022) leverage LinkedIn to reach out to a specific group of professionals: internal and external auditors. Their survey aims to develop and subsequently validate a comprehensive evaluation framework specifically designed for auditing automation activities. By selecting participants who are actively engaged in the auditing profession, the study benefits from the practical knowledge and expertise of individuals directly involved in automation processes, thereby ensuring that the framework is both practical and applicable in real-world settings.

6. LinkedIn for Other Purposes

LinkedIn also has other uses. Chan et al. (2022) explore the extent to which data from BoardEx can be augmented and verified through the use of LinkedIn and Google, aiming to enhance the accuracy and comprehensiveness of their dataset. On a different topic, Belnap (2023) adopts LinkedIn as a strategic tool to identify key individuals responsible for disclosing firms' tax strategies. These studies underscore the versatility of LinkedIn as a valuable resource in academic research, particularly in the context of improving data collection methods and identifying specific professional profiles relevant to specialized areas of study.

7. Conclusion

The use of LinkedIn data has become increasingly prevalent in accounting and financial research. This literature review presents a variety of studies that have leveraged LinkedIn to explore diverse aspects, including the impact of profile photos on analyst credibility, the importance of social skills in financial analysts' performance, the influence of teamwork on forecast accuracy, and recruitment for surveys. Moreover, LinkedIn data have been employed to investigate the relationship between ownership concentration and human capital disclosure, cultural diversity among analysts, labor market movements, and disclosure practices in public companies. The continued utilization of LinkedIn as a valuable data source promises to advance accounting and financial studies, shedding light on important phenomena in the industry.

References

Amiram, D., Huang, S., & Rajgopal, S. (2020). Does financial reporting misconduct pay off even when discovered? *Review of Accounting Studies*, *25*(3), 811–854.

Aslan, H. (2022). Personal financial distress, limited attention. *Journal of Accounting Research*, *60*(1), 97–128.

Belnap, A. (2023). The effect of intermediary coverage on disclosure: Evidence from a randomized field experiment. *Journal of Accounting and Economics*, *75*(1), 101522.

Bogdani, E., Causholli, M., & Knechel, W. R. (2022). The role of assurance in equity crowdfunding. *The Accounting Review*, *97*(2), 51–76.

Bradley, D., Gokkaya, S., & Liu, X. (2017). Before an analyst becomes an analyst: Does industry experience matter? *The Journal of Finance*, *72*(2), 751–792.

Bradley, D., Gokkaya, S., Liu, X., & Xie, F. (2017). Are all analysts created equal? Industry expertise and monitoring effectiveness of financial analysts. *Journal of Accounting and Economics*, *63*(2–3), 179–206.

Cadman, B., Carrizosa, R., & Faurel, L. (2014). Economic determinants and information environment effects of earnouts: New insights from SFAS 141 (R). *Journal of Accounting Research*, *52*(1), 37–74.

Campbell, D., Loumioti, M., & Wittenberg-Moerman, R. (2019). Making sense of soft information: Interpretation bias and loan quality. *Journal of Accounting and Economics*, *68*(2–3), 101240.

Chan, E. W., Evans, J. H., III, & Hong, D. (2022). Losers of CEO tournaments: Incentives, turnover, and career outcomes. *The Accounting Review*, *97*(6), 123–148.

Chen, X., Cheng, Q., Chow, T., & Liu, Y. (2021). Corporate in-house tax departments. *Contemporary Accounting Research*, *38*(1), 443–482.

Do, T. P. T., & Zhang, H. (2022). Styles of regulators: Evidence from the SEC's comment letters. *Contemporary Accounting Research*, *39*(2), 789–825.

Eulerich, M., Wagener, M., & Wood, D. A. (2022). Evidence on internal audit quality from transitioning to remote audits because of COVID-19. *Journal of Information Systems*, *36*(3), 219–234.

Fang, B., & Hope, O. K. (2021). Analyst teams. *Review of Accounting Studies*, *26*, 425–467.

Guo, F., Lisic, L. L., Pittman, J., Seidel, T. A., Zhou, M., & Zhou, Y. (2022). Fool me once, shame on you; fool me twice, shame on me: The long-term impact of Arthur Andersen's demise on partners' audit quality. *Contemporary Accounting Research*, *39*(3), 1986–2022.

Hendricks, B. E., Landsman, W. R., & Peña-Romera, F. D. (2022). The revolving door between large audit firms and the PCAOB: Implications for future inspection reports and audit quality. *The Accounting Review*, *97*(1), 261–292.

Jiang, L. (2025). *Three essays applying machine learning to improve audit risk and audit quality*. Doctoral dissertation, Rutgers The State University of New Jersey, Graduate School-Newark.

Klein, A., Li, T., & Zhang, B. (2020). Seeking out non-public information: Sell-side analysts and the Freedom of Information Act. *The Accounting Review*, *95*(1), 233–257.

Lang, M., Pinto, J., & Sul, E. (2024). MiFID II unbundling and sell-side analyst research. *Journal of Accounting and Economics*, *77*(1), 101617.

Lee, G., Naiker, V., & Stewart, C. R. (2022). Audit office labor market proximity and audit quality. *The Accounting Review*, *97*(2), 317–347.

Li, C., Lin, A.P., & Lu, H. (2020). *Analyzing the analysts: The effects of technical and social skills on analyst performance and careers*. Singapore Management University School of Accountancy Research Paper No. 2023-165.

Li, S. X., Nagle, F., & Zhou, A. (2023). *Mapping organizational-level networks using individual-level connections: Evidence from online professional networks*. Harvard Business School Strategy Unit Working Paper No. 24-010.

Libby, R., & Rennekamp, K. M. (2016). Experienced financial managers' views of the relationships among self-serving attribution bias, overconfidence, and the issuance of management forecasts: A replication. *Journal of Financial Reporting*, *1*(1), 131–136.

Merkley, K., Michaely, R., & Pacelli, J. (2020). Cultural diversity on Wall Street: Evidence from consensus earnings forecasts. *Journal of Accounting and Economics*, *70*(1), 101330.

Peng, L., Teoh, S. H., Wang, Y., & Yan, J. (2022). Face value: Trait impressions, performance characteristics, and market outcomes for financial analysts. *Journal of Accounting Research*, *60*(2), 653–705.

Pisano, S., Lepore, L., & Lamboglia, R. (2017). Corporate disclosure of human capital via LinkedIn and ownership structure: An empirical analysis of European companies. *Journal of Intellectual Capital*, *18*(1), 102–127.

Renschler, M. E., Ahn, J., Hoitash, R., & Hoitash, U. (2023). Internal audit competency and financial reporting quality: Evidence from LinkedIn human capital data. *Auditing: A Journal of Practice & Theory*, *42*(3), 1–30.

Stewart, C. R. (2023). Appraisal rights and corporate disclosure during mergers and acquisitions. *Journal of Accounting and Economics*, *75*(1), 101527.

Printed and bound by CPI Group (UK) Ltd, Croydon, CR0 4YY
16/09/2025
14736841-0003